The Art

THE ART

*A Grimoire of
Traditional Witchcraft*

by

Kerry Wisner

TROY BOOKS

Published by Troy Books
www.troybooks.co.uk

Troy Books Publishing
BM Box 8003
London WC1N 3XX

Cover design: Gemma Gary

Contents

Chapter One – Weaving the Willow   9

Chapter Two – Dragon, Cauldron, Cloak & Star   25

Chapter Three – Spirit on the Hearth   56

Chapter Four – Setting the Wards   70

Chapter Five – Watchers of the Night   107

Chapter Six – The Secret Seal   142

Chapter Seven – Through the Looking Glass   157

Chapter Eight – Mist and Glamour   178

Chapter Nine – Candle and Cord   200

Chapter Ten – Footsteps in the Night   228

Chapter Eleven – Salt and Iron   244

Chapter Twelve – Horn and Stone   255

Chapter Thirteen – Full Moon Ritual   277

Chapter Fourteen – Spokes and Flame   285

Chapter Fifteen – Between Hand and Foot   310

Chapter Sixteen – Invocations, Charms and Words of Power   317

Conclusion – The Lady and The Falcon   330

Bibliography   333

Index   337

Photoplates
between pages 168 - 169

All photos by Kerry Wisner

Chapter One

❖ WEAVING THE WILLOW ❖
THE ART OF PRACTICAL MAGIC

Magic, the ability to change or bend reality through occult means, has been with humanity throughout history. Beyond all else that we as a species have carried with us, magic has remained the one constant. The reason for this is simple: because it works. No matter where one looks, in any given period of time, magic has always been a vital tool for many people, whether they practiced this themselves or sought out those who did. Behind all of the rich traditions and systems filled with symbols and rites, all forms of practical magic follow a consistent pattern, a series of procedures that cause it to work. As such magic is a real art and discipline allowing for individual expression yet working within a set framework of measures that rest at its foundation.

When I speak of practical magic, it is important to understand that this is the art of applying occult techniques to enhance one's life, helping to overcome the challenges that the daily struggle of existence can bring. Some ceremonial magicians as well as 'armchair occultists' often call this *low magic*. Their thinking is that magic should only be used for their version of 'spiritual' pursuit and that all other uses are, at best misguided, and at worse, debased or even evil. I disagree.

The Traditional Witch views reality in very different terms than her would be noble counterpart, the ceremonial magician. The path of the Traditional Witch is not one of denial or suffering, and we certainly don't accept the difficulties presented in material life as some form of punishment that we can't do anything about. Further, we see no virtue in abstaining from the joys and pleasures that this world has to offer. On the contrary, the Witch sees life as a great adventure to be experienced and enjoyed. In doing so she seeks a balance, and yet, she can and does indulge in the delights of the material world. There is nothing 'evil' or 'low' about this. While in this physical world we should seek beauty and pleasure as part of the expression of what we experience in this incarnation. My teachers in the Art have always been quick to point out that *before* one can address spiritual concerns, one must first have their material needs taken care of.

As part of this, the Witch uses magic, and in doing so she actively engages with otherworld beings. Further, she does, on occasion, function in other realms. It is unfortunate that our limited language lacks the terms necessary to accurately describe exactly what these otherworld beings and different worlds are. As such, much of the work of the Witch is nearly impossible to explain in terms that the average person can understand. Perhaps the closest I can come is to define these states of being as 'transcendent' and 'experiential'. Yet even these words lack the real depth needed to understand how even the simplest of spells can enrich the inner life of the Witch.

What I can say is that it is through this exchange with these other realms that the Witch experiences the deeper essence of who she is at her core. Beyond incarnation, beyond the limitations of this realm, the Witch experiences the spiritual through her magic. So, for the Witch, magic is magic. There is no 'high' or 'low'. In fact, I will say from the outset that to not use magic to assist one in meeting material needs is an afront to nature. The ability to do magic is *natural* and something we all possess. It is the development of this talent that defines the Witch. To deny the use of magic in meeting daily needs is the same as deciding not to use any other skill one possesses. So never let anyone tell you that practical magic is 'low magic', that it is 'evil', or that magic should never be used for everyday purposes or personal gain. I suspect that many of those who say these things either don't have the training and skill to actually make real changes occur in their material condition, or they lack the courage to try because of their fear of failure.

Today, what we now call 'Traditional Witchcraft', or 'folkloric cunning' techniques, has its roots in the magic of the common people: those who worked the farms, lived close to the land, eking out an existence from the raw elements of nature itself. For them, spells, charms, talismans and all else that accompany these practices were as much a part of their life as tilling the soil or slaughtering livestock in preparation for the day's meal. The fact that these magical techniques have survived in one form or another over the centuries, having been handed down from generation to generation, is a testament to their effectiveness. Magic wasn't just part of the culture; it was a vital tool that enabled people to survive and ultimately thrive.

One could argue that, with the advent of the material sciences, much of the old folkloric magic has faded, being replaced by technology. However, this really isn't the case. If anything, magic has continued evolving over time, with more people seeking to learn and practice this now than ever before.

Like any of the other arts or sciences, magic has changed. With each successful spell, working or ritual performed, new techniques emerge that are found to be effective. This is as it should be. Magic isn't a static dogma, rather, it is a living system. It is for this reason that we now find elements of Hermetics, Astrology, Numerology and so many other occult sciences interwoven into the fabric of Traditional Witchcraft.

This blending began centuries ago as ritual magic developed in the Middle Ages. Born of Hermetics with strands of wisdom inherited through older sources including Arabic, Greek, Roman and Ancient Egyptian, the methods found in ritual magic soon joined with the folk pagan practices of rural regions. With this came references to planetary magic and the otherworld beings who resonate with these. From my research, it would appear that it was from this union that the techniques embodied in Traditional Witchcraft came to life. It is through this that cunning folk practices began to use elements found in various grimoires. Conversely, this exchange led to certain grimoires containing very real elements of pre-Christian folk magic. The Folger Elizabethan 16th century magical text is an excellent example of this. Despite the obvious Christian influence in major portions of the text, this work shows the clear incorporation of Hermetics as well as having direct references to a number of Pagan Goddesses and Gods. Even more telling is its evocation of the Queen and King of Elphame.[1]

My training in the Art has developed over several decades, beginning with Traditional Witchcraft through a woman whom I introduced in the first book: Julie. Shortly before her passing she connected me with a coven that, while more contemporary in its structure, had certain elements of Traditional Witchcraft in its teaching as well.[2] I spent ten years with the coven as an initiate and, in time, leader.

Beyond this I went on to become very active in the study of academic texts in order to learn and practice Ancient Egyptian magic. I have had a lifelong interest in Egypt, finding it to be one of the primary roots of western esotericism. It would appear that it was partly out of Egyptian magic that Hermetics was born. I am not going

---

1. Harms, Daniel; James Clark, Joseph Peterson. *The Book of Oberon: A Sourcebook of Elizabethan Magic.* 2021.

2. Julie spent quite a bit of time sifting through the many different local groups whom she was aware of before introducing me to this particular coven. She was well known in the community and had firsthand access to many different group's private practices. For her, it was vital that she find a group that was aligned to her core beliefs. As such, while this particular coven functioned more or less in a Wiccan fashion, there were essential facets within the group that resonated with her own tradition.

to go into the historical evidence that has been steadily building, indicating the manner in which Egyptian wisdom was eventually incorporated into Hermetics at the collapse of the Egyptian civilization.[3] That is a subject for another book. I mention it here though to show that for me it was a natural progression to then seek training in Hermetics through a structured magical order.

I mention my training here as, inevitably, the techniques I am presenting in this volume are influenced by all three disciplines. Here you will find direct reference and use of Gaelic *and* Ancient Egyptian words of power, otherworld beings, as well as the practical application of talismanic images drawn from medieval grimoires, all coupled with traditional folkloric magic. The folk magical practices that will be discussed are drawn from a variety of sources with an emphasis placed on Welch Traditionalist magic, Basque folk magic and enchantments, as well as elements of Strega Witchcraft, simply because these were some of the systems that my teachers understood and taught. As I do this, I will be careful to cite my sources whenever possible so that the reader can determine for herself what she may want to apply in her practice.

Whether one wants to admit it or not, over time there was a blending of different teachings as cultures from the Mediterranean moved into Europe. This was seen very early on in the Roman era, when Celtic deities were incorporated into the Roman pantheon and vice versa. It was during this era that rites dedicated to Diana and Isis moved into Europe. Eventually, Hermetics traveled into European cities through a series of books, the practices of private magicians, as well as through various esoteric schools and orders. In particular such cities Toledo, Spain and Prague in the current Czech Republic were known for their scholars in ritual magic and Alchemy. It was inevitable that there

---

3. Dr. Alison Roberts explores this in her book *My Heart My Mother: Death and Rebirth in Ancient Egypt*. 2000.199.

would be a mixing of these disciplines with the magic of rural folk and pagan practices.

It may be important to note that while Julie's teachings were strongly centered on her family's practices which she inherited through her Basque lineage, she was an avid reader and did incorporate Hermetics into her teachings. In fact, she had required her students to read a number of books on ritual magic, encouraging us to experiment with these while also using her practices.[4]

There is yet one more source that needs to be considered when we look for the origins of Traditional Witchcraft. Beyond all of these different, seemingly competing elements, it is important to understand that when one lives close to the land, drawing directly from the environment, one becomes aware of an underlying current ... a living consciousness of wisdom inherent in all of nature. It is from this that the Witch gains much of her insight, knowledge and power. This is one of the ways that the Traditional Witch differs dramatically from the magician. The magician can spend countless hours in study, analyzing techniques from different esoteric schools of magical philosophy. Yet he will seldom make that innate connection to this deeper natural current. The Traditional Witch on the other hand will often do the same study and research, yet, for her, the greatest asset in her Art is her ability to move between worlds, merging with the living power and consciousness of nature itself.

This consciousness, this power in nature, continues to emerge in new and transformed ways. Traditional Witchcraft is a natural expression of this living pulse in the land, a pulse that is often referred to as the *Serpent's Breath* or *Dragon's Breath*. In our small group we have also come to call it 'the Bond', the Geassa. It is because of this link to the land that Traditional Witchcraft continues to develop and grow.

---

4. In particular I recall her high praise for David Conway's book *Ritual Magic* as well as the classic Victorian era book *The Kyballion*, and strongly recommending both to me.

I would be willing to go so far as to say that this living consciousness is the primary organic generation of magical wisdom in all rural, magical practices.

It is through this connection that the Witch creates a direct communication with the otherworld beings inherent in the environment in which she lives. It is from such encounters that alliances with familiar spirits are formed. And so, we see that a portion of the work of the Traditional Witch can clearly be understood to be shamanic in the sense that she does, in time, interact with spirits in other realms and dimensions beyond the material.

There is a significant body of historical reference confirming the relationship of familiar spirits with Witches. The case of Isobel Gowdie from the 17th century is an excellent example of this. It is in this same manner that spirits continue to be an important source of information teaching the Traditional Witch today. This, too, has formed a vital part of my practice.

As mentioned, magic was part of the daily life of common people reaching back to very ancient times. There is significant evidence that these practices did survive and continued to be passed down in small groups and through families into the current era. I know that there are historians who will argue against this. I have personally encountered academics who vehemently state that any accounts of Witches and their gatherings during the persecutions cannot be considered credible because these were taken from individuals under torture. These same historians go on to state that any accounts of Witches after the persecutions must be people simply copying the false narrative given from accounts of those earlier tortured individuals. So, we find that when following this line of 'logic' it becomes almost impossible to prove the existence of the historical Witch no matter the evidence.

When one points out to these same historians that many accounts given during the persecutions were taken from people who apparently had not been tortured and who freely admitted their practice (such as Isobel Gowdie), the historian's retort is that *'obviously those folks were innocents who were deluded, mentally ill or were seeking attention'*.[5] In presenting this 'logic' it would seem to me that these well-meaning academics are, in fact, throwing the baby out with the bathwater. We have reached a point in which no matter the evidence provided, whether oral accounts, folkloric stories, actual written historical manuscripts containing clear elements of pagan spells and rituals, independent eye witness testimony describing occult gatherings, to artifacts dating well before the modern era, it has become vogue among academics to unquestioningly state that the historical Witch didn't exist. Yet, as was shown in the first book of this series, evidence does exist. In the time since I first wrote *The Willow Path* I came across an interesting book that documents a number of rural practices and folklore from Cornwall England dating to before 1880. In this the authors cite the following account which is particularly interesting:

> *"You ought to have known, as any old 'pellar' (conjurors) would have told ye, if you had deigned to talk with such without preaching to them, that the secret of secrets, the unwritten words which make this book of use are the names of powerful and benevolent spirits, by whose aid fiends are expelled. These secret names, by which alone they may be invoked, are only taught by word of mouth, to the few who are initiated, after long probation.*
>
> *Not so very long ago, the learned in occult sciences met, at stated times, on lonely downs, and at the same places in which sages were wont to confer in days of yore for examination of such as sought admission into their fraternity, and for the preservation of the mystic lore".*[6]

---

5. Wilby, Emma. *The Visions of Isobel Gowdie*. 2013.55-57

6. Bottrell, William & Joseph Blight. *Stories and Folklore of West Cornwall*. 1880.30

The implications of this account are staggering. This was written well after the persecutions, and certainly wasn't taken from the testimony of someone being tortured. Yet, it clearly makes reference to occult teachings and practices, as well as initiation and training into small groups meeting in secret rural locations at appointed times. The 'pellar' is the Cornish term used for cunning folk, those who practice rural magic.

No matter how one looks at this, the account has all the ear marks of a Witches' gathering. I am reminded of the old saying "if it walks like a duck and quacks like a duck, it's a duck".

Keep in mind that this was published in 1880. This was only thirty-seven years before the birth of Sybil Leek, and approximately forty years before the birth of my first teacher in Traditional Witchcraft, Julie. Both these women claimed to come from families who practiced Witchcraft, and to have been involved with close knit groups, i.e. covens of Witches and occultists going back generations. Further, both claimed that on certain occasions these covens would meet in secret places deep in nature. I see no reason not to suppose that this would be possible, especially in light of written records such as the one noted here. These gatherings certainly wouldn't have been in the form portrayed in many contemporary Wiccan practices. However, the fact is that small groups of people, bound by initiation, did meet in secret rural locations to practice their Art. It seems clear that the Art has been with us, and continues to this day, surviving centuries of persecution and then denial.

Thanks to the work of such important teachers as Sybil Leek, Robert Moser, Julie and so many countless others, today we find Traditional Witchcraft has emerged as one of the most important manifestations of western magical arts. Drawing the attention of serious-minded occultists and academics alike, practical folkloric systems of magic are quickly forming the foundation of a vital and rich system that will likely influence deeper currents of esoteric practice for generations to come.

This book is the third in the Geassa series, a set of books intended to document the Art as I have come to understand and practice it. In no way am I implying that this is the only way to practice magic. Far from it. Rather, these books are meant to be a distillation of what I have learned and found effective over the course of my lifetime. My intention in writing these books is to put these teachings into a form that would make them accessible to the sincere student, while ensuring that these techniques continue on.

The first book, *The Willow Path*, laid the foundation of these teachings covering the concepts, tools, and different realms of the Traditional Witch. In the second book, *Horns of the Moon*, I explored specific techniques surrounding traveling in spirit, interacting with otherworld beings, and reaching the realms those beings inhabit. This third book is meant to be a listing of specific spells, workings and techniques that I and associates of mine have found to be effective.

It is important that the reader clearly understands that while these all are drawn from older sources, this is a living, evolving system that is meant to adapt to the challenges of life here and now. And while many of the spells are historically accurate, they have been applied to situations today, being adapted to life in this era to meet personal goals. I present them here as examples and guidelines for how you can apply the Art in your life. Naturally, each person's results will vary depending on one's talent, skill, training and ability to use these to meet one's needs.

To get the most out of these techniques it is best that the reader become familiar with the first two books in the series, as there are a number of rituals and incantations in this present volume which directly relate to the concepts described previously. Many of the physical tools that will be needed in some of these rites were discussed at length in the first two books along with the methods for making and enchanting these. In addition, before embarking on these workings, please revisit the chapters in the prior books related to the use and differences between imagination and fantasy, how to set obtainable goals, knowing your own motives, and gaining confidence without self-delusion. Also, be certain that you understand the role of otherworld beings in Traditional Witchcraft and the alliance of the Witch with familiar spirits. All of this was covered in-depth in the first two books.

You are going to find that a large portion of the magic presented involves the use of sigils and seals. Essentially a sigil can be thought of as the 'signature' of the force or being for which it represents. It is quite literally an outer expression and manifestation of the force. A seal has similar qualities except that it is the manifestation of the 'function' of that force. The difference between the two is subtle but important. Yet, quite often the two cross over and are used interchangeably.

The question then becomes, where do these symbols come from? Some are derived through mathematical procedures involving the harmonics of numbers embodying the forces sought. Many others though were presented directly to Witches and magicians by the spirits themselves. Whether through scrying or direct manifestation, otherworld beings will reveal the sigils that are their signatures.

Yet, there is a third method by which sigils and seals come into being. In a state of 'becoming'[7], the Witch allows herself to gently focus on the force or spirit with whom she seeks to partner. As she does this, she needs to have at hand a means of recording the sigil. This can be paper and pen, quill and parchment, her Fe or staff tracing the dirt on the ground, it doesn't really matter. In this state she gently begins to move the pen or staff as she 'experiences' the force through her trained second sight, letting the image form more or less spontaneously.

---

7. See *Horns of the Moon* for a clear description of 'Becoming'.

The interesting thing about these types of sigils is that, once completed, the Witch can place her finger, Fe, staff or even the quill directly on any single spot on the drawing and bring back the essence of that force as it was expressing itself in that point of the symbol. Thus, the sigil as a whole becomes a conduit manifesting the entirety of the being involved. However, each individual spot on the drawing gives access to a particular aspect of this same force.[8] It is for this reason that sigils and seals have long been a part of the magical arts and should always be treated with great care.

Witchcraft as I practice it is a way of life. It requires focus, study and above all else unrelenting practice. Fortunately, the subject embraces so many different avenues of knowledge that one never gets bored. On the contrary, after more than half a century of practice I still feel that I have barely begun.

All I ask of the reader is that you approach the Art with care and discretion. These are tools that have real world effects and with them real consequences. In performing even the simplest forms of magic you are altering reality, and with that comes great responsibility. Perhaps the following gives a good example of understanding the consequences of practical magic.

Early in my training I decided to cast a spell. It was to be something simple and direct, nothing too complex, and certainly nothing anyone would consider 'unethical'. It was

---

8. During experimentation in remote viewing conducted through Stanford University and later the U.S. government a very similar technique was used by having the person in trance doing the viewing trace a spontaneous symbol while in contact with the viewed objective. Rather than being a drawing of a place, these tracings were found to act as 'triggers' that accessed specific qualities of the places, or people whom the viewer was connecting with. See David Morehouse's book *Remote Viewing: The Complete User's Manual for Coordinate Remote Viewing*.

the early 1980's and I had just moved from California to a small town in North Carolina; the heart of the 'bible belt' of the USA. Quite literally there was a church on every corner, and virtually everyone I met would ask which church I belonged to. When I explained that I had just arrived in town they would invite me to join them, seeing an opportunity to increase their flock while potentially saving my soul. It was in this atmosphere that I landed a job with a local book distributor. They supplied books and magazines to a number of stores up and down the coast of the Carolinas.

Perhaps I was a little too young, and certainly too naïve. Julie had died. However, beforehand she introduced me to a small coven which she felt would be a good fit for me to continue my training. Within a year following my initiation circumstances occurred uprooting the leader of the coven, which in turn brought her and I to this small community thousands of miles away and as distant in its culture and acceptance of anything non-Christian. Yet, conversely, what had drawn her to this area of the country, in part, was the opportunity to work with a group who were practicing a form of Welch magical arts, and it was from them that we both gained more training in Traditional Witchcraft.

It was in this environment that we began reconstituting the original coven as people began learning of our talents. Being a small town, I knew it was only a matter of time before rumors would fly and my new employer would learn of my occult interests. In addition, the leader of our group had been invited to speak to a large gathering and it would require that I take time off of work to attend. So it was that I decided that I would take the lead and explain the situation to the owner of the company . . . that is only after performing a work on him first.

In the days leading up to the actual spell, I arranged to spend some time near him in the building where we both worked. This was my opportunity to 'get his feel', to begin to create the link needed to enter his second skin.[9] Too, it was in these days that I managed to learn his birthdate and secrete away a small sample of his handwriting.

The rite itself was done over a series of three nights. My intention was to form a link in ritual, merging with his mind, and plant the clear and definite impression that I was his equal, that he respected and valued me as vital to his organization. This would be accomplished in part by calling on the spirits of Mercury and the element of air. Keep in mind that I had only been employed a few months and had never had any real interaction with him except basic politeness and greetings. So it was that I cast my spell:

> "(name of person), listen well
> Harken to this Witch's spell
> By swiftness of Mercury
> Power of Air,
> You will know that I am there,
> I am your equal strong and proud,
> (name of person) respect me now!"

After the third day offerings, ashes and leftover wax from the rite were scattered over the walkway where he would pass. Then, mustering my courage, I approached him, asking if we could talk. We sat in his office and as carefully and professionally as I could explained my practices to him and that I had wanted him to learn of these directly from me rather than hear any rumors in the community.

He listened intently but seemed almost stunned. He then said he understood and appreciated my honesty. After a moment he looked me square in the eye and granted me the time off needed to attend the gathering.

In the days after returning, he moved my work station, assigning me to one directly next to his. He then began showing me different tasks that only he, himself did for

---

9. See *Horns of the Moon* for information on the second skin.

the company. Soon he began inviting me to lunch where we would have long conversations about the business and his goals for the company. It soon seemed as if we were inseparable, working side by side, and constantly discussing business ventures. All I had wanted was to ensure I wouldn't lose my job when the day came that he found out I was a Witch.

I was so young and inexperienced. I can almost hear Julie laughing now. Traditional Witchcraft is a practical system for gaining real results. Yet one needs to be so careful in how one approaches this. The poor owner of the small book business never knew what hit him. And I, as a fledgling Witch, had thrown the entire gambit of my occult skill at him. He not only accepted my practice without question, he then went on to view me as a business partner . . . an equal, just as I had clearly stated in the spell.

I wanted to recount this incident because it illustrates that, first, this is real. Magic works in very powerful ways. Second, one needs to think through the consequences of any rite performed. You may know what you want, but the spell may be creating a different effect depending on the forces and words used in the rite. Finally in all magic, like everything else in life, there is a price, or rather consequences for the act, that have to be paid. There is a reason we call spells 'works'. They take time, careful planning and a tremendous amount of energy. In the example given here I ended up working side by side under the owner's direct supervision and scrutiny. If I had wanted to just be a staff member, flying under the radar, that simply wasn't possible after this spell. Virtually every action I made was now carefully watched by the head of the organization. So, think very carefully about the magic you do because it will have repercussions.

In Traditional Witchcraft, in the strictest sense word, there is nothing symbolic involved. Rather, when one begins a working one is actually performing the resulted desire in real and practical terms using very powerful forces that most people don't know of, or understand. This isn't faith. Nor is it religion, at least not in the sense that most people think of it today. Again, if anything, Traditional Witchcraft can best be understood as an Art, a practice and a way of life. Witchcraft empowers the individual to reach beyond themselves and take control of their own destiny. This is the Art as I have been taught and have come to practice it.

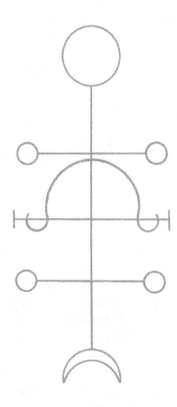

Chapter Two

✣ DRAGON, CAULDRON, CLOAK & STAR ✣
PREPARATION FOR RITUAL

One of the most important and powerful
talismanic images is that of the dragon, a creature
preserved in myth, song, symbol and countless
tales. We find dragons and serpents memorialized in
sacred art, temples, carvings, and earthen mounds the
world over. In Asia the dragon has always been seen as
representing luck, prosperity, as well as divine authority.
In Central America the dragon appears as the feathered
serpent, personifying power and wisdom particularly
among the Aztecs as the God Quetzalcoatl and the
Mayans as Kukulkan.

One of the oldest earthen structures in North America
is the serpent mound located in Ohio, USA. More than
1300 feet in length this representation of undulating
snake dates back to sometime between 800 BCE and 100
CE. Clearly this was a sacred site, yet no one is quite sure
why it was built.

In European cultures the dragon takes on a more
dualistic and often sinister nature. As we will see, this
is largely because of the later influence of Christianity.
Prior to the influx of Abrahamic theology, the dragon
appears to have been a totem embodying the innate
energy and primal awareness of nature itself. In many
ways the dragon and snake were seen as one of the
symbolic images of Pagan practices. In my opinion, this
was one of the reasons that, when Christianity began to
take hold, the church quickly demonized both the dragon

and snake, depicting these as images of their 'devil' while portraying Christian heroes as defeating them.[10]

A classic example of this can be found in what remains of a sacred site dedicated to the Roman Moon Goddess, Diana, at Lake Nemi, Italy. Hers was a spiritual practice that, for several centuries, rivaled Christianity. Diana's influence reached deep into Europe with artifacts dedicated to Her being found as far away as Great Britain. Lake Nemi is located a few miles outside of Rome, and is one of the oldest sites dedicated to this great Goddess. In fact, evidence has been found indicating that worship in some form or another took place here as far back as 10,000 BCE. At the lake a path winds through the forest leading to a cave that was once a pilgrimage for those seeking Diana.

However, with the advent of Christianity, they reconsecrated the site naming the path after Saint Michael. He, of course, is perhaps the primary Abrahamic entity ascribed to slaying dragons. The grotto itself was then renamed "The Cave of the Devil". The intent could not be more obvious; the demonization of the Great Queen and equating Her and Her religion to the image of the dragon[11] as a representation of their 'Satan'.

So, we find that in European cultures the dragon and serpent have taken on a complex bearing. For some their image conjures a sense of terror with tales of knights sent out to kill these creatures. For others the dragon remained as a symbol of a sacred, ancient wisdom. But for all, the dragon has come to be a symbol representing immense power. In Celtic and pre-Celtic myths dragons and serpents can be characterized as the unbridled force of nature itself.

---

10. MacMullen, Ramsay. *Christianity & Paganism in the Fourth to Eighth Centuries.* 1997.93.

11. Tejeda-Moreno, Manny. https://wildhunt.org/20021/07/re-opened-trail-in -nemi-echoes-christian-conquest-of-pagan-areas.html, last accessed 25/1/2022

The dragon was neither good nor bad, rather it was the embodiment of the pulse of life.

This is described in a number of legends. For example, in the accounts surrounding Conall Cernach a great snake guards a courtyard. But when Conall encounters the beast it leaps onto his belt, thereby conveying its power to him [12].

It is important to understand that snakes are quite often tied directly to the power of women, Goddesses, magic, healing and female sexuality. This was hinted at in the Christians equating the dragon to Diana. Another example can be found in the lore surrounding Queen Sybille, Sybil, Sibyli or sometimes known as Sebile. In the medieval era she was seen as Queen of the Underworld, an otherworld being or Fae, who was particularly revered by Witches in Italy. Legend explains that she lives in a cavern that is accessible only by crossing a deep abyss in which a fast-flowing river is found. The path leads one to a narrow stone bridge crossing the chasm. On the other side, the entrance to Sybille's kingdom is sealed by a crystal door that is guarded by two dragons. [13]

If one gains entrance, they find them self in a rich world of pleasure where the Queen rules as a beautiful woman. She was portrayed as a great sorceress and seductress. There, so the lore explains, one enjoys the delights of this realm much of which is spent in long sessions of making love. The legend goes on to recount that every Friday night the Queen would shapeshift into the form of huge dragon like serpent whom the Christians equated with their devil. What is so intriguing here is that several medieval sources also equate Sybille with the Moon Goddess Diana. [14]

The symbolism couldn't be clearer: a powerful sorceress who rules the underworld, in an obvious representation

---

12. Paice MacLeod, Sharon. *Celtic Cosmology and the Otherworld* 2018.119

13. Howard, Michael. *Liber Nox: A Traditional Witch's Gramarye*. 2014.84.

14. Scot, Reginald. *Discoverie of Witchcraft*. 1584/1972 is one such reference connecting the two.

of the Annwn. This is only accessed by moving across the abyss separating our realm from Hers. The entrance is guarded by the very pulse of nature itself in the form of the twin serpents. Yet, the crystal door harkens back to the Castle of Glass found so often in the esoteric imagery of European Pagan magic. The Lady herself is the essence of the land: beautiful, seductive, powerful. Then on the night ruled by the planet Venus, the planet of feminine beauty and sexuality, the Queen transforms into the dragon itself as the life force of nature. The very same Queen who is also identified with ancient Moon Goddess images and the dragon force, demonized by the Abrahamic traditions. This is such a powerful image of transition and initiation, awakening to the true spiritual essence of life itself.

I find this particular legend to be very interesting, not only because of the power of the imagery involved, but also by the fact that direct evocations and spells involving Sebile/ Sibyli made their way into English and Scottish books of magic.[15] These include spells to cause her to appear while scrying in a candle flame or a show stone crystal. In others she is listed as one of the many otherworld beings appearing at the magician's circle. I find it at once immensely important that She appears in these texts, yet, when one considers the legends surrounding her, it seems so clear that much was lost by the time these manuscripts recorded these spells. I suspect that much lore and many potential ritual practices may have existed around this powerful Pagan otherworld being that is lost in time. Especially so when one considers that an elaborate, ancient carved grotto near Naples, Italy exists that appears to be directly linked to this same being. But what this also shows is a clear, though fading, lineage of Pagan beliefs surviving into manuscripts that directly relate to Witchcraft. No matter what one wants to think regarding

15. Harms, Daniel; James Clark, Joseph Peterson. *The Book of Oberon: A Sourcebook of Elizabethan Magic*. 2021.

the historical survival and influence of older pre-Christian practices and their said influence on Witchcraft, the fact is that this being, with Her links to Pagan beliefs, the dragon force and ancient pagan Goddesses, is there in documents directly related to Witchcraft during the height of the Witchcraft craze.

There are further examples related to serpent power and its connection to Goddesses and healing. This simple Celtic spell exemplifies one of these:

> "I invoke the three daughters of Flidias,
> O Serpent, heal the swelling!"[16]

Similar motifs also emerge from Ancient Egyptian practices. Here magic itself is deified in the form of the snake Goddess Heka. Neither good nor bad in nature, She represents the spiritual power hidden in nature ruled over by the divine feminine. She was considered to be so powerful that 'Heka Wands' in the form of serpents were vital tools used by the Egyptian priesthood and local sorcerers alike.

Egyptologist, Dr. Alison Roberts explains that the serpent force was seen as both fiery and feminine, being embodied in the Goddess Hathor/Sekhmet.[17] In this regard the serpent corresponds to the raw feminine force that creates and destroys. Further Dr. Roberts goes on to show that this force is the driving influence that guides both the Sun God and the spirits of the deceased through the underworld toward a state of transformation and rebirth.

In late period Egypt we also find temples and specific rites surrounding the Agathodaimon, or 'the good spirit'. This is an otherworld being portrayed as an androgenous winged serpent bringing wisdom and enlightenment through ritual practice and esoteric teachings. Also known as Knouphis,

---

16. Paice MacLeod, Sharon. *Celtic Cosmology and the Otherworld.* 2018.147

17. Roberts, Alison. *My Heart My Mother: Death and Rebirth in Ancient Egypt.* 2000.168

this dragon-like being remains a powerful influence in certain Hermetic Orders to this day.[18]

To this day the snake is considered to hold considerable power in magic. One of the most prized possessions of the Traditional Witch is the discarded skin of a snake. When found this is usually kept in a special wooden box. It is used to encourage health and regeneration by gently wrapping this over the part of a person that needs healing.[19] It is also carried in charm bags to enhance the power of the Witch in all of her operations.

Throughout my writings I have continued to express the teaching that there is a living power and consciousness in the land, the sea, in fact in all of nature. As noted earlier we call this the Geassa, the Bond. It is the living wellspring of wisdom that is behind all of nature. It can be felt most readily in the liminal spaces dividing contours and changing the rhythm of natural places. These can include the meadow that ends at a line in the forest, a cliff, cave, an isolated pond or spring, lakes, brooks and rivers, the top of a mountain, or a deep valley. Wherever there is a distinct 'edge' or change deep in an isolated part of the natural world. It is in such places that the consciousness of nature, this power in the form of the serpent's breath, the dragon force, can be felt the strongest.

In Celtic mythology there is a strong tradition surrounding twin winged dragons. Traditional Witch Michael Howard explains that, according to lore, King Aurthur's sword, Excalibur, was emblazed with the images of two entwined serpents or dragons on its blade. This sword, so the legend indicates, was given to him by the Lady of the Lake; again, showing the link between the divine feminine and the dragon force.[20]

---

18. Denning, Melita and Osborne Phillips. *The Magical Philosophy, Book V, Mysteria Magica*. 1981.92

19. Patterson, Steve. *Cecil Williams Book of Witchcraft*. 2014.93

20. Howard, Michael. *Liber Nox: A Traditional Witch's Gramarye*. 2014.34

The theme of the twin serpents continues with the images of the red and white dragons of Welch tradition. On the surface the story surrounding these appear to be as symbols representing the struggle between the Welch people and the invading Saxons. Yet to the Witch, these dragons have always corresponded to very distinct energies in nature that, while of the same essentially quality, are very different from each other. They both correspond to the power within the land, yet there is a complementary quality to these, each making the other whole. As Michael Howard explains, the twin serpents represent "'earth energy' and 'dragon energy' that flows in the enchanted landscape".[21]

Looking back once again to Ancient Egypt, we find very similar imagery. For example, the king was often depicted as wearing a red and white crown. In one sense this crown represented the lower and upper regions of Egypt. Thus, in wearing this the king was seen as sovereign of the entire country. But, as with so much in Egyptian magic, the red and white crown had another purpose. Each corresponded to a distinct Goddess. The white crown was seen as the embodiment of the Goddess Nekhbet. She could be portrayed as a vulture, but more often than not She could be shown as a winged serpent. The red crown, on the other hand, was the talismanic object of Wadjet, also sometimes referred to as Buto, the cobra Goddess. Together these two otherworld beings became the essence of divine power linked intrinsically to the very land of Egypt itself. In wearing this the king was endowed with the sheer power of these two great Serpent Goddesses within him or herself.

This same imagery is also found in the dual headed crown depicting the Cobra and the Vulture, worn by Egyptian royalty and the Gods themselves. Again, the purpose was the embodiment of the powerful serpent force of nature bound in this talismanic image of the Ureaus.

---

21. Ibid, 2014.34

In the centuries that followed the collapse of the Egyptian mysteries, portions of these teachings were carried forward, many of which were concealed in the science of Alchemy. Within this there are teachings surrounding the symbolism of the red and white roses. In Alchemy the red rose is seen as representing active, solar energies; while the white rose is the embodiment of receptive, lunar power. These can be seen portrayed in a number of esoteric works including the highly important Splendor Solis paintings and texts from the renaissance period.

My point is that these two forces are inherent in all of nature. They were known of and a vital part of Pagan esoteric systems the world over. As such, in the Art the use of these in ritual today is highly effective.[22]

In the system that we practice, the red dragon is the active, vital, solar force pulsing through the land, while the white dragon is receptive, creative energy that answers to and is embodied in lunar tides of power. For the Witch it is the merging of these two distinct composites that that give her a measure of her power.

As we saw in *The Willow Path*, the serpent is one of the four familiar spirits that is vital in the practice of Traditional Witchcraft. In one sense this can be seen as the combined essence of the red and white dragons, merged as a single unified force. And so, we find a number of techniques are used to seek out the serpent breath, the red and white dragons in nature, gathering their energy into oneself and one's tools.

Of course, there are three other spirits that hold equal importance, and like the dragon, they are found in the liminal places of nature. I discussed these at length in *The Willow Path*, as such, the reader may want to go back and review the sections surrounding the "Four Familiars"

---

22. The reader may recall that these two forces were incorporated into the ritual "The Castle and the Cauldron", in the second book of the series *Horns of the Moon*.

before proceeding. The three other spirits are the crow, the hare and the toad. All four of these will be called on in the practices that I am presenting here. However, the underlying current of the serpent force is perhaps the most critical of the four.

The following are a series of three techniques that I use on a regular basis to align myself with the forces involved in this system of magic, opening my senses to the realms beyond those normally perceived, and to gather a measure of power through a connection with nature. This power, in turn, is then available for magical workings. As you read through these you will find that the first two are drawn from Traditional Witchcraft sources, while the third pulls directly from Ancient Egyptian techniques. As with all of my teachings use what you find to be practical for you. All three can be employed in tandem, or you may choose to use them individually depending on your needs and predilection. Ideally these should be done each day, and if possible, in the same place and time. Of course, the reality is that we all lead very hectic lives and find ourselves in a variety of places. Nevertheless, do your best to try to perform this on a regular basis.

The Serpent's Breath
Stand facing the hearth. If you don't have a hearth, face north. Have your feet slightly apart, and arms at your sides. If your situation allows, it is best to wear loose clothing, or nothing at all. The main point is to keep the solar plexus region unrestricted during this. Begin by calming your mind as you breathe slowly and evenly: four counts in through the nose as you fill your diaphragm. Then hold this to the count of two. Follow this by breathing out slowly through the mouth to the count of four, gently releasing the air from the diaphragm. Hold your breath to a count of two, then begin the process again. Do this several times as you allow yourself to relax. Then, when ready, recite the following:

"I call you Serpent of the Land,
Awake, arise ye from thy stead,
By Dragons Red and White,
By Crow,
By Toad,
By Leaping Hare,
Rise in me O Serpent Breath!"

As you do this envision the earth beneath your feet and allow a sense of energy to begin to well up, as if pulsing through the connection you have formed. Even if you find yourself performing this in a room several stories above ground, the reality is that directly below you the earth remains as the realm in which you are living, in this time and in this incarnation. Your body is of the earth, being part of the land and all of nature. So simply allow yourself to be aware of the surging force that is the dragon energy as it begins to rise in you while reciting the first three lines of the enchantment. See a scarlet red energy flow up through your right leg, while a brilliant white pulse of energy floods the left leg.

At the genitals the two dragons meet. But rather than merge, envision these entwine around each other in a courtship of complementary forces. Like two serpents spiraling around one another, the red and white streams of energy steadily rise up the spine. Take some time as you allow this process to take place. When they reach the base of the skull the two will slip over your head and come to a point of power at your brow. It may be helpful to envision this as the head of a serpent, similar to Egyptian renditions discussed earlier. In this moment simply allow yourself to merge with the serpent force that is alive within you.

After a moment recite "by crow". With this envision a crow or raven centered either within, or just above, your head. As you do, recall that the crow is known for its intelligence, and yet it is highly intuitive being seen as a messenger between worlds.

In reciting "by toad" turn your focus to your chest, the home of your heart and emotions. This is the meeting point between the body and the spirit. By visualizing the toad here, you are connecting this spirit to the liminal center of yourself, becoming aware of its power in you.

Now turn your attention to your genitals as you state "by leaping hare". This totem is known for its proliferation, its ability to reproduce. Your genitals are the part of you most connected to the life force, fertility, creativity, pleasure and the transition between worlds; for sex is the vehicle that brings those who have passed back into this world.

Then, once again become aware of the serpent pulse rising up from the ground, through your legs, continuing to spiral around the spine and eventually merging as a complementary force over your head, poised as the serpents resting on your brow. It is here that you recite the final line of the enchantment. For with it, the very power of nature itself is now centered within you, at the ready whenever needed.

The concept of attributing specific beings and spiritual forces to centers in the body is very old. We see this in ancient practices from India involving the seven centers that are tied to the endocrine glands. Similar centers are referred to in Ancient Egyptian texts, with the enigmatic referral to the rite of "swallowing the seven cobras" found in the Coffin Texts.

Closer in time and culture we find similar Druidic teachings surrounding the three "Cauldrons of Poesy" that were introduced to students in the first book. As described, a Druidic poem from the seventh century discusses three centers or 'cauldrons' in the body. The 'cauldron of warming' found in the genitals and solar plexus corresponding to the Hare, the 'cauldron of motion' situated in the chest where we find the toad, and the 'cauldron of knowledge' found in the head, the place that the crow perches.

In addition, some teachings in Traditional Witchcraft speak very clearly about the ability to hold or house familiar spirits in one's chest or solar plexus. In doing so, the spirit is then given expression and form through breathing energy and life out through the mouth.[23] No matter how you wish to think of these, whether as "chakra centers" described in eastern practice, sephiroth centers from contemporary Hermetics, or in the more traditional image of the three cauldrons found in ancient European teachings, the reality is that there are areas of the physical body which, when worked with, do produce changes in energy and consciousness.

In my experience this has become one of the fundamental practices that I have found exceptionally powerful. By performing this simple rite daily, you are becoming aware of the forces inherent in nature, and that the same forces reside within you. You are also beginning to learn how to move energy through the body. Remember, *force follows will* and this is frequently carried through the breath. Lastly, you are aligning yourself with the four familiar spirits who watch over this system of magic. With practice you will find that your second sight develops through this procedure, opening your perception and intuition.

Donning the Cloak

Like the dragon, the cloak has long been associated with magic. We see this in a number of legends, from the Celtic God Lugh and His cloak enabling Him to remain concealed, to the cloak of the Lady of the Lake in grail legends casting a veil over Avalon. I find it interesting that there is a long tradition of Witches being able to raise storms by waving cloths and cloaks in the air, suggesting the power contained in the cape effects the wind itself when needed.[24] Folklorist Claude Lecouteux draws a link between the Old English term 'hacele' meaning cloak and 'haechel' which refers to Witchcraft and sorcery.

---

23. I will be discussing the use of breath in magic later in this work.
24. Lecouteux, Claude. *The Tradition of Household Spirits*. 2000.45

The cloak has always been a tool giving anonymity and protection, yet holding within itself power and magic. This of course stems in part from the ancient art of weaving and enchanting articles of clothing while they are made. Yet the essence of the cloak is much more. At once it conceals that which is sacred or esoteric from those not ready to perceive it, protecting that which it is hiding, and yet it holds within it a sum of power conveying this to whomever dons the cloak. It is for this reason that we see images of royalty wearing capes. In these instances, the person is "assuming the mantel" which the cloak or cape presents.

In Traditional Witchcraft, when an actual cloak is worn, to my knowledge these are generally either black, red or green.[25] These are made of natural material such as wool and are worn when working out of doors. In some traditional covens these form the only ritual attire worn in initiation rites.[26] The black cloak is primarily used to help conceal and protect. It can be worn very effectively when meeting at night in secret, allowing one to move more or less unnoticed when in woodlands. The other two cloaks have a more esoteric meaning.

The green cloak embodies within it the fruition of nature and is worn by groups that work extensively with nature spirits such as the Sidh as well as in those covens which Julie used to refer to as 'field and forest' groups. There are a number of Irish ballads that speak of men donning a green cloak and calling to their female lovers to wear their red cloaks.[27] This may harken to the old traditions of the Green Man as the embodiment of masculine virility and the growth of vegetation in the summer. Yet, green also strongly resonates with the Moon, Earth and the feminine power in nature. Like all else in the Art, much depends on the context and purpose applied at the time of ritual.

---

25. I have seen references to blue cloaks as well, however the meaning appears less clear then these three.

26. Howard, Michael. *Liber Nox: A Traditional Witch's Gramarye.* 2014.35

27. "Pretty Moirin O!" Sean Bhean Bhocht, Volumes 1 - 4

The red cloak is very powerful, being worn primarily by women in the Art. Like any cloak it is meant to hold and conceal, and yet it is also the outward expression of the very power and raw life force of nature. In looking into lore from Ireland, documentation from the early 1900's and before indicates that certain women known for the abilities in the Art often wore red cloaks. This was in recognition of their status as leaders while also representing the Goddess of the land itself. Michael Howard explains that women who practiced the Art in East Anglia England also wore red cloaks as part of their magical attire.[28]

This is important, in part, because it shows a measure of continuity with certain covens today. In these a red cloak is worn on certain occasions by the Mistress or by the Maiden showing her power as the living expression of the Witch Queen. In addition, for me this is important as I have had a number of encounters with an otherworld being, a Lady here in the forests of New England, who always appears entirely cloaked in red.[29] For all of the reasons just given you can choose to wear an actual physical cloak in ritual, however, it isn't essential by any means.

Rather, the procedure given here speaks more to the ability to cloak oneself in the essence of nature, or more specifically, the vital force that resonates through the otherworld being whom we refer to as the Great Queen, the Witch Queen, Lady of the Moon, or as the Mistress of this Art. In this technique an interesting parallel can be found in a quote given by Sybil Leek. At the time she was in a hypnotically induced trance. During this, parapsychologist, Hans Holzer, began questioning her about her coven meetings. She stated:

> "*I don't often work with others, [only] certain times of the year. I go first, because I know the way very well in the woods,*

---

28. Howard, Michael. *East Anglian Witches and Wizards.* 2017.23
29. See *Horns of the Moon* for my account of these experiences.

the others come, sometimes we are ten, sometimes thirteen, we draw energy from the trees ... We always succeed because we know the powers ..."

When asked about these powers Sybil said:

"They come from the Moon. The trees go up toward the Moon. The Moon comes down from the sky ... between the trees ... it makes you feel warm. Moonlight is warm."[30]

There is so much hidden in this simple quote. This interview occurred in the early 1960s. First, it shows that her coven gatherings were fairly rare, only occurring at "certain times of the year". This is in keeping with most Traditional Witchcraft groups. These groups tend to be independent Witches who largely practice on their own but are tied through initiation and gather at certain seasonal tides of power, often at the Full Moon closest to the cross quarter corresponding to the traditional Celtic Fire Festivals. When they occur, they are usually in remote areas.

Perhaps what is more telling is Sybil's description of where and how her coven got their power . . . from nature . . . the trees and the Moon. Clearly this was highly experiential, and one could say that it borders on what academics have come to call 'shamanic' in nature.

I cite Sybil's quote as similar imagery is used in the following technique, 'Donning the Cloak'. Through this one learns how to gather this natural force around oneself, and like a cloak, wear this as a mantle of power that can be used in ritual, no matter the purpose. Or, conversely, it can be a magical covering protecting and hiding one as needed. Beyond this though, the cloak can become a vessel which is molded and shaped, producing a glamour that alters how others see and react to you. Thus, this technique is one of energizing and renewing the second skin.

---

30. Holzer, Hans. *The Truth about Witchcraft.* 1969.

It could be argued that the cloak as described in this technique is analogous to what contemporary occultists and parapsychologists have come to call the 'aura'. Both Sybil Leek[31] and Julie did acknowledge the existence of the aura, with Sybil stating that it was the visible appearance of the 'etheric body' or what other teachers have called the second skin. In my experience this energy can be seen and felt by the Witch. Generally, it exists around people, animals and certain objects, though it varies in strength depending on the tide of power in place at the time, as well as from person to person and item to item. The following technique is meant to vitalize and manipulate this field of energy however you choose to think of it.

In performing this, it is important to understand that, while the techniques of the Serpent's Breath given earlier awakens and gathers power, Donning the Cloak preserves, embodies and shapes this. As such the two can and should be used in tandem whenever possible.

As with the Serpent's Breath stand with your feet slightly apart and your arms at your side. Begin with slow, rhythmic breathing using the same pattern as before while you allow yourself to enter a state of Becoming. When ready, envision yourself standing in a forest clearing on a starry night with the Full Moon overhead. Feel the ground beneath you, allowing your awareness to reach down into the earth merging with the energy there. Then gently draw this up through the legs. But rather than seeing this as the red and white dragon currents, instead think of this more as clear water or a silvery energy, flowing upward through the legs, into the torso, and filling the entire body. Let yourself become saturated with this nourishing force. Then, as this seems ready to overflow, allow this to reach out through the top of your head, seeing this as branches of a tree reaching high into the night sky. Or, if preferred

---

31. See Sybil Leek's books *ESP: The Magic Within You* and *The Sybil Leek Book of the Curious and Occult* for her views on the aura.

see this energy as being similar to a fountain, with the energy flowing upward and then flowing around you, encircling you at a distance of about two feet, creating a cocoon of light.

Take your time with this vision. As you do, be aware of the forest around you. The deep roots of the trees; the strength of their trunks and the wonderful canopy of branches stretching toward the sky. Let yourself become aware of these wonderful beings as they too pull energy from the ground. In this one moment allow yourself to feel the connection flowing between yourself and the trees, their energy merging with yours. For, in essence, you are both part of the natural flow inherent in this place.

Now shift your attention to the Moon itself, whether envisioned or, if outside, the actual Moon. Allow its translucent light to flow down over and through you, at once enveloping you and yet becoming one with you. As you do this begin to gently enchant this Gaelic incantation:

"Bandia Gelach,
Airgead Calla,
Dlúthuigh liom."

This is pronounced somewhat like this:

Banjeeah Geloch
Arregot Calla
Dluthuigh Liom (similar to 'lion' but replace the 'n' with an 'm').

Roughly speaking this translates to:

Mistress Moon,
Silver cloak,
Embrace me.

Take as long as you need, reciting the incantation repeatedly in a gentle, rhythmic manner. In doing so see the energy flowing up from the ground and out reaching toward the Moon, and, in turn flowing down from the Moon filling and surround you as powerful cloak.

For obvious reasons, this is much more powerful when actually performed in a forest. But, remember that imagination is the faculty of the mind that is at once able to perceive energies and forces in other realms, yet it is also the means by which we form connections and matrix on an occult level. As such, the act of envisioning, when done with care and discipline, can be highly effective.

At this point one can immediately move on to whatever spell or ritual one is preparing for, using the natural force collect in this. Or, as alluded to earlier, this cloak can be manipulated to affect how others may perceive you. I will be discussing this when we examine the art of 'fascination' and 'overlooking' further in the book.

A Star in the Well

Some may recognize the name of this third technique from the conclusion of *Horns of the Moon*. In that I attempted to tie the book together showing the deeper connection to the worlds and realms beyond this, pulling them into the deeper essence of the self, the well of one's consciousness. The following technique is meant to be a ritualistic means for achieving this. This draws almost exclusively from Ancient Egyptian practices, using names of otherworld beings as *Charms of Power* and linking these directly to oneself. This, of course, ties to the Ancient Egyptian teaching in which the initiate addresses the Gods and states "there is no part of me that is not of thee".

As in the previous two techniques, stand facing the hearth or, barring that, face north.[32] Using the breathing method

---

32. Egyptians saw the north as the realm of the Gods as the 'imperishable ones', because the northern stars never rose or set.

discussed earlier, allow yourself to enter a state of becoming, then visualize a clear, starry night sky overhead. As you do enchant the following:

"Nebet Hetepet"

As the word fades, become aware of a star directly overhead becoming brighter and brighter, growing in size as it appears to come closer. The light from this star increases to a brilliant magnesium fiery white. It is then that you need to clearly say:

"Atum"

As the word leaves your lips, envision the brilliant light of the star merge with you, flowing down from the top of your head and flooding your entire body. Take some time to allow this to build in your awareness. Then, when ready, draw your attention to your feet and the ground that lies beneath. In doing so, imagine the rich green, fertile earth. Then recite:

"Hwt-Hrw" (pronounced 'Hoot-Heru')

As you say this name envision the beautiful horned Goddess Hathor standing before you. Let this image build in form, becoming as clear as possible.

Next, place the tips of your left hand on your right shoulder, your left arm crossing your chest. In doing so picture a large cobra rearing up, with red light emerging from around it just behind and to the right of you. Enchant the name:

"Wadjet"

Now bring your right arm over your chest and across your left arm as you touch your left shoulder. Here a field of white energy encircles the image of a vulture, the totem of the following Goddess whose name you will now intone:

"Nekhebet"

Next spread your arms wide to the sides, envisioning the wings of a great falcon. At your heart the golden Sun shines in radiant glory as the center of your being. Enchant the following name:

"Ra-Horakhty"

This next, final step, is perhaps the most crucial. Let the golden light of the Sun expand out from your chest, reaching out beyond your body becoming a golden sphere surrounding you. Take your time with this visualization as this grows in brilliance and clarity. When this has reached a point of creative reality enchant this last, and most important, Word of Power:

"Iusaas"

Then lower your arms as you let yourself bathe in this orb of gold light. You can then turn your attention to whatever magical working you are now about to perform.

You will notice a distinct pattern emerging when using all three of these techniques in succession. In the first the serpent power of the nature is awakened and pulled into oneself while acknowledging the four familiar spirits tied to the Willow Path of Traditional Witchcraft. In the Donning the Cloak the emphasis is on accessing the lunar force of the Witch Queen as the Moon itself, merging with this. Then in the final step, solar energies tied to the celestial sky are combined in the ritualist, flooding out from the center of one's being. Yet, in this no less than five distinct Egyptian Goddesses are enlisted in this process. Earth, Moon, Sun and Stars all combine within the Witch linking her to the realms and worlds which she accesses in her rites.

Passing the Power

In traditional magical arts ritual passes of the hands play a tremendous role. Repeatedly one will find spells as well as complete rituals that require certain passes and gestures be done to activate the forces evoked. Generally, the right hand is considered that which is most active, evoking positive forces. It is dominant in rites of abundance, prosperity, building up and creating positive change in one's life. The left hand is more receptive, but lends itself generally to removing unwanted influences. I use the term 'generally' because, like so much else in the Art, intention and application are everything. Some will state that the left hand can only be used for negative works such as cursing, while the right is used only positive magic. This is an over simplification and I suspect that those who stick strictly to such an assertion don't fully understand the subject. Rather, either hand can be used in either type of magic. It largely depends on how the Witch approaches her Art. For example, one may cure someone of a disease using the left hand if it is used to remove the unwanted illness. Or one may use the right hand in a hexing, directing the driving force of their will to stop or block another.

As such one can see that perhaps it is best to look to the left and right more for their association in *how energy is delivered* as opposed to imposing a moral standard on either. The right hand is active, solar or martial in nature, working toward material and external goals. The left is more receptive, Lunar and Venusian in nature, functioning on internal, emotional and even spiritual levels. Yes, the left hand can be, and often is used in negative magic, but equally it can work well with creative processes providing it is employed in a manner that is consistent with how it best functions.

It is important to understand though that the simple act of passing one's hand over an object is not in itself sufficient to cause an occult reaction. Rather, it is in the technique of moving energy through the body and out through the hands that causes this. The following is the technique I have been taught for doing this. Traditional Witches call this "Passing the Power", however, I prefer to use the term "The Dua". This is an Egyptian name describing the ritual hand gesture of adoration to the Gods, while in the process, extending energy to these beings as well as to the objects and people important to them.

To perform this, you will need to begin by performing the Serpent's Breath technique. If you also want to incorporate the Cloak and Star, so much the better. Once you have drawn the power into yourself with these enchantments focus your attention on the center of your chest. Envision the heart region as gently but steadily glowing with power, as light. The color will vary depending on the working. The color should correspond to force you are seeking resonance with. If you are not forming resonance with a specific type of planetary or elemental force, brilliant gold or a crisp electric blue are both excellent and highly effective.

Let this power increase as it rides on the rhythm of each breath you take. Then, when you feel as if the energy has reached a peak, allow this to move up into the shoulders, down the arms, and pass out through the palms of your hands. If working with only one hand, envision the flow of power going through that arm and out through the hand in question.

As you do this gently exhale at the same time. If you are using a Charm of Power allow the energy to flow out through the hands with the utterance of the charm. Again, remember, force follows will. By envisioning the power moving through the arms and hands while it rides on the current of your breath, the force *will* follow.

The final step in this is in the recognition that the power gathered has now centered into the object which the hands had directed it to. This process should be maintained for several moments. If you have an incantation or a single

Word of Power that you are using, repeat this over and over while envisioning the power permeating the object. This will increase the effectiveness of process dramatically. You will find that this same process figures highly in the art of fascination though it must be used in a much more subtle way so as not to arouse suspicion. Again, this will be discussed further in the book.

This is the same process used when projecting power by pointing or extending individual fingers. As was shown in *The Willow Path* each finger is ruled over by one of the four elements: the thumb relates to earth, index finger as air, the middle finger is spirit, ring finger is water, while the small or pinky finger resonates with fire. When doing a working involving a specific elemental force, or a goal that clearly falls under the influence of one of these, this energy is sent streaming through the appropriate finger and hand. As such, it is easy to see how one can 'tune' their working accordingly.

It may be important to note that a similar technique forms a part of most Traditional Witchcraft initiation rites. In these, once the candidate has passed the transition through the worlds as represented by key components in the ritual, there comes a point when the Mistress and Master "Pass the Power" to the initiate. This is done by both placing their hands on specific parts of the candidate's body, as well as using the "Charged Breath" on certain centers or cauldrons of the body.

Final Preparations

The Serpent's Breath, the Cloak, and the Star are each meant to be used as a means of attuning oneself to specific forces on a consistent, if not daily, basis. However, once one has settled on a specific rite or spell, there are certain additional steps that can be taken to further enhance one's effectiveness. The following are taken directly from oral teachings given to me. I have seen some of these in print elsewhere, but never all of these together. Keep in mind that these are guidelines.

How strictly you adhere to these is up to you. Some may be harder to follow than others. My advice is to stick with these as closely as possible. However, if you don't or can't follow these, for whatever reason, don't assume your spell won't work. These steps are meant to increase the power of the rite and your sensitivity to the forces invoked, but not following these doesn't necessarily negate the effectiveness of the ritual itself.

Three days (72 hours) prior to the working:
• Avoid eating any red meat or dairy products.
• While sexual stimulation can be a very powerful means of arousing raw psychic energy, refrain from orgasm during this time.

Two days (48 hours) before hand:
• Avoid eating any meat including pork, fish or poultry.
• Refrain from drinking any alcohol.
• Refrain from any caffeine during this time.

One day (24 hours) before hand:
• Drink only water.

Six hours before hand:
• Refrain from eating any solid food.

One hour before the rite:
• Take a ritual bath involving a hand full of salt added to the tub. Incense and a candle should be lit in the room during the bath.
• Drink a small glass of red wine or fruit juice one hour before the working.

Immediately after the bath anoint yourself with an oil that resonates with the working. A good 'all-purpose oil' that we have found to be effective is Vervain. As noted elsewhere traditionally thirteen key points of the body are addressed.

Note that you are only lightly anointing each spot with a 'dab' of oil. There is no need to add excessive amounts of oil:

- The soles of the feet;
- The knees, front and back;
- Genitals;
- Base of the spine and buttocks;
- Navel or solar plexus;
- Breasts;
- Wrists and hands;
- Nape of the neck or under the chin;
- Forehead.

One then dresses or not, depending on the rite involved, and proceeds to perform the ritual.

Again, not all these guidelines may be possible or appropriate for every situation. Nevertheless, the more you can incorporate these into your practice the greater your ability to be aware of and manipulate the energies needed for the rite. While going through these guidelines with me Julie made an important observation:

"Think of the typical football game. In this you have the strongest and most fit young men meeting in a circle, the stadium. Around them is an enthusiastic audience projecting all of their emotional energy into the game. The players have been put on a careful diet and told to refrain from sex in the days leading up to the game. Then, on the sidelines are beautiful young women dancing for the sole purpose of arousing further passion and excitement. It would be the perfect magical ritual if there was someone there directing the energy in a purposeful way."

She made a very real point. In essence, this is exactly what the Witch is doing when she is preparing for ritual. She cleanses her system and opens her centers through diet and bathing. She increases her own passion by at once denying this and yet purposely entertaining the idea of a certain amount of stimulation without allowing this to be fulfilled in the days leading up to the rite. That energy, passion and raw sexual tension is then transferred into the goal of the spell itself.

After the ritual is done, it is essential to just 'let go'. Forget about the spell and go ahead and indulge in the pleasures that were denied. It is for this reason that Witch gatherings were and are often followed by feasting and 'merry making'. If working solitary, by all means treat yourself to a good meal and relaxation, no matter how simple this might be. This helps you to move your focus away from the ritual work, allowing those forces to go and achieve the goal at hand without interference, while helping to bring you back into balance allowing for personal pleasures.

The Serpent Fe

Earlier I spoke of the 'Heka Wand' as a primary Egyptian magical tool that embodied the serpent power itself. In our system, we too have come to use a similar object. This is not unlike the Fe wands discussed in the earlier books but with a few distinct differences. While those were made to correspond to different purposes and uses, this Fe is tied directly to the dragon force in the land linking this to the will of the Witch herself.

This can be of traditional length, from the crook of the arm to the tip of one's middle finger. Recently however, I was introduced to a smaller, more portable version that can be easily concealed. Sometimes known as a "Keppen" these, too, are tailored to match a specific measurement on the Witch's body. The most common length appears to be from the wrist to the tip of one's middle finger.

Whether this is to be full length or that of a Keppen, the Serpent Fe should be made from a live Oak. As always, thanks and offerings to the tree itself and the spirits of the land need be made. Ideally this should be done in the days leading up to the Full Moon when the serpent force is flowing the strongest. This is then carved in the shape of a snake. Because of the strong connection to the raw creative force of nature, this can take on a clearly suggestive shape, often phallic in form, embodying this force. The 'head' of the snake should be obvious, while a small hole is drilled several inches deep into the tip of the wand.

In this hole you will need to place the spine bones of an actual snake. Please, do not hunt down and kill a snake for this purpose. We are very strong animal rights advocates recognizing the spirit that lives in all things. Rather, you will need to find a snake that has already passed. This is actually easier than you may think. For us in New England snakes are prevalent and can be found in most fields, wood piles, stone walls and rotted trees. Their skins and bones are powerful objects which naturally embody the dragon force of the land. As such, bones found in the land on which you live, like the oak that provided the wood, are exceptionally powerful talismanic objects.

Place the dried snake bones deep into the hole. Then, gather the herb Vervain. This can be traditional European Vervain, American Blue Vervain or even Lemon Verbena. On the Vervain place several drops of your own blood, then pack the tip of the wand with this. The hole is then sealed with beeswax, preferably from local bees.

If desired, on the sides of the head mark or carve serpent eyes where these would normally be on a snake. On the lefthand side of the Fe carve or mark sigil of the 'Power of the Lady' with the arrow pointing toward the head. On the righthand side do the same substituting this with the 'Power of the Master' sigil. On the top of the body of the snake the 'Sigil of the Dragon' is also marked. If desired the wood can then be stained with the Witch's own fluid condenser. This, along with the blood in the tip of the Fe, helps to form the distinct link between one's will and the serpent force that the wand will embrace.

The Art

Power of the Lady

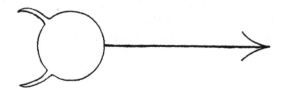

Power of the Master

Sigil of the Dragon

On the night of the Full Moon return to the Oak tree from which the limb was cut.[33] You will need to bring the serpent Fe, your black hilt knife, a bone used in your rites to call the ancient ones, your wind roarer, a small bowl or goblet, wine and either bread, a biscuit or other baked good. You will also need a small spade for digging, three white candles, and your Stang.

At the tree begin by calling on the spirits. This should include the use of the wind roarer and your own personal enchantment which can involve your familiar.[34] Plant the base of the Stang in the ground so that it stands straight up. If needed this can be propped with rocks. Then dig a hole deep enough to place the Fe on end without its head extending above the surface. If available you may want to set some white quartz stones inside the hole or around the rim of the opening.[35]

Then, if space permits, with the black hilt knife trace an equal sided triangle around the well, and set a candle at each of the three corners. At the left side of the triangle place the bowl or goblet filled with wine. On the right set the bread. In front of the triangle place the bone. Holding the serpent Fe in both hands pointing at the crook of the Stang, envision the power of the land and trees flowing into the Fe as the dragon force of nature itself. When ready recite:

"Master of the Wild Wood,
Horned One in the night,
Janicot, Janicot, (pronounced "Hanicot")

---

33. It is completely fine to return on the following month's Full Moon to perform this next step. In this way you have an entire lunar month to carve and prepare the Fe.

34. See *The Willow Path* for information on this.

35. We have made a permanent 'crystal well' at the site that the Lady in Red first appeared. It is in the Well that different offerings, workings and the enchantment of different objects - including the Serpent Fe - have been done.

Janicot, Janicot.
Serpent power and dragon's breath,
Arise, awake this Full Moon night."

Now raise the Fe to the Full Moon. As you do let the light of the Moon flow into the wand seeing this as a steady stream bringing it to life with the Lady's breath:
"Silver circle and crystal well,
She who rides in the night,
Witch Queen & Mistress
Bandia Gelach, Bandia Gelach,
Bandia Gelach, Bandia Gelach,
Dragon's power in Full Moon's light."

Place the Fe in the well, its head pointing toward the sky. Then, using the Dua, pass the power you have summoned into the wand, creating the resonance and link between yourself, the serpent's breath in the land and the light of the Mistress above. In doing so you may want to recite the following Words of Power:

"Bandia Gelach, Bandia Gelach,
Janicot, Janicot"

This is then followed by repeating this enchantment over and over until you feel the distinct merging of the red and white dragons into the Fe:

"Anál nathrach
Bandia Gelach
Draiocht dénmha"

Pronounced:

"Onal NathRack
Banjeeah Geloch
Dray-aht de-N-may"

When done, hold the Fe in your hands as you state:

"By Dragons Red & White
By they who ride in Full Moon's light,
From Crystal Well and woodland deep
This Serpent Fe my will to keep."

The Fe is now ready for use. Remove the Fe from the well. Then, holding up both the wine and the bread, make an offering of thanks to the Mistress and Master, spirits of this place, and to the forest itself. Be sure to drink and eat some of this yourself then pour the rest in the well. If you are not planning to use the well in the future fill this in. Be sure to remove your candles and then return home.

Chapter Three

✤ SPIRITS ON THE HEARTH ✤

For the Traditional Witch, the place one practices the Art is immensely important. Whether this be a clearing in a forest or standing before the hearth in one's home, forming a relationship with the land, the locale and more importantly the spirits who reside there is vital. Ceremonial magicians generally pick which spirits they prefer to work with, depending upon which grimoire they are referring to. The Witch can do the same. Yet more often than not, she will first seek to form alliances with those spirits already present. This can and often does include spirits who are tied directly to the home. The tradition of household spirits is very old.

This should not be confused with familiar spirits. Rather, the spirits of the home and land on which one lives form a different layer of magical partnership, one that I have only briefly discussed so far. The extent to which you are able to practice this is going to vary greatly depending on your living conditions. Needless to say, much depends on the building itself and its location. Urban settings hold very different energies and attract different types of spirits than country dwellings. Also, the age of the home matters. Older homes have history, with many years of people living and dying in them. Whether urban or rural, over time homes do attract forces and spirits to them. Most are fairly benign, having only a subtle influence on the occupants, while others can be quite potent, making their presence known in very tangible and sometimes disturbing ways. These were often referred to as revenants – spirits who have returned to haunt the living.

Houses also tend to build up an 'atmosphere' of sorts: a distinct character and personality. This is largely made up of the emotional energy projected by those who have lived there. Whether positive or negative, this can be thought of as a type of psychic 'soup' composed of lingering thoughts and feelings coalescing in home. Through the years this tends to seep into the very fabric of the building itself. It is through this that the house begins to take on a life of its own manifesting as its own rudimentary spirit and character.

To understand this it is important to recall that in the Art we recognize the animistic nature of reality. That is, at its core, all is consciousness. This consciousness tends to 'collect' or 'pool' forming identity and personality. This is not unlike the way in which different tools of the Art take on power. For example, one's Fe, once properly prepared becomes its own separate entity that is specifically attuned to you. So too the home takes on life and power. It is in this regard that the Witch uses her knowledge to work with the innate consciousness of the house and land it is situated on, as well as any spirits who reside there, again, forming an alliance with these.

Ideally, if one is able, the actual building of a new home can be the best way to ensure the optimum practice for drawing in and shaping the identity of the eventual spirit that will inhabit the place. But this comes with a measure of work. Still, if one has the means this can be very powerful.

The first step in such a task is in choosing the right location. My recommendation is to look for some place rural, fairly far from the influence of larger cities and neighborhoods. In doing so, look to the natural features of the land itself. Take long walks on the property and surrounding area. Let yourself wander in a state of becoming, experiencing the 'feel' of the place. Look for any signs or omens that may tell you that this is the right place for you.

For example, in selecting our place in New England we looked at multiple locations. However, the land we eventually settled on had several dramatic features. These included a number of natural 'signs' that we found that spoke directly to us. These included a small cliff face covered in moss that has the distinct profile of the Green Man, a clearing in the trees at the top of the highest point in the forest, a number of clefts and small caves, and on our first exploration of the property we found a set of bear bones.[36] In nature, these are fairly rare to find as the scavengers quickly remove all remains. Beyond this, though there was an unmistakable sense of power and presence only found in the hidden places of nature. For us, this was the perfect place to reside.

Whether one is building a home or moving into an existing building the process is essentially the same. Take the time to get the feel of the place, inside and out. Look for the signs that this may be the right place for you. Whenever possible try to spend a night in the location. This was a common practice in preindustrial times. In doing so, if one could spend the night peacefully without having disturbing dreams or visitations the place was often deemed as suitable.

If you are planning to build, before doing so, folkloric tradition strongly suggests seeking permission from the spirits of the locale itself. This can be through simple acts of leaving food offerings with a modest verbal statement explaining what you intend to do and specifically asking permission of the forces inherent in the space. If desired more elaborate rites of evocation can be performed. The ritual of *Calling the Sidh* [37] can be an excellent means for gaining this permission. The point is to take some time to become aware of the forces and spirits of the specific plot itself, introducing yourself, and forming a relationship right from the beginning.

As for what type of spirit or spirits these may be, this can and will vary greatly. Again, much of this depends on the

---

36. Interestingly, in Slavic practices bear fur and presumably bones were often placed in new homes to ward off evil spirits.

37. See *Horns of the Moon* for this.

location of the property and its history. If deep in nature where there has been little in the way of human occupation, the spirits are going to be more of a loci genii intelligence. That is, spirits tied directly to the land itself. In Witchcraft the environment is seen as being filled with spirits. Oral traditions around the world speak of the Sidh, brownies, elves, elementals, dwarves, djinn and so much more.

On the other hand, if the place is one that humans have readily occupied it is common for spirits of the dead to be present. Your task will be to communicate with these entities, gaining their acceptance and, over time, their partnership. For obvious reasons, old cemeteries and burial grounds should be avoided. Also, former battlefields and other places in which violence or the restless dead may still be active can be troublesome. This also applies to animal slaughter fields. These should be approached carefully as these spirits may remain as part of the fabric of the place.

If you find that you simply have no choice but to build on a location that did have some unfavorable past, it was often customary to purify the plot by 'salting the land'. That is, sprinkle salt over the site to help dispel any residue negative influences. This is a very old custom, and one which some today may be resistant to do. Yet clear documentation exists showing that, at least in some cases, it was quite common to salt the plot in advance of most construction.

Once the site is chosen it is customary to mark the basic outline of the foundation with a trench or hedge, as if working the land like a farm field. This was often done with the hearth hook that would later be used in the actual hearth. The reason being is that, once built, the hearth itself becomes the point in the home where the spirit will settle.

When one begins building the actual home the foundation is critical. In many older homes across Europe and Colonial America it was common to place 'deposits' of magical items in the walls, or directly in the foundation. In fact, this is a very ancient technique reaching at least as far back as Egypt. There, specific sacred objects and talismans were placed in pits at the four corners of temples during construction.[38]

When looking to medieval buildings some of the items placed in deposits included coins and tokens representing prosperity, talismans to attract happiness, as well as protective amulets to keep the house safe. It was also very common to seal the remains of an animal inside the foundation or walls. The intent was that the spirit of the animal was meant to be a guardian protecting the home. In time, it was often common to substitute fertile eggs for animal remains. These were placed in cavities inside the foundation.[39]

One of the most intriguing items placed in home deposits were old shoes. It is very common to find shoes walled up inside older buildings. Shoes were long seen as representative of prosperity and abundance. This was in part because of the effort and cost involved in making and purchasing shoes, particularly during medieval periods. Many of the common people wore rags on their feet for much of the year simply because they couldn't afford shoes. Too, shoes took on a sexual connotation. They were often seen as symbolic of the vulva. Thus, they represented fertility, love and pleasure. This association with sexuality and fertility is, of course, seen thinly veiled in the tales of Cinderella and the glass slipper, as well as such old nursey rhymes as the *"woman who lived in a shoe, who had so many children she didn't know what to do"*.

Whether building a new home, or moving into a house that you have purchased it is a simple matter to physically install magical objects into the actual structure of the house. On the other hand, if you are renting these can be placed strategically in the home living space (as opposed to the structure itself) without drawing undue attention. In such cases placing these in basements, high up on

---

38. Wilkinson, Richard. *The Complete Temples of Ancient Egypt*. 2000.38-39

39. Paul Huson gives an excellent adaption of the use of a fertilized egg for home protection in his book *Mastering Witchcraft*.

closet shelves, on rafters in an attic, concealed above ceiling tiles, under loose floor boards; all can be excellent places to hide these.

Home Prosperity Deposit

This is a simple technique which we have used quite successfully. During the Waxing Moon, on either the day of *The Lady of the Fe, The Lady of Abundance*, or *The Lady Whom the Gods Adore*,[40] or barring these chose the day and hour of Jupiter, draw the *Seal of Sustained Wealth*[41] shown below. We often use small Birch Bark squares, parchment, or small mounted canvas squares for our talismans.

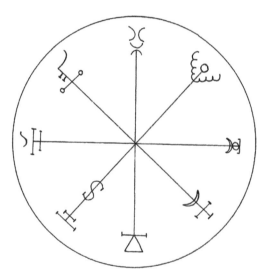

Seal of Sustained Wealth

---

40. See *Horns of the Moon* for these dates.

41. It can be challenging to get all of the timing to coincide with many spell instructions. Do the best you can. You are seeking to gather in the energies from the various tides of power available. For this spell, at a minimum, it needs to be performed during the waxing Moon with a Jupiter influence (hour and/or day).

Some may recognize this from the 7th pentacle of Jupiter found in the *Key of Solomon*. We have found that the patterns found in this and other medieval Grimoires can be exceptionally powerful.[42] In our practice we purposely do not include the mottos that were sometimes placed around the edges of these talismans, finding them distracting at best. Rather, repeated experimentation has shown that it is the patterns themselves and not the mottos which bring power to the image.[43]

When finished place the talisman in a Triangle of Art, the edges of which can be marked by sprinkling Vervain, Juniper and Bayberry. While not essential, if desired, blue or purple candles can be placed at each point of the triangle. A green candle is then set inside the triangle. The talisman is placed at base of the green candle. Anoint the green candle with either Olive Oil or Vervain Oil. Then light this.

Next, power is passed into the talisman using the *Dua* described earlier. In doing so recite the following incantation while envisioning money and prosperity coming to you and the home. Be as creative and expansive as you can in this visualization. In doing so allow this to flow as energy down through your hands and into the talisman. Remember that your imagination is creating the matrix through which the forces can flow. So, envision this to the fullest. However, do not specify how the prosperity will manifest. Like water, magic follows the lines of least resistance. You don't want to limit your opportunities. Rather, be open to letting good fortune come by whatever means it can best manifest in your life.

---

42. Interestingly, many of these texts often contain a mix of ritual magic and Hermetics while also describing clear folkloric rural practices.

43. This is discussed further, in detail, in the chapter involving talismanic images.

"baH HAw, baH HAw,[44]
Prosperity in abundance
Comes through the door!
baH HAw, baH HAw
Money and Good Fortune,
Riches Evermore!"

This incorporates the direct use of Words of Power coupled with a simple rhyming chant. Repeat this over and over as the power moves through your hands into the talisman. Once you feel the transfer is complete leave the talisman in the triangle, allowing the green candle to burn itself out. The talisman is then placed in a small wooden box along with any number of coins or other denominations of money[45] as well as the herbs and any wax left over from the triangle. This is then concealed in the far-left hand corner of the house as one faces the entrance looking in. It should be noted that historically examples have been found of similar talismans tacked into the corner of homes. These are often accompanied by a written copy of the incantation used when it was enchanted.

Witch Marks
Whether you build your own home, or move into a preexisting residence you may want to place specific markings in important places. Traditionally these were known as 'Witch Marks'. Currently there is much controversy surrounding these as some historians feel that these would not have been used by Witches at all, as they were intended to protect the home from Witchcraft. Such arguments however miss the point of these sigils entirely.

---

44. Ancient Egyptian Words of Power which mean 'Wealth in Abundance' – pronounced 'Baa Haoo'.

45. Because our talisman was going directly into wet cement we wrapped this in plastic with a number of rare silver coins and paper denominations of money.

Not only were these meant to provide protection, but they were also intended to bring good fortune. Further, these same historians seldom consider that many documented cases of Witchcraft involved people who were, for the most part, practicing positive magic. It seems only logical that these same wise women and men would be called on to protect a home while also bestowing good fortune.

I addressed the use of one of the most famous of these markings previously;[46] that is *The Mare* and its connection to the many horse Goddesses of Europe. By carving or burning this into the actual structure of the home the essence of the Witch Queen as the Mare Goddess was evoked.

Mare "Witch Mark"

Another mark that is very common and quite powerful is what we call the *Sigil of Warding*.

Sigil of Warding

---

46. See *Horns of the Moon* for information on this.

This appears in many older homes and buildings across Europe and into Colonial America. From being stamped directly into metal door handles, to being carved into door lintels, the sigil of warding was used to protect the home by stopping all negative forces and entities from encroaching on the space. Often the mantel of a fireplace, or a post in the center of the room was made of Rowan, a wood known for its protective properties. On these, the sigil of warding was frequently carved, enhancing the protective qualities of the wood itself.[47]

Other Witch markings that were placed near doors and windows included those known as *Spirit Binding Knots*. There are several different examples of these. However, each essentially serves the same function, that is to protect the home from evil spirits, influences and curses. When a spirit encounters a binding knot it becomes transfixed or enchanted by this to the point that it is bound by the sigil and thus, is under the Witch's control. In Traditional Witchcraft one of the most commonly used binding knots is:

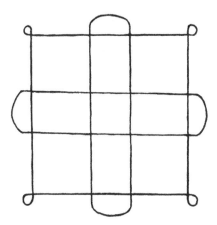

The Binding Knot

---

47. Lecouteux, Claude. *The Tradition of Household Spirits*. 2013, photo insert.

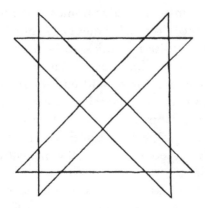

Common variation of the Binding Knot

In Germany a similar pattern is used. This is frequently referred to as a "Schratterlgatterl".

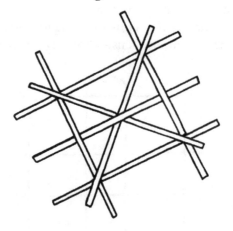

The Schratterlgatterl

The Witch's Foot, or pentagram, has been used in a very similar way for centuries. One technique that I use regularly is to seal the home by first performing the Dua and then carefully tracing a pentagram over the door of the house or at the edge of the property. This creates a barrier sealing the entrance.

Beyond these there are many other Witch Marks that are used in Traditional Witchcraft. Each can be craved into the home itself. They can also be carried as individual sigils acting in the role of amulets. Too, I often employ these in ritual itself, tracing these over objects or during specific spells to enhance the working's effectiveness. These markings are pulled from many different historical sources, possessing a variety of purposes. I will be giving examples of many of these throughout this book.

It is important to know that each of the workings given so far are meant to enlist the services of various forces and spirits. By asking permission, giving food offerings, placing the deposits in the building itself, and inscribing protective sigils on the structure, one is approaching the spirits of the house and the land, asking them to accept their new role as aid and protector of the house and family.

The Hearth

Throughout these books I have repeatedly expressed the importance of the hearth. Without a doubt this stems from my training with Julie and her family. For it was here that they performed much of their magic. The fact is that the hearth has always been critical to the practice of rural expressions of the Art. Seen as the center of the home, it was the hearth that acted as the point of contact between worlds.

Earlier I had mentioned the hearth hook, which is normally used in the hearth to hang pots or the cauldron over the coals. This also plays an important role in hearth magic as it was seen as the embodiment of the house spirit. As such a common custom is to place a hand on the hook while swearing an oath or evoking the spirit. Wine is often poured over the hook as an offering to the home spirit. In some older rural practices when a new bride entered the home for the first time she would touch the hook as a gesture binding her to the family spirit residing in the home.

Unfortunately, most newer homes don't have this luxury. If yours does have an actual hearth you should take full advantage of this. Today woodstoves are beginning to take the place of the traditional hearth. These can be a wonderful alternative, serving very much in the role. However, if your situation is such that neither is possible there are other options.

Early in my training I had the opportunity to learn from some Welch Traditionalists. To avoid prying eyes, they practiced their craft in the attic of their home. There they had a separate room on which they had laid the triple circle representing Annwn, Abred and Gwynfyd. As a hearth they placed a large flat stone in the center of the circle on which they laid four rectangular blocks interlocked in the pattern of a 'solar cross', similar to a Bridget's Cross, yet forming a square opening in the center. Inside this they would build a small fire. This was their hearthstone or 'altar'.

One can easily adapt similar practices in lieu of an actual fireplace. For example, one can place the Table of Art in a discreet yet accessible spot in the home. On this a single candle may be set near the back of the table with a small Stang measuring between twelve and eighteen inches high, standing just behind this. Gemma Gary uses a similar arrangement with a 'Hood Lamp'[48] made with an iron horseshoe attached to a small shaft. Between the two horns of the horseshoe a candle is placed. In both examples, these act very similar to the hearth, while also drawing in the energies that the Stang brings through. Keep in mind that Julie had often explained that the hearth was the meeting point of all five elements, yet she also made it clear that the candle also held these same elemental features.[49]

In a similar vein, I have known of some Witches who place a candle to either side of the Table of Art at the back corners, then a third, taller candle was place at the rear center of the table, directly between these. This was meant to act in

---

48. Gray, Gemma. *Traditional Witchcraft: A Cornish Book of Ways*. 2008.
49. See *The Willow Path* for a detailed discussion on Julie's teachings regarding the hearth and candles.

every way as the flame between the Horns, and as the spirit
of the hearth itself.

On a more conventional level, in any home, those spaces
that provide heat or where one cooks food have long been
seen as the equivalent of the hearth. In whatever form a
home's hearth takes, it is here that traditionally the house
spirits normally reside making their presence known. As
such food offerings may be presented to them here. This
should be done not only during ritual, also on a regular
basis showing gratitude while keeping communication
with them open. It is advisable to address the spirits daily,
always showing respect.

Some Witches will place a small poppet on the hearth
inviting the spirit to enter and use this as a home. I am also
aware of some who will place ceramic or actual skulls on
hearth with the same purpose in mind. In doing so these will
often be inscribed with sigils of spirit summoning.

Once one has established a relationship with the spirits
of the home, the Witch can then move on to other practices
to ensure the place is at once protected and yet is inviting
positive influences that will bring prosperity.

Chapter Four

SETTING THE WARDS
PROTECTION & COUNTER MAGIC

Having discussed some of the means by which spirits can be enlisted to aid in the protection of the home, it is important to understand that there are times when one is confronted by some otherworld beings who simply aren't interested in such alliances. In fact, it is very likely that you will encounter entities who become hostile. This can lead to hauntings with all of the classic phenomena associated with them.

Beyond contact with discarnate entities, there are other types of occult interference that the Witch needs to contend with. Earlier I mentioned that we literally live in a type of 'psychic soup'. The emotions and thought-forms generated by the internal motivations of others, along with the unintentional general psychic energy people leave, surrounds us. It permeates our environment, increasing exponentially in highly populated areas. For those of us who practice the Art, consciously seeking to open our senses, this can be a big problem. Because of the increase in sensitivity there is the real possibility that these energies will affect one in very tangible ways.

Finally, make no mistake about it, once you set foot on the path of the Witch or magician inevitably someone will take notice. Unfortunately, human nature being what it is, at some point there will be those who will seek to challenge you through occult means. Whether out of fear, jealousy, anger, or the mere fact that they can, there are people who are far too willing to cast hexes and curses without thinking twice about it.

Setting the Ward

The questions then become how do you recognize occult interference when it is happening? How does one identify its source? And, lastly what can you do to either repel, or at the least, isolate the forces involved?

The first thing that needs to be realized is that not every piece of bad luck or unusual coincidence is an indication that one is somehow under psychic attack. I have known far too many people who have pushed themselves into self-fulling prophecies of personal 'doom' by believing that they were under a hex with no clear reason other than they were having a 'bad day'. As psychologists will be quick to point out the mere perception of being cursed can cause some people to become frantic with worry, drawing the very misfortune they fear to them through their own negative attitude and actions. The reality is that sometimes life is tough. Challenges and misfortune can and do happen. They are part of what helps us to grow and evolve as spiritual beings. There doesn't have to be a nefarious reason, sinister person or evil entity behind these.

Having said this, occult interference is very real. I have experienced this myself on several occasions. This has ranged from situations in which I intuitively knew that I needed to avoid specific places, to experiencing very real poltergeist phenomena while living in haunted houses. Then there were those time when I have been the direct target of curses and blastings cast by some very talented members in the Art. Psychic attack can and does happen.

Learning to recognize the signs that accompany psychic interference early on is critical. Fortunately, there are specific 'symptoms' you will want to become aware of. The more of these symptoms that occur, as well as their severity, the greater the likelihood of them being the result of occult causes.

Some of the first symptoms that one may experience include a growing sense of unease. This can be accompanied by sleeplessness. When one does sleep it tends to be restless and is often punctuated by nightmares. Pay close attention

71

to these dreams as clues will emerge revealing whether the interference is caused by an entity, energies in the location itself, or if it is the result of a well-placed curse. Dreams can also help to reveal the identity of the person who may be trying to influencing you.

From these dreams you may be able to infer the motive of the person or entity involved. Keep in mind that they may not be meaning any harm at all. In fact, in some cases the person may not realize that they are causing you any disturbance. For example, you may find that you are having repeated dreams of an acquaintance. The dreams may take on a vivid and pointed nature. This doesn't necessarily mean that the person is casting some type of spell. Often it may be something as simple as the person secretly being an admirer to the point that they may have been indulging in personal fantasies. These fantasies, in turn, may be projected unconsciously by them manifesting in your dreams.

In such cases the energies involved are essentially the same, yet when fantasy is involved this is generally meant as a private affair with no real intention of influencing the other. Of course, on the other hand, it could very well be that this person is purposely targeting the Witch with spells. In either situation, if the interference is unwelcomed the Witch has every right to repel the interference, or better yet isolate this energy for her own use later.

It is important to know that there are a number of otherworld beings who are known to sometimes manifest in dreams. These can vary greatly. Much depends on the occult work one may be involved with at the time. I have had many occasions when I have been steadily evoking different Gods and Goddesses ritually, only to find that they communicate later in dreams immediately after the rites. This is part of a very old technique used in Ancient Egypt.[50] In this the goal

---

50. Finnestad, Ragnhild Bjerre. "Temples of the Ptolemaic and Roman Periods: Ancient Traditions in New Contexts". *Temples of Ancient Egypt.* 1997.236

is specifically to gain such communication with these being through dreams.

But there are other entities who can be quite bothersome in dreams. If not dealt with they can drain vitality away from one in very real ways. These of course are vampiric in nature. I discussed these to some extent in *Horns of the Moon*. While romanticized in literature and contemporary culture the reality is that these types of entities literally gain their sustenance by drawing energy from one's second skin, or etheric double. Classic examples of these can be found in the form of vampires, incubi and succubae and any number of skin-walker forms. Too, folk teachings surrounding 'riding the second skin' of another person fall into this category.

Keep in mind that dreams alone don't always indicate that one is experiencing some form of psychic influence. On the contrary, the subconscious speaks to us in highly symbolic ways through the healthy process of dreaming. Don't confuse your own deep mind and its methods of cleaning out the cobwebs of the past in natural sleep with the influence of someone or something else. Generally, you will find that dreams that have their root to genuine occult influences are very vivid, carrying a lucid quality about them that stands out as different and powerful when compared to those that are simply the mind cleaning its closets. Even in those cases when one does experience repeated lucid dreams remember that this is just one of the signs indicating possible interference. You must also see if any other symptoms are occurring as well.

In decidedly malicious attacks, whether from human or otherworld entities, a steady pattern of misfortune over an extended period of time frequently takes place. This can manifest both in your personal and professional life. When psychic attack is occurring it is common to have problems with electrical and mechanical devices breaking down or simply not working. This can also include glassware inexplicably cracking and breaking.

Under such attacks you may begin feeling ill, coming down with perfectly normal afflictions but they then become severe, taking longer to heal. You can experience aches, pains, nausea, dizziness and general fatigue beyond what you normally are used to. A very common symptom is the unexpected death of a beloved pet who, as far as known, was healthy beforehand. If the curse was directed specifically at you, oftentimes a pet that is very personal to you will take the brunt of the attack.

Repeated clumsiness and accidents can be a symptom of negative influences. Excessive arguments and tension with others, as well as periods of confusion, forgetfulness and inattention to detail beyond what one normally experiences; all of these can be indications as well.

If an entity is involved, whether of its own design or sent to do the bidding of someone else, you will begin seeing shadowy forms out of the corner of your eye. They can appear as being very fleeting yet distinct. As soon as you turn to look directly at them, usually, they will be gone. Yet, you know you saw something. Rather, it is better to continue to keep your gaze forward, while observing the forms as they appear in the corner of your eye.

You may begin experience haunting in the house. This can be as minor as hearing voices or odd knockings but eventually become full blown poltergeist phenomena. I recall one situation when living in an old home in North Carolina. We experienced footsteps on the stairs, furniture moving, doors opening on their own, lights turning on by themselves, candles lighting with no apparent cause and more. At one point, the woman I was living with felt hands on her back as she was pushed down a set of stairs. She experienced major bruising, but no bones were broken. It was at that point that we decided to use our Art to remove the unwanted influence.

When entities are involved it is very common to have everyday objects suddenly disappear despite having been placed in the same spot they have always been kept for years.

These are usually objects that have personal meaning, or are items used on a very consistent basis. You may search the entire area, backtracking your steps and not find them. Then, oftentimes days later, these will reappear out in the open, in a place you had searched or a place you regularly use, with no apparent reason for how they got there. For example, the item may suddenly appear in the middle of a table, on the bed you made just that morning, or on the kitchen floor that you had cleaned and walked through countless times in the days that the object was missing.

You will find too that if you wear silver jewelry on a consistent basis, when you come into contact with harmful energy, the silver tarnishes very quickly. Much more so than normal. I have seen black splotches of tarnish literally appear within minutes of encountering people who were very angry and putting off a lot of energy. Perhaps it is for this reason that silver has always been seen as a mineral that at once purifies and protects.

Again, any of these alone or even combined with another don't necessarily indicate that one is under some form of curse. However, the more of these that occur over a short time, as well as the intensity involved in their manifestation, the greater the probability of some form of cunning interference.

Pay attention to the time in the lunar month when these different phenomena occur. You will find that visitations and full visual manifestations of entities occur more frequently during the week leading up to and following the Full Moon. This includes dreams involving vampiric entities. The reason is that the Dragon's Breath, as well as the Nephesh of Hermetic teachings is readily available. As such, entities who work in the Abred using astral currents can gather this easily at this time of the month. Having said this, hauntings of a negative sort tend to occur more during the waning Moon.

Curses are most likely to be directed at one during the waning Moon, particularly during the last quarter. If you suspect that someone is going to blast you the most likely time that this will be done will be in the days leading up to Dark Moon. Be particularly mindful of the Tuesday or Saturday just before the Dark Moon as both are days that a baneful curse would be highly effective.

In magic the best defense begins by ensuring that you yourself are protected on a personal level. This involves ensuring that you maintain your health through all normal physical means including diet and exercise. Beyond this, the regular use of the Serpent, Cloak and Star techniques helps to keep your energy healthy and strong while sealing the second skin so that entities and negative forces have a harder time of influencing you without your consent.

Oftentimes a relaxing, cleansing bath can help tremendously in removing negative influences while strengthening one's natural defenses. A simple method for this is to burn Rosemary as an incense while taking the bath. To the water add a handful of Hyssop, crushed or chopped pine needles and salt. You can also have a black candle burning to negate any negative energy that may be present.

Beyond this there are specific objects that the Witch will frequently carry on her. I already spoke of the power of silver. Silver rings, bracelets and necklaces are very useful for this. They also have the added benefit of relating to the lunar essence of the Witch Queen Herself, drawing Her power to one.

The Nata or Elf Bag

Another item that is highly effective is the Nata Bag; sometimes referred to as an elf bag,[51] charm bag, mojo bag or, among native American people, as a medicine bag. This is highly individual. Ideally this should be durable as you will carry this on you throughout the day, and keep it nearby when sleeping. Like all of your tools this will also take on a life of its own and you will learn exactly what it needs

---

51. Howard, Michael. *East Anglian Witches and Wizards*. 2017.136

to continue to act as both a protector and as a force that attracts good fortune.

I have seen these made of cloth or from animal hide. My own was made by a local Abenaki native American woman from deerskin. It is very robust, yet it is also soft to the touch. In this I have placed a number of herbs and minerals. Some of these include Vervain, Solomon Seal root, Beth Root, Rosemary and Mugwort, a small piece of silver taken from a talisman dedicated at my initial initiation more than forty years ago, some Oak, a small Jet stone, a small topaz, the first wild violet of spring each year, and a few other personal ingredients that tie the bag to me.

As I mentioned, this should be carried at all times. They are small and compact, sliding easily into a pocket, or worn on a cord around the neck. The best time of year to start your own is during the waxing Moon following Beltane. Think carefully about the items you want to put in this. You don't have to use the same ones that I listed above. Rather, find those that resonate well with you. However, be certain to include traditional herbs and minerals that relate specifically to both protection and good fortune.

Don't underestimate the power of this simple bag. It has proven to be a valuable tool. Just carrying this brings with it the influence of these plants and minerals. However, I have found that it can be used ritually as well by placing this on the hearthstone to lend power to the rite. When I am having a particularly stressful day, I find it calming to take a moment to pull the bag from its keep and gentle rub this, sometimes holding it to my nose to inhale the scent of the combined ingredients.

You will want to feed this on a fairly consistent basis. Feeding the Nata consists of placing a pinch of fresh herbs in the bag. Then, each year at Beltane I will empty the contents, replacing the herbs with fresh but keeping the minerals and other objects.

The Hag stone in Protective Magic

In *The Willow Path* I spoke of the Hag Stone. This natural object is considered by most Traditional Witches to be a powerful talismanic aid. Wearing this as a necklace brings both protection as well as the regenerative essence of the Great Queen Herself. For me, I find it to be very similar in effect to the more ritually created Lamen of ceremonial magic. In this way it at once resonates with, and acts as, a focal point of power for the Witch. It is one of the most potent items that the Witch owns, embodying her craft while also carrying with it the authority to conjure or banish as she wills.

The unique thing about the Hag Stone is that each has its own personality. As I may have stated elsewhere these stones tend to find the Witch, rather than the Witch finding the stone. A clear relationship forms with the spirit of the stone and it is through this spirit's aid that the power of the Queen comes through. This can be an exceptionally powerful item to wear either openly or under one's clothing so as not to attract undue attention. I am seldom without mine.

These are often incorporated into protective amulets, strung together with other items and placed near doors and windows. Frequently they will be hung on bedposts to ward off evil, helping to keep nightmares away.

Seal of Protection

Another powerful object that is used extensively by Traditional Witches is the *Seal of Protection*. One of the earliest representations of this appeared in Reginald Scot's *The Discoverie of Witchcraft* published in 1584 CE. Undoubtedly Scot took this from earlier sources. There are any number of ways that one can incorporate this into an amulet that is easy to carry on oneself or placed in the home. The following is the formula we use for making and enchanting this.

Ideally this should be done on the third day of the Waxing Moon. This is the day of the *Lady of the Besom*. While this day relates directly to joy, fertility and pleasure, there is a second name given to the energies that come through here – *The Lady who fights for Her Lord.* As such, this is one of the most powerful days in the lunar month for protective works because it evokes the energies found in many of the ancient warrior Goddesses.

Barring this, you can choose to perform this ritual on a Tuesday or Saturday during the Waxing Moon. You will want to have set up a Table of Art or use your normal Hearthstone. On this trace an equal sided triangle. This can be drawn in chalk, flour, or even permanently painted onto a cloth that you then place on the table. If you are performing this outdoors, the triangle can be traced on the ground, or you may use herbs or flour to mark this.

If working in the Roth Fail (circle or maze) the Stang is placed in the north with a candle between the horns. As an alternative you can place a smaller Stang at the rear of the hearthstone, standing this up. In front of this, just outside of the furthest point on the triangle place a red taper candle.

You will want to have a small fireproof dish or incense burner on the hearthstone with a burning coal in this. This can be an incense charcoal block, available at many metaphysical and occult shops, or if you are working outside you can build a small fire and use the embers from this for the rite.[52]

As an incense, gather equal parts of dried Elecampane, Mugwort and St. John's wort. If desired, include White Sandalwood to give it a more pleasant scent. These are then powdered and mixed together. As an alternative you can mix Sandalwood and Vervain in equal portions. Or, if you are in a pinch, dried cedar wood and needles are excellent for protection.

You will also want an oil for anointing the candle. Like the incense, you may make this yourself from the same herbs

---

52. Do not use barbeque charcoal when working indoors as this is very toxic and can be deadly.

just listed. If you are uncertain on how to do this, you can purchase a vial of Sandalwood oil and place dried Vervain in this. Then allow it to steep for a lunar month.

In addition, you will need either a quality paper, parchment, or a small piece of clean Birch Bark. Birch Bark has a paper like consistency and yet is silky soft on the underside, feeling very much like skin. It is a wonderful medium for the creation of talismans, with the added advantage of holding up to the elements far better than paper.

With these you are going to need a quality pen and ink. If you would like you can make your own. There are several excellent traditional recipes that you can use for this.[53] However, I have found that using a normal good quality pen purchased just for your spell crafting works very well. This will need to be present for this working. If desired you can draw the seal out in advance. I will often trace this carefully in pencil first and then go over this in ink afterwards. This ensures that no part of the design is missed or drawn incorrectly. On the other hand, you can elect to draw this in the actual rite itself. The choice is yours.

Along with these items you will want your normal ritual tools, including a small offering of wine and food to be given to the spirits at the end of the rite. At the appointed time, perform the Serpent, Cloak and Star. Then call the spirits as normal. If working in the Roth Fail establish this now. Once all is ready focus your attention on the triangle. Scatter the protective incense on the coals and anoint the candle with the protective oil. Placing the candle at the furthest point of the triangle, or in the crook of the Stang (if working with a large Stang), light this as you intone:

"Between the horns lays the path we keep"

Then, if you haven't done so already, draw the seal of protection to the best of your ability. This needs to be

---

53. See the chapter on mirror working giving the recipe for Lampblack ink.

in your own hand; not a photocopy or printout from a computer. Examples of this seal have been found going back hundreds of years. Many of these are crude in form but clearly served the purpose. So much so that they have survived the years hidden away tacked to rafters in homes, protecting these structures that are still standing.

Seal of Protection

When finished place the seal in the center of the triangle. Then perform the Dua/Passing of the Power, breathing life into this, while you chant:

"Neamhshaolta (pronounced *NAV-HEALTA*)
Neamhshaolta
Neamhshaolta
By my breath I conjure you,
By these words I conjure,
By this seal I conjure you!
No evil, no curse, no spirit can cross
This seal of protection,
This shield embossed!
By my will I conjure you,
By the spirits of the Art I conjure you!

Neamhshaolta
Neamhshaolta
Neamhshaolta
Sciath (Pronounced *SHKEEA*)!"

Leave this in the triangle for an hour, with the red candle burning. While this is taking place offer food and wine to the spirits. Then take some time to have some food and enjoyment yourself forgetting about the seal. After the hour is finished return to the triangle. Thank the Witch Queen, the Master and the spirits for their presence. Put the candle out. Wrap the seal in cloth or place it in an envelope. Clean everything up. The seal can then be carried on your person, in your bag, pocket or wallet, however you want to keep this with you. I can envision some placing this in a locket and wearing this around the neck for protection. Or, if desired, this can be placed in the home – either over the main entrance or in the highest point of the house.

Rowan Amulets
A number of powerful amulets used in the Art for centuries surround the application of the wood and berries of the Mountain Ash, also known as the Rowan. This beautiful tree has a long history of being highly protective. Some of the easiest amulets to make include drying the ripe red berries and then stringing them into a necklace or bracelet. This can also be hung near doors, windows and the hearth to help keep evil away. In New England there are written accounts from the 1800's speaking of people cutting small branches of Rowan wood and stringing these into either beads or small pieces of wood which, in turn, were made into necklaces that had to be worn against the skin. It was often common to carry a small piece of Rowan in one's hand bag or pocket for the same affect. Walking sticks and staves can be made of Rowan to ensure safety and luck while traveling or hiking.

One of the most popular and powerful objects used for home protection is the equal armed Rowan cross. These are extremely easy to make. During the waxing Moon collect two pieces of Rowan cutting these so that they are the same length. Generally, I cut these approximately four inches long. You can either leave the bark on these or peel it off. Then, crossing these so they form an equal armed solar cross or 'X' tie these with red wool thread or yarn. As you do chant this simple charm several times:

> "By Rowan wood
> By wool's red thread,
> Protect my home,
> Defend our stead!"

Then you may place this in a triangle of Art and Pass the Power into this through your hands as described earlier while reciting:

> "Rowan beams, sturdy walls
> No evil can enter, fly or crawl!
> Wool's red thread ties and binds,
> No evil can endure this four-fold sign!"

Now, trace the sigil of warding over this, envisioning it as a fiery electric blue flame.

Sigil of Warding

The Rowan Cross is then ready to be placed in the home. Like the others this is often placed above or near doors, windows and fireplaces. I frequently will make several of these, placing these strategically throughout the house; over each door, hanging over beds, as well as setting them in windows. Oftentimes when I suspect the direction from which a curse or malicious intent is coming, I place a Rowan Cross in the window facing that direction.

If you don't have access to actual Rowan an excellent substitute is Oak. We have used this very successfully in several situations. If using Oak simply change the wording in the chants from 'Rowan' to 'Oaken'.

House Protection Bag

A rather simple amulet that can be another level of protection for the home is to combine equal portions of dried Trefoil (Clover), Vervain and Dill in a small bag. This then is hung at the entrances of the home. This is particularly useful in repelling curses.

The Fire Cauldron

If you suspect that the home itself has malicious spirits present, that the psychic atmosphere of the place is negative and filled with ill intent, or you feel that someone has directly targeted you with a curse there is a simple but very effective technique for removing these. It is called the *Fire Cauldron*, or *Fire Pot*. I mentioned this briefly in the first book but wanted to give detailed instructions here.

For this you will need a fire proof metal pot or small cast iron cauldron small enough that you can carry easily, unless you are planning to only cleanse one room, in which case you would leave this on the floor. In the cauldron place a small layer of salt. Over this pour just enough rubbing alcohol to ensure the salt is wet. While not necessary you can also add a small amount of herbs used for power or banishing. Angelica Root, Dragon's Blood Resin, Rue, Rowan; any of these would be good for this. Oftentimes I use Vervain as a general all-purpose sorcerer's herb primarily because it adds power to any rite it is part of.

If you know that someone is purposely attempting to hex you place a taglock of theirs in the cauldron as well. On the other hand, if this is a general cleansing of the home, obviously no taglocks are needed. This is then set on fire. Be careful though as the flames can be quite dramatic and the pot will become very hot. As the fire burns enchant:

> "All curses and evil are banished,
> All unwanted spirits gone!
> Only the forces and powers we wish,
> Will be with us from this moment on!"

More often than not you will find that the flames themselves will grow in intensity and height. In my experience this is dependent on the amount of energy it is encountering. I have had times when the flames reached several feet high and burned a sickening greenish color. This was during a time when we were the subject of what we suspected was a particularly nasty blasting.

You will find that when you do this the energy in the room seems to get pulled into the fire itself, and you experience a sense of weight almost being lifted away from you. Once the flames burn out you will almost certainly find that the atmosphere will feel 'clear' or clean. It is an interesting and powerful experience. Essentially it is setting everything back to zero.

Ancient Egyptian Home Protection
While the technique of using the Fire Cauldron is one which we were taught by Welch Traditionalists I have found that it is often prudent to use this in conjunction with an Ancient Egyptian spell that I have adapted directly texts. This acts as an excellent way to set protections in place in the home and

then essentially burn any malicious influences out with the flames of the cauldron. Standing before the cauldron begin by reciting the following Egyptian spell:

"I conjure the windows of this house, for I am a wild cat.
I conjure the locks of this house, for I am a female falcon.
I conjure the bolts of the doors, for I am Ptah.
I conjure the bolt holes, for I am Nehebkau.
I conjure the hiding place, for I am the one whose name is hidden.
I conjure the cross timbers, for I am the Master of Mysteries.
I conjure this house, these rooms, the beds.
I conjure the four noble Ladies in whose mouths are flames,
Whose fire chases away all evil, all enemies, male and female, living and dead,
Within this house and without, within my body and without,
No evil and no enemies can come for me.
No evil and no enemies can come to this house,
Not by day, nor by night, not at any time.
The four noble Ladies with flame in their mouths protect this place!"[54]

Now, carefully light the alcohol on fire. Be sure that you have a means to smother this if needed. Once the fire is lit begin chanting:

"All curses and evil are banished,
All unwanted spirits gone!
Only the forces and powers we wish,
Will be with us from this moment on!"

Maintain the chant until the fire burns itself out. Then let the cauldron cool. Once the fire is out you may want to recite this simple Egyptian closing:

---

54. Borghouts, J.R. *Ancient Egyptian Magical Texts*. 1978.

"Djehuty (Thoth) has come.
He has delivered the Eye of Heru (Horus).
No evil shall enter this house.
Ptah has closed the door,
Djehuty has set it fast.
The door is closed, the door is set fast with the bolt."

Several things are happening in this procedure. The Egyptian incantation is a clear example of evoking the cooperation of the spirit of the house itself while enlisting specific otherworld beings whom the Egyptians worked with regularly. The four 'Noble Ladies with fire in their mouths' describes the female serpent power protecting the home. The Fire Cauldron stems from Welch practices but fits beautifully into this, bringing actual flames to bear in the invocation of the fiery serpent power. Finally, the closing is taken from the end of temple rites used across Egypt when any building or home was meant to be sealed from evil. I can't over-emphasize how simple and powerful this spell has proven to be.

Salt, Garlic, Onions, and Sage

Salt continues to be a theme in many protective spells and rituals. I recall that before doing any occult work Julie would rub a small amount of salt in the palms of her hands to cleans them. Similarly, she would cleanse Tarot card decks that had become unusable over time, due to others projecting too much negativity into them. This was a simple matter of laying the cards out on a sheet and then scattering salt over the cards. These were then left overnight. In the morning the cards are picked up and put away, ready for use. The salt was then discarded, having absorbed the negativity that had been in the cards.

An excellent technique for basic psychic protection in the home involves the use of salt and onions. For this an onion is cut into quarters. Each quarter is placed in a small bowl and is then covered with salt. Then each bowl is placed in the four corners of the room or home. What I have found is that these tend to absorb etheric energy, the same energy that is used in creating astral forms, the fetch and when projecting the second skin. As such, only use the onion and salt method when you suspect that there may be negative spirits present, or that someone may be maliciously seeking to send entities to you. This is also effective when you suspect someone may be visiting you themselves while traveling in spirit. The onion and salt will tend to draw any excess energy away from these beings making it harder for them to manifest.

The bowls can be left for a few days, until the onions either dry out or begin to rot. In either case, be sure to remove them before you, yourself decide to do any type of workings in which you will be projecting the second skin. This includes sending the fetch or, traveling in spirit. Also, if you attempt to evoke any otherworld being while the onions and salt are in place this will prove difficult because ritual evocation involves gathering this type of energy so that the entity can manifest.

In a similar vein, garlic can be very effective. When one is trying to root out a particularly persistent negative force that is permeating the home you may want to use this simple method. Sybil Leek wrote that she often would use garlic, presumably dried, mixed with salt and scatter this throughout the house.[55] In native American traditions the burning of White or Silver Sage, allowing the smoke to waft through the living space, is a frequent means of aiding in removing negative forces. As such, one could easily combine these techniques, scattering the salt/garlic mixture and then censing the area. As an added protection I will often mix Vervain and Salt together, forming a simple powder. This is then scattered on the door step and windowsills to help keep negative forces and people away. Often one's work environment can be quite toxic. As such I have found this

---

55. Leek, Sybil. *Driving Out the Devils.* 1975.

particular powder to be very effective when scattered at doorways to an office.

Protection from Slander

Like the Seal of Protection, there are many other written symbols that have long proven to be very effective for turning away unwanted forces. This is a very old sigil used as protection from enemies, as well as turn any slander, scandals or "evil reports" away from the person who carries this. Draw this on a piece of quality paper, parchment or Birch Bark. It can then be placed in a purse or wallet, inside a locket, the Nata Bag, pinned to one's clothing, etc. As simple as this seems I have found this be uniquely impressive in its performance.[56]

Sigil of Protection & Averting Scandal

Square of Protection

Tablets made from numbers have long been seen as being very potent magically. These are frequently known as "Magic Squares" or Kamea's. Part of their power comes from the fact that when added together in any direction they will total to the same sum. Overtime, specific squares have been found to resonate with different planets. However, there are

---

56. This sigil and it use as a protective sign comes from the Newberry Library's "Book of Charms" dating to the 17th century. Interestingly a very similar sigil can be found in Sloane MS 3851 manuscript dating to the same century. However, that sigil is used primarily to "invoke a dream specifically identifying a thief". I have only used the sigil shown here and then for protection. To learn more about the sigil for invoking a dream see: Baker, Jim. *The Cunning Man's Handbook.* 2013.201

also several that work independent of planetary influences. Rather they have been found to have specific magical effects on their own. The reason for this is that everything moves in patterns of vibration and frequency, resonating with different forces in a variety of states of being. The numbers in the square form a direct link to those patterns.[57]

This particular square is found in cunning folklore and is used solely to protect the home. As with the other sigils you will want to draw this on parchment, a good quality paper, or Birch Bark. While tracing this pass the power through the Dua procedure. Then tack this to the highest point in the home.

5	10	3
4	6	8
9	2	7

The Witch Bottle

One of the most widely used traditional forms of protection is the Witch Bottle, sometimes referred to as the 'Bellarmine Bottle'. This latter term comes from the name of the company who had made a specific type of stoneware jug throughout the 16th and 17th centuries. This was one of the favorite bottles used for this purpose. Essentially, a Witch Bottle is meant to act as a decoy, drawing curses or evil entities to it rather than the intended person. Once this happens the bottle then turns the curse back onto the one who cast this.

The preparation of the Witch Bottle should be done on a Saturday during the waning Moon. For this you will need a small bottle with a stopper or tight-fitting cork. This can

---

57. See *The Willow Path* for a detailed discussion on the use of numbers in the Art.

be of glass or it may be earthenware. In this you will want to place bent needles and pins along with some of your hair. Then urinate into the bottle. Stop this up tightly. It is helpful to seal the stopper with black wax. This is then deposited in a place where it won't be disturbed.

These have been found in the foundations of old houses, under the doorsteps of the main entrance, or hidden in walls. However, there is a long tradition of burying these away from the home in a secret place where they won't be found. This is done to draw the curse or entity away from the person and their house altogether. The entity is drawn to the bottle because of the personal taglocks within it, but then, so the logic goes, the spirit or curse is repelled by the steel pins. Being bent and sharp, these turn the force back onto itself. While I have not used this technique, I do know of Witches who swear by this as a powerful means of protection.

The Stag's Antlers
A simple technique that I use to clear a space of negative forces quickly is one which I call "The Stag's Antlers". I need to explain that this is my own technique drawn directly from my training in both Hermetics and Traditional Witchcraft. Those of you familiar with Aleister Crowley as well as Ogdoadic practices will recognize the overall pattern, though the spell given here is far simpler, being stripped down to its most basic format and using different Words of Power. For my part I find this to be a relatively easy procedure that requires little preparation and virtually no special equipment, yet it is very effective:

- Perform the Serpent, Cloak and Star.
- Envision brilliant light increasing in intensity in the center of your forehead.
- Form an upward triangle with the thumbs and forefingers of both hands, placing this over the forehead with the opening of the triangle focusing the power and light that is building.

• Now picture the light forming into the pattern of the Witch's Foot, the pentagram, inside the triangle.
• When the energy is at its peak 'throw' the pentagram forward, thrusting your arms out in front of you while spreading your fingers wide as if forming the antlers of a stag.
• At the same time mentally see the pentagram fly forward, becoming larger and eventually standing at the edge of the area.
• When casting the pentagram intone the Word of Power: "Sciath" (pronounced *SHKEEA*)!

As a side note, if you are using this to clear the four cardinal directions of a given space it is very effective to intone the Elemental Ward names given further in this chapter that are associated with the different directions while forming the pentagram in the triangle. Then when actually 'throwing' the pentagram recite the Word of Power noted above.

The Stag's Antlers can be used very effectively when confronted with a specific otherworld entity that you wish to banish. In such cases the exact same process is followed, except that you will be facing the entity as you throw the pentagram. While doing this enchant the Gaelic Word of Power for banishing:

"Deoraidhin" (pronounced JER-rid-hin)

In looking to the procedures given so far in this chapter, the goal has been to create a series of protective layers surrounding oneself, and one's home. Each is powerful and quite effective. Yet, when one is confronted by a serious magical assault launched by a seasoned occultist, anyone of these alone may not be enough to repel such an attack completely. However, in combination they can be quite formidable. This is why I strongly advise using different techniques in tandem. This leads us to the next level of protection; the boundaries of one's property.

Setting Boundaries – An Egyptian Curse

Much of protection on an occult level involves setting distinct boundaries both in the structure of the home and at the hedge that marks one's property. Even if these lines aren't clearly demarked physically, it is important that magically the distinction is very clear. It is in this regard that I like to use two very unique magical workings. The first is a classic Ancient Egyptian curse meant to afflict any being, otherworldly or not, that is intending to enter the boundaries of the property and do harm to the Witch or her family.

This can be done during any phase of the Moon. I prefer to perform this during the day as it requires making a potion that is then sprinkled around the border of property. As such, for practical reasons, daylight helps to avoid tripping when walking the property line.

For this you will want to chop at least four bulbs of fresh Garlic. Once these are cut up place the Garlic in a large bowl. To this add beer. The greater the boundary that you need to sprinkle the more Garlic and beer you will need. As the beer is being mixed with the Garlic, recite the following enchantment four times:

"O hdw, protect this house as you protect Ausir!
The arms of Ra, the arms of Heru, the arms of Djehuty, the arms of each of the company of the Neteru will destroy the enemies of this household through you!
You will ravage their heads in your name of hdw,
You will turn their mouths against them in the name of Wpw-R,
You will consume them in the name of Wnmw.
You will crush their bodies in the name of ndrh.
O white Eye of Heru that comes from the ground,
Protect this house, protect this land and all who live here!
You will close the mouth and turn back any evil person,
Spirit, thought or curse that tries to enter here.
They cannot enter this house,

They cannot enter this land.
For it is protected as you protect Ausir!
The heat of your flame is directed against them and you destroy them completely,
For they will wither and be repelled by your awesome power!"

Starting at the northeast edge of the property, begin sprinkling the potion at the boundary as you walk in a sunwise, deosil, manner. You will want to circle the entire property, or if this is too large, ensure that a large area around the house itself is sealed with the potion. As you do chant the following:

"The White Eye of Heru,
Protects this house,
Protects this land,
And all who live here!"

Be sure that you have enough potion to make a complete circuit around the area. You will note that this spell employs a variety of Ancient Egyptian names and Words of Power. Don't alter these as they are a major part of what makes this spell so potent. This particular spell has proven to be highly effective for us.

Setting the Wards
This working evokes very specific forces at the four quarters of the property, enlisting their protection. On the surface these forces may seem basic in nature as they do relate to the energies or "modes of being" associated with the traditional elements. However, what the Witch is actually doing is evoking otherworld beings who resonate strongly with these elements but are not necessarily limited to them. These and similar beings were discussed in the second book, *Horns of the Moon*. These are beings of a complex and powerful nature who are tied directly to specific currents

that cross between worlds. Where the previous spell was taken directly from Ancient Egyptian sources, this working is an original piece drawing from European folk magic and Irish Celtic mythology.

The rite itself starts with some important preparation. You will want to begin this during the Waxing Moon. Choose a day when you can be alone or with a trusted associate in the Art. Then take some time to become intimately familiar with the boundaries of the property, becoming aware of areas where the Serpent Breath gathers and flows freely. Look to the features of land itself. You want to find a place on the border of the property where the Serpent Breath is very strong, yet relates strongly to the elemental qualities normally associated with the direction itself. Thus, in our system we call on the essence of air in the east, fire in the south, water in the west and earth in north.[58]

In European folk tradition normally a large stone that is naturally present is chosen. If not, one was often erected. Today, however, this may not be practical or even possible. In such cases it is perfectly acceptable to mark this in a less obvious manner so as not to draw attention to the site. Much will be dependent on individual preference and your situation. At the least you will need to find, or put in place, some way of tying the forces evoked to the spot. This then will become a focal point through which these energies can readily manifest. You may mark this with something as simple as placing a Stang in the ground, or against a tree. A small pile of rocks, or a specific tree that has resonance with the energy can be effective. Any number of possibilities exist. This is where your own intuitive ability needs to guide you. Here in New England it is very common to find stone walls and similar clusters of rocks at the edge of property lines. As such, a small stack of rocks placed in a simple

---

58. Some Traditional Witches have different patterns associated with the elements. See *The Willow Path* for discussion on these.

form won't attract attention in the least and can serve the purpose of housing the Ward quite well.

Once you have chosen and prepared the marker proceed with this simple rite. I have divided this into four distinct elemental rituals. Depending on the size of the property involved you may want to perform this over a series of four days, one for each Ward. However, this certainly isn't necessary.

East Ward

Proceed to the eastern border marker. Bring with you a sword or your black hilt knife, a means to burn incense (for convenience a bundle of dried herbs tied together in a stalk or 'smudge stick' is easiest), a small amount of wine, a food offering, your wind-roarer, your personal Stang, and a small vial of ritual oil (I prefer Vervain). You will also need your Serpent Fe, or barring that, your own personal Fe.

Clear a spot at the base of the marker and place your ritual items. Take some time to slip into a state of becoming, as you let your awareness merge with the element of air itself while breathing in the Serpent Breath. Call on the spirits using the personal invocation you had created.[59] Then circle the marker three times tuathal as you spin the wind-roarer. Next light the incense and carry this around the marker three times scenting the air in a tuathal direction.

Facing the marker and the east, place the incense on the spot cleared. Lift your Stang and recite this invocation:

> "From the realm of Findias, the Mighty One comes, dressed in yellow and violet,
> His sword flashes in the morning Sun as the falcon calls.
> Ravens caw and the wind begins to rise,
> Uscias, Uscias,
> From the east He now comes.
> Uscias, Uscias
> Watcher on the Wind.

---

59. See *Horns of the Moon* for a description of this.

Ward of this property,
Protector of this land.
Come! Come Uscias,
From the realm of Findias,
Come! Come Uscias,
I ask, watch over this land!"

Replace the Stang, setting this against the marker. Then with the Fe trace the Witch's Foot (pentagram) beginning at the topmost point and proceeding deosil. When finished trace the sigil of Air:

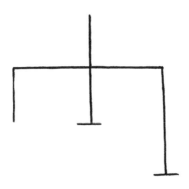

Sigil of Air

Then recite the following:

"Come O Mighty One, by sigil and line,
Watcher on the Wind, bound in this sign.
I conjure and call
Uscias, Uscias,
Keeper of the Wind, Protector of this land,
I conjure and call
Uscias, Uscias,
From Findias He comes, the Ward at this stand."

With the Fe trace the invoking Witch's Foot of Air, beginning at the lefthand upper point and proceeding deosil.

As you do, intone:

> "Come Uscias,
> Come to this Land"

Then, with the Fe trace the Crossroad sigil.

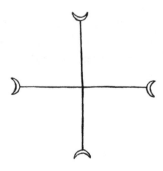

Recite:

> "The Gate is Open! Come!"

Replace the Fe and then, with the oil, trace a spiral on the marker itself. This should begin at the bottom and spiral inward, in a tuathal manner. Pick up the sword or knife, holding this high as you envision the Watcher approaching. He is cloaked in yellow holding a sword high as its edge gleams in the morning light of the Sun. Then address the Ward directly:

> "Uscias, Uscias,
> Uscias, Uscias.
> By the sword of Findias, realm of the Gods,
> I ask, watch over this land as Ward and Protector that no evil can enter,
> Whether person, spirit, thought or curse.
> By the winds of Findias, this land and all who live here are safe in your keep!"

Replacing the sword, it is essential that you now pour an offering of wine over the marker while giving thanks to the spirits and to the Ward itself for their presence.

South Ward
Moving to the south, follow essentially the same preparation. However, rather than the sword or knife you will use the Fe. Also, rather than using incense you will want a candle that is in a container and able to stay lit. When walking around the marker three times you will carry the lit candle instead of the incense.

Facing the marker and south, place the candle on the spot cleared. Lift your Stang and recite this invocation:

"From the realm of Gorias, the Mighty One comes, dressed in red, orange and green.
His lance held high in the noonday Sun as the wild cat roars and the sacred flames burn bright.
Esrus, Esrus
From the south He comes.
Esrus, Esrus
Watcher of the flame.
Ward of this property,
Protector of this land.
Come! Come Esrus,
From the realm of Gorias,
Come! Come Esrus,
I ask, watch over this land!"

Replace the Stang, setting this against the marker. Then with the Fe trace the Witch's Foot (pentagram) beginning at the top most point and proceeding deosil. When finished, trace the Sigil of Fire:

Sigil of Fire

Then recite the following:

"Come O Mighty One, by sigil and line,
Watcher of the Sacred Flame, bound in this sign.
I conjure and call
Esrus, Esrus
Keeper of the light, Protector of this land,
I conjure and call
Esrus, Esrus,
From Gorias he comes, Ward at this stand."

With the Fe trace the invoking Witch's Foot of Fire, beginning at the righthand lower point and proceeding deosil. As you do intone:

"Come Esrus,
Come to this Land"

With the Fe trace the Crossroad sigil. Recite:

"The Gate is Open! Come!"

Then with the oil, trace a spiral on the marker itself. This should begin at the bottom and spiral inward, in a tuathal manner. Pick up the Fe, holding this high as you envision the Watcher approaching, cloaked in red and orange with flecks of green, holding a lance high while the noonday Sun shines above him. Then address the Ward directly:

> "Esrus, Esrus,
> Esrus, Esrus.
> By the lance of Gorias, realm of the Gods,
> I ask, watch over this land as Ward and Protector that no evil can enter,
> Whether person, spirit, thought or curse.
> By the Sacred Flame of Gorias, this land and all who live here are safe in your keep!"

Pour an offering of wine over the marker while giving thanks to the spirits and to the Ward itself for their presence.

West Ward

Moving to the west follow the same procedure. This time though you will want to bring a goblet with fresh water. In walking around the marker you will hold the goblet filled with water.

Facing the marker and west, place the goblet on the spot cleared. Lift your Stang and recite this invocation:

> "From the realm of Murias, the Mighty One comes, dressed in blue.
> Her Goblet in hand, as the great orm swims in oceans deep.
> Semias, Semias
> From the west She comes.
> Semias, Semias
> Rider on the waves.
> Ward of this property,
> Protector of this land.
> Come! Come Semias,
> From the realm of Murias,
> Come! Come Semias,
> I ask, watch over this land!"

Replace the Stang, setting this against the marker. Then with the Fe trace the Witch's Foot (pentagram) beginning at the topmost point and proceeding deosil. When finished trace the *Sigil of Water*:

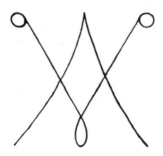

Sigil of Water

Then recite the following:

"Come O Mighty One, by sigil and line,
Rider on the Waves, bound in this sign.
I conjure and call
Semias, Semias
Silver Cauldron, Protector of this land,
I conjure and call
Semias, Semias,
From Murias She comes, Ward at this stand."

With the Fe trace the invoking Witch's Foot of water, beginning at the righthand upper point and proceeding deosil. As you do, intone:

"Come Semias,
Come to this Land."

With the Fe trace the Crossroad sigil, recite:

"The Gate is Open! Come!"

Then with the oil trace a spiral on the marker itself. This should begin at the bottom and spiral inward, in a tuathal manner. Pick up the goblet, holding this high as you envision the Watcher approaching across the surface of the ocean, her hair a rich copper as she is cloaked in blue. In her hands she holds a silver goblet, and about her feet, just breaking the surface of the water the great orm of the sea swims among the foam crested waves. Address the Ward directly:

"Semias, Semias,
Semias, Semias.
By the Cauldron of Dagda that comes from Murias, realm of the Gods,
I ask, watch over this land as Ward and Protector that no evil can enter,
Whether person, spirit, thought or curse.
By the Silver Cauldron of Murias, this land and all who live here are safe in your keep!"

Be sure to pour an offering of wine over the marker while giving thanks to the spirits and to the Ward itself for their presence.

North Ward
Moving to the North, again follow the same preparation. This time you will want to bring either a natural flat stone, or a plate that is used in ritual to represent earth. Many Traditional Witches will use a copper plate that they have engraved with the Witch's Foot in the center. Ours is made of wood. One could easily use a flat stone for this same purpose. On this place the food offerings. In walking around the marker you will hold the plate/pentacle.

Facing the marker and north, place the plate on the spot cleared. Lift your Stang and recite this invocation:

"From the realm of Falias, the Mighty One comes, dressed in green and indigo,

Her shield of gold.
With sickle in hand, Her foot resting on the Stone,
The great stag emerges from forest old.
Fessus, Fessus
From the north She comes.
Fessus, Fessus
Lady of the forest, Maiden in the field.
Ward of this property,
Protector of this land.
Come! Come Fessus,
From the realm of Falias,
Come! Come Fessus,
I ask, watch over this land!"

Replace the Stang, setting this against the marker. Then with the Fe trace the Witch's Foot (pentagram) beginning at the topmost point and proceeding deosil. When finished trace the sigil of Earth:

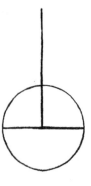

Sigil of Earth

Then recite the following:

"Come O Mighty One, by sigil and line,
Lady of the forest, bound in this sign.
I conjure and call
Fessus, Fessus

With the Stone of Fal, Protector of this land,
I conjure and call
Fessus, Fessus,
From Falias She comes, Ward at this stand."

With the Fe trace the invoking Witch's Foot of Earth, beginning at the lefthand lower point and proceeding deosil. As you do intone:

"Come! Fessus,
Come to this Land"

With the Fe trace the Crossroad sigil. Recite:

"The Gate is Open! Come!"

Then with the oil trace a spiral on the marker itself. This should begin at the bottom and spiral inward, in a tuathal manner. Pick up the plate/pentacle, holding this high as you envision the Watcher approaching across a rich field on a summer day. Behind her the mountains rise high, and in the background the tree line of an ancient forest can be seen. In the field a bull grazes lazily while a great stag emerges from the forest. The Ward has long blond hair and is clothed in green. On her left arm a great shield of pure gold shines like the Sun, while in her right hand she holds a razor sharp silver sickle. Her right foot rests on a sacred stone, while the left stands in the lush grasses of the meadow. Address the Ward directly:

"Fessus, Fessus,
Fessus, Fessus.
By the Stone of Fal that comes from Falias, realm of the Gods,
I ask, watch over this land as Ward and Protector that no evil can enter,
Whether person, spirit, thought or curse.

By destiny's stone found in Falias, this land and all who live here are safe in your keep!"

As with the others, be sure to pour an offering of wine over the marker while giving thanks to the spirits and to the Ward itself for their presence.

Like all connections with otherworld beings, you will want to continue to engage with the Wards on a regular basis, bringing them offerings and reaffirming their role as guardians over the boundary that they are stationed. The more often you do this the stronger their presence will become. At a minimum this should be done at the Spring and Autumnal Equinoxes. In fact, you will find that it is best to reset all protection then. The reason is that the tides in the Abred reverse themselves at these times. As such, the barriers set in one tide tend to weaken once the shift occurs.

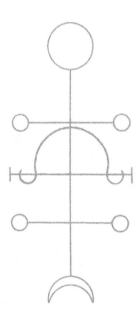

Chapter Five

✣ WATCHERS OF THE NIGHT ✣
PLANETARY MAGIC IN TRADITIONAL
WITCHCRAFT

Both Sybil Leek and Traditional Witch, Michael Howard, use an interesting and obscure phrase in their writing. They both describe the "Watchers of the Night" or the "Night Watchmen". In Sybil's case this was part of a line taken from an exorcism she did in which she was calling on different otherworld beings to assist her. In this she chanted "Spirits of the Watchers of the Night, I conjure it".[60] Michael Howard references the "Night Watchmen" when discussing the warding spirits at the quarters as summoned by Witches in northern Italy.[61] Perhaps this is no coincidence. While Sybil was an English Witch, her family had connections throughout Europe. In fact, her initiation and at least some of her training, was conducted in the south of France very near the region Mr. Howard described. I mention this because these spirits are seen as gatekeepers to the realm of the Gods. Yet, this term implies a probable reference to those who watched over and studied the stars and planets.

The simple fact is that Astrology has been a part of magical practice for a very long time. In Celtic culture we know that various artifacts, monuments and stone circles across Europe were aligned with different astronomical events. One of the oldest Celtic artifacts is the Nebra sky

---

60. Leek, Sybil. *Driving Out the Devils.* 1975.236
61. Howard, Michael. *Liber Nox: A Traditional Witch's Gramarye.* 2014.51

disc dating to approximately 1600 BCE. Unfortunately, whatever Astrological knowledge that the Celts had is lost in time with only hints surviving in artifacts and myth.

When we turn to Traditional Witchcraft itself, we find that planetary lore fills grimoires and cunning folk books well before the industrial era. References to specific planetary spirits, talismans, the timing of spells and more form an important body of texts and lore reaching very far back in history.

Western Astrology itself almost certainly has its roots in ancient Babylon. It was there that the zodiac with its twelve signs appears to have been first recognized. Yet, it wasn't until the Persian invasion late in Egyptian history that Astrology as we understand it began to develop. According to Egyptologist Dr. Richard Parker, during the period in which Persia ruled Egypt there was considerable cross-culture and exchange of esoteric knowledge between the two societies.[62] This began approximately between 521 BCE through 486 BCE. It was after this that we begin to see beautifully carved, clear representations of the zodiac in some of the most sacred areas of different temples. Perhaps the most famous is the circular ceiling panel found in Hathor's temple of Dendera.

Important to our discussion, though, is what happened once the Egyptian priesthood embraced this new science. For while the basics of rudimentary Astrology were imported into Egypt, research of temple records and other ancient texts indicate that the Egyptians really took Astrology to a new level of understanding. Researcher Robert Hand extensively examined the evidence surrounding this. Through this he has come to the conclusion that very important advances occurred in Egypt including the discovery and use of Astrological aspects, the thirty-six decans, the different 'lots' or 'parts' as well as the concept of planetary rulership and

---

62. Parker, Richard A. "Egyptian Astronomy, Astrology and Calendarical Reckoning". *Dictionary of Scientific Biography* 1978.723

correspondence.[63] This last development marks a critical step in magical practice. For it is from this that the entire system of using the planetary forces in magic stems.

In essence the Egyptians realized that everything in nature is related to and resonates with greater or more complex powers, beings and intelligences. With this understanding they found that these forces could be cataloged under the rulership of different celestial objects.[64] It was from this pattern that a systematic understanding of these forces came into being, including the numerical association of the planets which have come down to us via the Hermetic Qabbala and the Pythagorean systems. One can argue that they are both linked, stemming from this single Egyptian source.[65] It was a simple step to then begin forming ritualistic magical procedures for addressing and controlling different events by calling on the forces and spirits associated with the planets that ruled over the goal at hand. Of course, much has changed and evolved over the millennia since, yet essentially, this was the birth of planetary magic as practiced in western esotericism.

During Hellenistic times Astrology and planetary magic began to spread from the mystery schools of Alexandria and other areas of Egypt into Turkey, Arabia, Greece and Rome. From there it was only matter of time before this knowledge

---

63. Hand, Robert. *Project Hindsight*. 2004

64. It is quite possible that at least the basic concept of planetary rulership may be far older, reaching back into early Egyptian history. We know that specific planets and stars were seen as the embodiment of different Goddesses, Gods and spirits. Each temple was aligned with specific astronomical settings. Further, both pyramid and coffin texts from very ancient times speak of the different stars and planets. Yet, it would seem that this knowledge was kept fairly esoteric and didn't develop into the magical systems we would recognize today until the late period of Egypt.

65. See *The Willow Path* for a detailed examination of these different numbering systems and how they interact with each other.

was carried north into Europe. During the renaissance much Hermetic teaching involving planetary magic continued to spread through esoteric orders and individual magicians. As I noted in the first chapter, it was inevitable that this would find its way into folk traditions and the magical workings of those who still followed older pagan practices. Keep in mind that it is entirely conceivable that a certain amount of lore from Celtic and pre-Celtic teachings regarding planetary magic may have been incorporated into oral traditions and practices. However, if it did, it is so diluted and mixed with other sources that it is almost impossible to discern. No matter the case, it was through this process that Traditional Witchcraft came to embrace planetary magic.

In practice you will quickly find that planetary magic is exceptionally powerful, harnessing different natural tides that will add to your workings considerably. This is done through the use of a variety of techniques, symbols and objects all of which are linked through the principal of resonance and correspondence. This is where the genius of Ancient Egypt comes into play with their discovery of planetary rulerships. For planetary magic helps one to place desired goals, and with these, different types of workings and spells, into specific categories. In doing so one can begin to link these to tides of power and items of power that can be accessed to help with the spell. In *The Willow Path* I spoke of some of the correspondence between different objects, colors and numbers with the various planets. The following is meant to continue that examination in greater detail.

The Sun

The first of these to consider are the correspondences related to the Sun. By far this celestial body has the biggest impact on life on this planet. The Sun regulates the cycle of the seasons and without it there would be no life on Earth as we know it. But for the Witch the Sun is so much more. In general, the Sun is considered to be masculine, fiery, energetic, relating to the cycles of material existence and outward expression. Yet, like each of the planets its influence extends much further and is very complex.

As a Witch, there are a number of otherworld beings we partner with on various occasions who resonate well with the Sun. The first of these is the multifaceted being that many refer to as the Master, the Witch King, the Horned One, the Old One, the King of Elphame, and by so many other names. He is one of the primary otherworld 'contacts' who is directly tied to the systems which most Traditional Witches practice. Complex in nature, the Master necessitates that He can and does relate to several different planetary energies, yet the Sun is perhaps the most readily identifiable. It is in this regard that we find Him in the life-giving aspect of the Green Man of Summer, the Lord of the forests and fields, the joyful piper and the virile Horned God of pleasure providing for all. Yet He is also Lord of the Mysteries, the underworld, the secret voice of the wind, the rider in the night forests. In this regard He embodies the dying Sun at Samhain that sinks deeply into the womb of the Lady in order to be renewed and made ready in the spring. He can also be found as the King of Elphame, governing the underworld. He at once is the gatherer of souls, the Summoner, and then protects the spirits of the deceased. He rules magic and all things associated with the Mysteries of the Art.

His symbols and tools include horns, bones, antlers, hoofs, the stang, the staff, the sword, the upright standing stone, the black hilt knife, the stone of flint, the mineral of gold, and the metal bronze. Gold topaz and yellow sapphire resonate well with the Master and the Sun.

There are many different otherworld beings who closely resemble the Master. It is often tempting to suppose that these are but different names for the same being, and this may be the case. However, in practice I would caution against such an assumption. Rather, the seasoned Witch or magician quickly comes to realize that each name given almost certainly is individual, unique and sentient in how they present themselves. Some of these include the Celtic Gods Gwyn Ap Nudd, Cernowain and Cernnunos, the Greek and Roman Gods of Pan and Faunus, as well as several Egyptian Gods including Ra, the ram headed Khnum and Atum. Basque Witches often refer to Him as Janicot, in Italian Strega He is sometimes known as Tanus, while in Cornwall He is often associated with the Bucca. The legend of Esus and Tarvos exemplify the two main ways He is experienced. Other beings include Puck, Robin Goodfellow, Oberon, and Herne. I have, at one time or another, partnered with many of these.

Beyond those already given, there are several other beings who resonate well with the Sun. Two of my favorites are found in the Irish pantheon of the Tuatha de Danann. These include the solar champion, Lugh, who is master of all crafts. Also, Nuada, lover to the Great Queen Morrigan.

In the Egyptian pantheon the Phoenix as the Bennu is very powerful. He is the living flame in the heart of Ra, and is an exceptional being to partner with. There are also many Goddesses who embrace the solar energies. The dual Goddess of Hwt-Hrw (Hathor) as the lover, mother, and Great Queen along with Her alternate identity as the warrior lioness Sekhmet. Both are exceptional to form partnerships with. As the lioness She is the protector and avenger, the Eye of Ra, or Eye of the Sun.

While not quite Gods the Olympic Spirits can be very helpful, and are very powerful in their own right. These beings have been a part of magical practice for centuries. We see them particularly in German medieval Grimoires, yet they appear to have links to Greece – hence the name 'Olympic Spirits'. In my experience these otherworld entities can be very quick to act, bring unmistakable and tangible results when called on. However, to do so it would appear that they respond best when one's need is very great as opposed to calling on them when you simply 'want' something.

The Olympic Spirit that resonates best with the Sun is Och. He is called on to prolong life while giving excellent health. He helps to bring wisdom, riches and honor, promotes fame and admiration. He is best evoked on at dawn on a Sunday.

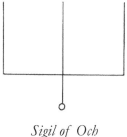

Sigil of Och

Another powerful solar spirit who has a long history in magic is Aspis. Like Och, He is part of a series of seven spirits each relating the seven different planets. Where the Olympic Spirits appear to have links to Ancient Greece, Aspis is one of the Archons appearing in Egyptian Gnostic texts. These Archons are part of a magical formula relating to Abraxas. I am personally aware of at least one magical order that evokes each of the seven Archons in their planetary workings.

The reality is that you will find literally hundreds of different spirits listed in old grimoires, cunning folk books, and Witches' notes. This can get rather confusing. The best advice I can give is to consider the planet that the spirit is listed under, along with the qualities of the planet itself. Then, when calling on any otherworld being treat them just as you would any guest you would normally invite to your home, with respect, but with an approach of taking the time to get to know each other to see if a partnership with this being is right for your situation. In many cases you may be very pleased with the arrangement finding that you can work well with them, gaining the results desired. And yet, there are some whom you may not be comfortable with. Be very wary of any otherworld being who requests blind allegiance to them, whether out of fear or promise of rewards, especially if this is meant to keep you from working with other beings.[66] In such cases it is best to end the contact right away. There are many, many other spirits whom you can work with.

Keeping in mind that, while a sigil is the spirit's unique signature embodying its essence, a seal is the condensed manifestation of how a specific spirit or type of spirits function. We often use a series of different seals for a variety of purposes. These are drawn from many different traditional sources. The following is one we use when evoking spirits of the Sun. In such cases we will often place this seal on the Hearthstone; recite our evocations and then trace the sigil of the specific spirit in the air over the seal. Beyond just general evocation of Sun spirits, this seal is also used to cause entities who were not previously visible to appear.

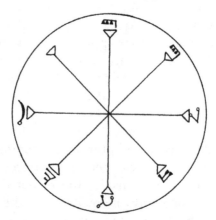

Seal of Evocation
Spirits of the Sun

---

66. An example of this type of otherworld being can be seen in the advent of a certain cult that has risen in prominence during the past 1500 years, surrounding an entity that insists it is the "one, true and only" deity.

Another seal that we use when working with the Sun is the traditional 'daisy wheel Witch mark'. These have been found throughout homes in Europe and Colonial America. While they have long been thought to be protective marks against baneful magic, the reality is that they are very old with exactly the same markings found in Egyptian tombs dating from 1492 BCE to 1473 BCE.[67] In Traditional Witchcraft this seal is used as a talismanic image of the Sun itself,[68] pulling in its light and positive life affirming power wherever it is placed. As such, it can be used in any solar related spell.

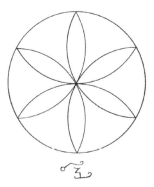

"Daisy Wheel"
Sun Symbol

One of the most ingenious developments in the magical Arts was the discovery of the Kamea, a numerical square that adds up to the same value no matter which row or column one chooses. What is intriguing about these is that specific squares were arranged to correspond to the specific energies embodied in the planets. As we saw earlier, these came to be found in rural practices, with these being written on parchment, scraps of bark, even on the walls and beams of buildings.

---

67. Tomb of Hatnefer, Egypt.

68. Glass, Justine. *Witchcraft, The Sixth Sense.* 1965. Melvin Powers, Hollywood, California, USA

In practical magic they have several unique properties. First, they can be used as talismanic images, placed on the Hearthstone itself during spells related to the planet to draw in the forces being evoked. These same squares can then be carried or hung in the home as talismans themselves.

The Kamea can also be used to help one move into a state of becoming simply by counting the numbers, allowing the eye to find each on the square. In this way, the act of counting becomes a meditative exercise while helping to align one with the planetary influence itself. Once this is completed, the Witch then moves on to the actual spell itself.

Yet another way that a Kamea is often used is to create one's own personal sigil that links one directly to the planet itself. To do so transfer the letters of your name into numbers using a numerological system that works best for you.[69] It is then just a matter of tracing a line on the Kamea beginning with the number that corresponds to the first letter of your name and following through to the remaining numbers. This then is your personal sigil when working with the planet. The sigil itself can then be placed on working tools and talismans. Or it can be traced in the air above seals. One could also trace this in an essential oil on doorways or windows to draw the planetary influence into your home.

6	32	3	34	35	1
7	11	27	28	8	30
19	14	16	15	23	24
18	20	22	21	17	13
25	29	10	9	26	12
36	5	33	4	2	31

Kamea of the Sun

---

69. See *The Willow Path* for a discussion on the numerological system which we use.

When considering these different sigils, seals and Kameas oftentimes can be used in conjunction with one another, either as different symbols placed in key points of the working space, or as the obverse and reverse side of a single talisman that is then worn. The following is the Seal of the Sun, along with its Sigil, adapted from 16th century magical sources.

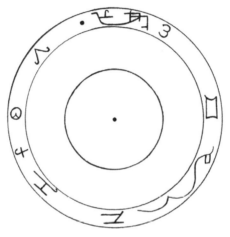

Seal of the Sun

Sigil of the Sun

You will find that as you get to know each of these different otherworld beings and forces, along with their sigils and seals you will develop your own practice, forming relationships with these intelligences. In my opinion it is best to work within the framework of the tradition as this is the foundation of the entire system. Yet, essentially, you are opening the lines of communication so that you can then use these in your daily life.

The Moon

In the Art the Moon holds immense sway. As shown previously, the timing of esoteric work is almost always centered around this orb, and with it the availability and type of energy it gives at different times. The Moon itself resonates with a number different otherworld entities, most, though not all, of whom are female. It is in this regard that the Witch Queen, the Mistress, manifests through the different phases of the Moon. Like the Master, She is very complex in nature covering a breadth of qualities. She has long been referred to as the Queen of Elphame. Like the Master, a number of beings are closely aligned with Her and may in fact be corresponding names for Her, yet again, I would caution the reader from treating these as such. Rather it is best to recognize each name as unique identities who resonate well with the Moon. The following are just a few names given to the Queen of Elphame: Sybil, Sebile, Janet, Medb, and many other names. In our system the Lady is the flame at the heart of the Mysteries. She is the Grail and Cauldron that all seek.

A number of Goddesses throughout history can also be seen as closely aligned with the Witch Queen. Among these is Diana whose worship, as we saw, spread far across Europe merging with the rites of other native Goddesses such as the Germanic Holda, and the Irish Flidais.[70] Artemis, Hecate, Aset whose name was later changed to Isis by the Greeks, Tana among Strega Witchcraft, Tanat/Tanit whose practices appeared among the Phoenicians and appears to have eventually spread to covens in England,[71] all resonate with the Moon. In Celtic mythology the Moon can be linked to such Goddesses as Arianrhod and the Druidess Tlachtga. Morrigan, Danu and Bridget all with their triple forms in myth can be thought of as resonating with the Moon.

---

70. Paice MacLeod, Sharon. *Celtic Cosmology and the Otherworld*. 2018.155
71. Patterson, Steve. *Cecil Williamson's Book of Witchcraft*. 211-214.2014. Troy Books Publishing. London, England.

In the Egyptian pantheon we find that the Moon resonates with both Goddesses and Gods. For example, we know that at different times in Egyptian history the crescent horns of the Moon were seen as analogous to the horns of the cow Goddess Hathor. The cat Goddess Bast was equally linked to both the Moon and Sun. Two male deities who manifest through the Moon include the protective Khonsu and the God of wisdom and magic Djehuty who is also known by the Greek name Thoth.

Among the Olympic spirits Phul resonates with the Moon. She can be evoked when seeking to gain the alliance of water spirits. She helps with healing and prolonging life, bringing fertility as well. She can be called on to aid with all things related to the Moon.

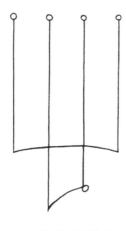

Sigil of Phul

The Archon from the formula of Abraxas corresponding to the Moon is Anaktor.

When it comes to Witch Marks, we use the symbol of the Mare as discussed in Horns of the Moon, finding that this has a resonance with the many different horse Goddesses of Europe including Epona.

Mare "Witch Mark"

We use several different lunar sigils in our work, many of which have already been portrayed in this series. The following though is a seal we use when working with spirits of the Moon generally:

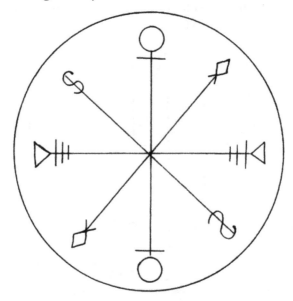

Seal of Evocation
Spirits of the Moon

As with the Sun, the Kamea of the Moon can be used alone as a talismanic object drawing in the essential qualities of the Moon to your ritual. It can also be used to trace your own personal lunar sigil, based on the numerical values of your name.

37	78	29	70	21	62	13	54	5
6	38	79	30	71	22	63	14	46
47	7	39	80	31	72	23	55	15
16	48	8	40	81	32	64	24	56
57	17	49	9	41	73	33	65	25
26	58	18	50	1	42	74	34	66
67	27	59	10	51	2	43	75	35
36	68	19	60	11	52	3	44	76
77	28	69	20	61	12	53	4	45

Kamea of the Moon

In practical workings I have found the following sigils and seals to work well:

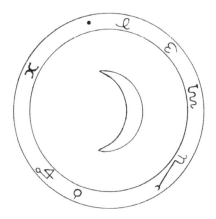

Seal of the Moon

Sigil of the Moon

Mars
In Mars we find dynamic energy in all its forms. This can range from the first burst of life in spring, to aggressive action, the urge to push forward and accomplish, to many of the most basic elements of life including fire, power, dominion and so much more. No matter the intent, works related to this planet all have one common denominator: raw energy. When the Witch evokes Mars the reason is to lend this planet's intense passion and power to the goal at hand. As such, Mars needs to be approached carefully for an imbalance here can wreak havoc. Nevertheless, Martial energies are very useful when starting new projects and in getting the power needed to achieve a task.

When it comes to otherworld beings related to Mars this can be complex and a solid understanding of the entity one intends to evoke is essential. Both the Witch King and Queen can manifest through Mars. In the case of the King, He can come through as the raw sexual impulse of nature itself. These same martial forces can be seen in the unbridled lust and desire of Pan or Cernunnos and is also displayed in the Egyptian ram headed God Khnum who, in his mating with Hathor, fashions humanity. Then again, the Master can be the hunter of autumn, slaughtering the food needed to survive the long winter months.

The Queen uses martial forces as the protectoress and avenger. Whether protecting Her own, or enraged in blind anger, the Witch Queen is the single most powerful force in nature. Yet like the Master, She is the embodiment of the living pulse of life as manifest in sex. So, we find Her in the Celtic Morrigan when She seduces Nuada, for it was through the embrace of the Great Queen of the Land that the Celtic Kings were chosen and renewed.[72]

In Egypt we find the same forces: Iusaas as the sexual feminine force that brings life to the universe, Nebet Hetepet as the "Lady of Pleasure", Anukis as "the embracer" and

---

72. Paice MacLeod, Sharon. *Celtic Cosmology and the Otherworld*. 127.2018.

of course, the Great Goddess Hathor. In each of these the pure urge of lust manifests in powerful and unbridled fashion. Yet, each of these can also resonate with Venusian and lunar forces depending on the rite involved.

Various warrior deities also manifest through their resonance with Mars. As such, they can and often are called on when blasting or cursing. I very rarely work with this side of Mars, finding that it should only be used when no alternatives remain.

The Olympic spirit that resonates with Mars is Phaleg. He brings honor and ability in any military matter, or martial art. He also provides assertiveness, power and strength.

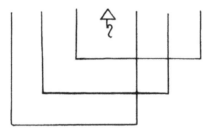

Sigil of Phaleg

In the formula of Abraxas the Archon Rutor works through the energies of Mars. As with the other planets, the following seals, sigils and kamea can also be used:

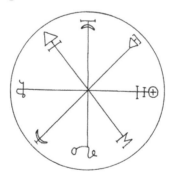

Seal of Evocation
Spirits of Mars

11	24	7	20	3
4	12	25	8	16
17	5	13	21	9
10	18	1	14	22
23	6	19	2	15

Kamea of Mars

Seal of Mars

Sigil of Mars

Mercury

Mercury is one of the most versatile and important planetary energies that the Witch can work with, for this is the great communicator, carrying information and ideas forward. In Hermetics this planet is seen as the repository and key to the Mysteries. For the country Witch though Mercury is more. This planet resonates with crossroads and liminal places, both being points of transition. It is in this aspect that the Master as the 'Man in Black' makes Himself known. Sometimes He is seen as the guide of souls, and yet it is He who challenges the candidate in initiation. Mercury is also the crow as messenger between the worlds, companion to the Witch aiding her as she moves through the different realms. As the crow He is the teacher and familiar.

The Queen, too, manifests through Mercury. For here we find the Lady who prepares the sacred potion of knowledge and inspiration. She is the wise one whose counsel we all seek, for only through Her skill and intuition can real wisdom emerge.

In practical workings any rites involving the influencing of others, presenting an idea, concept or prospect all fall under this planet. Writing, communication, knowledge and skill, memorization of data, as well as overall health and wellbeing resonate through this planet.

Some of the many otherworld beings who are easily evoked through Mercury include Hermes, as well as the Egyptian Goddess Seshat and Her mate Thoth. The Olympic spirit of Mercury is Ophiel. He gives knowledge of the sciences and arts, increases one's logic and intellectual ability. Writing and communication are aided through this spirit.

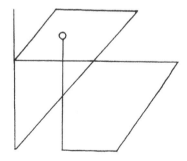

Sigil of Ophiel

125

The Gnostic Egyptian Archon of Mercury is Sthenos.

There is an interesting and very old talismanic spell using Mercurial forces. This is done to increase your odds of winning in games, as well as to obtain favors from people in power. During the Waxing Moon, on the day and hour of Mercury, trace the following symbol on paper, parchment or some other medium that you can carry easily. While tracing this intone the word of power "Yparon". This is then carried while participating in the game, or when meeting with the person you are seeking to influence.

Mercury "small face" of favors

For general spirit work related to Mercury we use this seal in our rites:

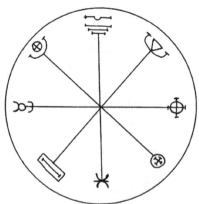

Seal of Evocation
Spirits of Mercury

The Kamea of Mercury can be very helpful when preparing for divination, particularly if the technique you are using involves a set system such as Tarot, Astrology, Numerology, Geomancy, and similar forms.

8	58	59	5	4	62	63	1
49	15	14	52	53	11	10	56
41	23	22	44	48	19	18	45
32	34	35	29	25	38	39	28
40	26	27	37	36	30	31	33
17	47	46	20	21	43	42	24
9	55	54	12	13	51	50	16
64	2	3	61	60	6	7	57

Kamea of Mercury

The following have also been found to be effective in rites involving Mercury:

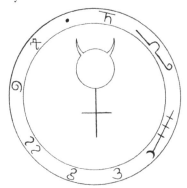

Seal of Mercury

Sigil of Mercury

Jupiter

Jupiter is such a wonderful planet to work with. Through its energy prosperity, friendship, deeper knowledge and wisdom develop. Jupiter works exceptionally well when combined with solar influences. Yet, even on its own it can bring lasting positive benefits.

For us, in our practice as country Witches, we find the Master in the form of generous provider and benefactor comes through very strongly when evoked under Jupiter's tides. In this regard Cernnunos, Faunus, Janicot and Khnum all resonate well with Jupiter.

The Great Queen too comes through in very positive ways. Here we find Her as the Earth Mother bringing forth bounty and life. Such Goddesses as Danu, Bridget, Heartha, Habondia, Hathor and so many others are easily evoked using Jupiter's influence.

You will find that a number of other classic deities resonate with Jupiter as well. In Celtic lore Dagda, as mate to Danu, is very consistent with this energy. With His cauldron of plenty from which none go hungry, Dagda is a clear embodiment of Jupiter. In Greek mythology the sky God Zeus easily corresponds with this planet.

When looking to the Olympic spirits Bethor falls under Jupiter's domain. He aids in bringing money, good fortune and general prosperity. Interestingly he also aids with the making of potions and medicines that prolong life. The older grimoires state that He responds quickly when evoked.

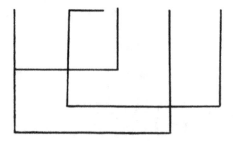

Sigil of Bethor

In the formula of Abraxas, the Archon of Jupiter is Balen.

An interesting spell found in cunning folk magic uses the following symbol as a talismanic sigil drawing on Jupiter's influence:

Jupiter Sigil of Luck

In particular this symbol is used in a spell meant to increase overall luck. On a Thursday night during the hour of Jupiter trace the above sigil on paper, parchment, or some other material that you can carry as a talisman. While drawing this chant the following Word of Power: "Phetomeus". This is then carried, particularly while participating in games, purchasing lottery tickets, and working on projects that you hope will bring money.

There are several other seals that traditionally resonate with Jupiter, depending on your purpose. Earlier the Jupiter seal of sustained wealth was given when we discussed house spirits. The following is another which we use generally in ritual for evoking spirits of Jupiter.

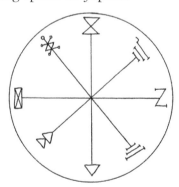

Seal of Evocation
Spirits of Jupiter

In using the Kamea of Jupiter, I have found this to be very versatile. It can be used in all of the ways already described for kameas, but I have also used this as a focal point in ritual to enhance the power of the rite by placing this in front of candles that were meant to draw very specific monetary rewards to us. This has proven to be very effective provided that all else involved has been attended to.

4	14	15	1
9	7	6	12
5	11	10	8
16	2	3	13

Kamea of Jupiter

In addition, the following seal and sigil have shown themselves to be very useful in practical magic.

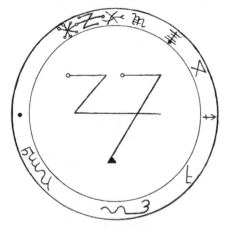

Seal of Jupiter

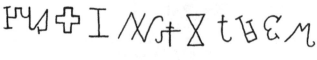

Sigil of Jupiter

Venus

When people think of Venus immediately the subject of love spells and seduction comes to mind. This is such a difficult topic to broach as perhaps no other type of spell carries with it the potential to bring so many unwanted consequences with it. For, essentially, one is entering into the most intimate aspects of another person's life. It is one thing to cast a spell to get someone's attention, having them notice you and appreciate you. But to cause, on an occult level, someone to fall in love with you is an entirely different and deeply personal affair. Think very carefully before you embark on such a working.[73]

For the seasoned Witch though Venus rules much more than romance. Venus brings pleasure and beauty in all forms. As such the arts are governed by this planet, as are social gatherings, friendships, peace, harmony, and companionship. While Mars represented raw lust, Venus is the erotic side of the same coin. She also aids with fertility and abundance. Like the Sun and Jupiter, Venus is also good for prosperity and money matters. As with so much in the Art, how Venus manifests depends largely on the intention, wording, symbols and focus of the rite itself.

In Traditional Witchcraft the Great Queen manifests in the natural desire for pleasure, that brings meaning to life. It is in such guises that She is seen in the May Queen of spring, the lover in the field bringing fertility to the land, or the

---

73. Please note that it is exactly for this reason that I am not including a chapter devoted to love spells. I believe that I am providing enough information that the astute reader will be able to discern the means to perform these should they desire. But again, I want to caution the apprentice that the consequences of a well cast love or seduction spell can affect areas of both your own and the other person's life in ways that often are unforeseen and unwelcome. If you still wish to pursue this aspect of the Art though, there are a number of excellent books that do give clear instruction in this.

Lady of the Earth itself who chooses, tests and then mates with he who would be King. Without Her, he is nothing. All comes from the Queen, and all returns back to Her.

We find that, when working with Venusian tides of power, such otherworld beings as Sebile, Arianrhod, Aphrodite, Astarte, Ishtar, Morrigan (as lover to the warrior), Hathor, Iusaas, Anukis, Nebet Hetepet, to name just a few, come through easily. As for male Gods, the Celtic God Angus is easily evoked under Venus. So too are the Egyptian Gods Min, Amun and Bes.

The Olympic spirit associated with Venus is Hagith. She is called on to aid with all matters related to love and romance, sex, beauty. She also helps to bring money and prosperity.

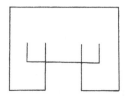

Sigil of Hagith

The archon in the formula of Abraxas corresponding to Venus is Alale. The pentacle used to evoke spirits of Venus generally is:

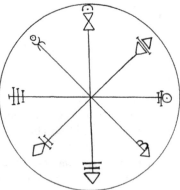

Seal of Evocation
Spirits of Venus

There are other seals used when evoking Venus. The following is used in traditional Arts when calling on any of the Goddesses of love, and is generally carried as a talisman to attract affection and adoration from others.

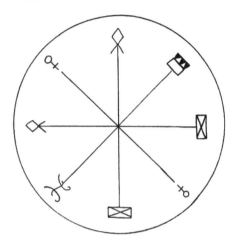

Venus Pentacle of Love

Like the Kameas of the other planets, this can be used in exactly the same way.

22	47	16	41	10	35	4
5	23	48	17	42	11	29
30	6	24	49	18	36	12
13	31	7	25	43	19	37
38	14	32	1	26	44	20
21	39	8	33	2	27	45
46	15	40	9	34	3	28

Kamea of Venus

Both the following sigil and seal are taken from older sources and have shown their value.

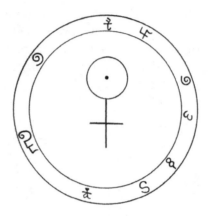

Seal of Venus

Sigil of Venus

Saturn

Among the seven traditional planets perhaps the most misunderstood and feared is Saturn. It has long been seen as the 'great malefic', bringer of sorrow and misfortune. As such, the tides surrounding this planet are favored by those wishing to hex or blast others. In fact, Saturn can be used for exactly that purpose. However, for the Witch, this planet is far more complex and can be quite positive to work with. Saturn brings structure and form, organizing and crystalizing that which is desired. Thus, it is used to bring into physical manifestation different occult forces. This includes the evocation and materialization of otherworld beings: spirits, elementals, astral forms, the second skin and fetch, and so much more. Saturn also corresponds with that which matures, as such it relates to wisdom that comes through experience and the ability to apply this through discipline.

In regards to otherworld beings who work through Saturn, we find that the Master, as the spirit of the forest in fall and winter, can work easily in this tide. The Great Queen, too, comes through in Saturn's sphere. Here She is the death crone who receives those who pass, the Dark Queen who gathers souls so that they too can be renewed. As the death crone She assists with spirit evocation, as well as Traveling in Spirit, sending the fetch, and work with the many different astral forms and beings. Yet, in Saturn, She is the Wise Woman, crone, teacher and guide.

The Olympic spirit who resonates with Saturn is Araithron, sometimes known as Aratron. The grimoires explain that he helps with all things related to the Earth, including the evocation of earth elementals. He is said to aid with making one 'invisible' – that is, not noticed by others as needed. Generally, he can be called on to assist with most anything governed by Saturn.

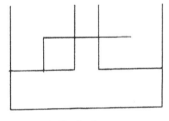

Sigil of Aratron

The archon associated with Saturn in the Abraxas system is Xais.

There are several seals that have emerged related to different functions of Saturn. Some of these are very dark, used in cursing or sending evil spirits to torment others. It is exceptionally rare that we use such tactics and I am not comfortable in presenting these in a public manuscript. Rather, the following seal can be used to evoke spirits of Saturn generally. However, the texts explain that this should only be done once your working space has been properly sealed and purified, and then only at night on a Saturday.

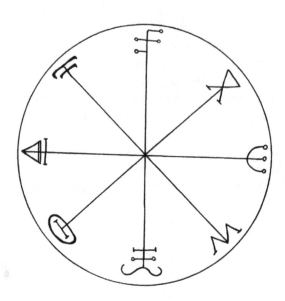

Seal of Evocation
Spirits of Saturn

The Kamea of Saturn has a long history in the Art as being very practical. Not only can it be used in each of the ways other planetary squares can be, it has the added benefit of being a protective shield of sorts. Whether worn, written on paper or parchment and placed in the home, or drawn directly on the beams of buildings; this square has a solid reputation of being highly effective for defense.

4	9	2
3	5	7
8	1	6

Kamea of Saturn

These last two images are included as they can be highly effective in the arousal of Saturn's influence in rites as needed.

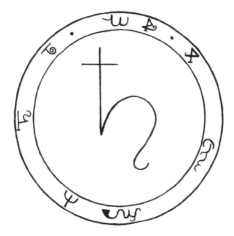

Seal of Saturn

Sigil of Saturn

Sigils of the Zodiac

Lastly, we need to consider the influence of stellar forces and the spirits who resonate with the signs of the Zodiac, because these form the backdrop and general means through which the planetary influences manifest. In doing so, the Witch or Magician can place the sigil of a planetary spirit alongside that of the zodiac sign desired to help channel how the planetary force will manifest the goal. For example, if one were working to bring monetary prosperity through a spell the Witch may combine the Seal of Jupiter with the zodiac sigil of Taurus.

Like the planets, each of the signs resonate with a number of different functions, governing many aspects of daily life. The following list of magical uses for each sign is far from conclusive. Rather it is meant as a quick reference that can be used in conjunction with the planets as you prepare your spells.

Aries

Aries brings power and attention to anything it is used for. However, this energy tends to be short lived. This influence is excellent when starting new projects. Any spell involving aggressive or assertive action, whether to create or destroy will thrive well under Aries. As this is a fire sign, the spirits of Aries work well with the evocation of fire elementals.

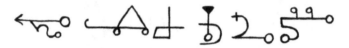

Taurus

The spirits of Taurus bring stability, harmony and physical pleasure. This can include monetary success as well as personal and sensual pleasure. As an earth sign, Taurus can be useful for all matters related to property and real estate, as well as banking. Love, fertility, steady growth all fall within these spirits' ability.

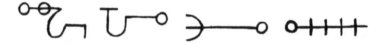

Gemini

Spirits resonating with Gemini work best with any goals in which one is trying to convey ideas and communicate out to others. Success in writing, public speaking, teaching, winning debates, convincing others, all fall with the realm of these spirits. Also, any matters related to transportation, movement of any kind, short trips can be influenced by the spirits here.

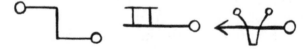

Cancer

All matters concerning the home and family, parents, safety and security can be strongly influenced by the spirits of this sign. Fertility, growth, abundance and prosperity all can be drawn in through these entities. Works related to finding a home, or obtaining property can be affected by these spirits. They can also influence other people emotionally on a deep, subconscious level. As this is a water sign, the spirits can assist with the evocation of water elementals.

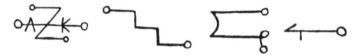

Leo

The spirits of Leo help to bring recognition and honor to any project you may be working on. They assist with spells meant to bring attention to oneself. As such, promotions, publicity, friendships, all fall in this category. Also, Leo works well with matters of love, as well as children. These spirits can be called on to aid in any creative pursuit

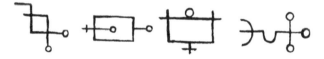

Virgo

The spirits here are best called on when seeking to bring intellectual pursuits into material manifestation. These entities aid with critical thinking, health and wellbeing. They can also be of help in the study and practice of Hermetic sciences and magical arts.

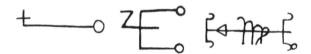

Libra

Relationships, both public and private, are influenced by the spirits of Libra. They control harmony, balance, and how one is perceived by others. The magical acts of fascination and glamour work well through these spirits. So too, these spirits work well in bringing and maintaining peace and cooperation. They also bring talent in the arts. As the cardinal air sign these spirits can aid with the evocation of air elementals.

Scorpio
These spirits are called on to aid with all forms of consultation with otherworld beings, particularly summoning the dead. The spirits of Scorpio aid in all acts of Witchcraft, enhancing one's intuition and skill. They can also be helpful in all matters related to sex and eroticism. They are very powerful and tend to having lasting effects when applied in ritual. As such great care should be taken. These spirits work well with that which is hidden or is meant to be kept secret

Sagittarius
Sagittarian spirits are called on in all matters related to education, philosophy, religion and science. As such they can bring knowledge of all of these. They also affect communication, particularly publication of books and manuscripts. They bring success in travel and foreign affairs. They also aid with selling of any kind. They tend to be generous in their benefits and can bestow a measure of prosperity and recognition.

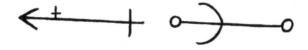

Capricorn

Capricorn, being a cardinal earth sign, has spirits who bring success and recognition in business. They can be called on to build one's public reputation and career, bringing respect from others. These spirits are useful in the evocation of earth elementals.

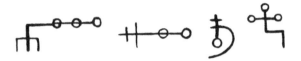

Aquarius

In Aquarius we find spirits who bring success in all social gatherings, aiding with popularity and friendships. These spirits can also bring knowledge, particularly of a technical or scientific nature. They also aid with the fulfillment of personal aspirations and lifelong goals.

Pisces

In Pisces we find spirits that can be called on to open paths between worlds. The spirits bring deep creativity and sensitivity. They enhance one's second sight, including abilities in divination as well as mediumship. They can also aid with recall of previous incarnations. These spirits can be called on to increase wealth if used in conjunction with Jupiter or the Sun.

Chapter Six

❖ THE SECRET SEAL ❖
AMULETS, TALISMANS, SIGILS AND SEALS

In the previous chapter a number of sigils, seals and related symbols were given in relation to the planets and zodiac. Each of these can be employed in many ways, from focal points in ritual meant to draw the power of the beings or forces involved, to markings placed on buildings or homes, or inscribed on objects to be carried or worn. Some of the sigils were accompanied by rites empowering these, but not all. The reason is that these markings are very flexible in how they can be employed. It would seem that at this point it is appropriate to present a clear understanding of how these are prepared, enchanted and used. In doing so, essentially these markings can be broken into two categories: amulets and talismans. There is a distinct difference between the two.

Amulets

As I was taught, an amulet is largely considered to be more or less passive or general in its effect, often being used as a protective device. In this capacity amulets are often thought of as creating a sphere of influence or 'field' around one that either attracts an influence desired or repels those that are harmful. Generally, the amulet draws its power from the items it is made of and the intent put into it by the Witch during the making. In considering their protective powers Cecil Williamson gives an excellent definition of the amulet:

"An amulet is an object which is endowed with magical power and which of its own accord uses these powers ceaselessly on behalf of the person who carries it, or causes it to be laid up in his house, or attaches it to his belongings, to protect him and his belongings from attacks from evil spirits."[74]

A good example of an amulet that both attracts and protects was seen in the Nata Bag described earlier. An amulet that is used solely to attract good fortune can be seen in the making of a Loadstone Pouch.

The Loadstone Pouch

Loadstones are natural magnetite, magnets found in nature. These are highly prized for their ability to attract virtually anything. This particular amulet is meant to draw good fortune and prosperity to the home. For this you will need a lodestone, either a High John the Conqueror Root or a Trillium Root (which is sometimes referred to as Low John Root, or Beth Root), a square of green cloth, red yarn or twine, and Vervain oil.

During the waxing Moon, in the day and hour of Jupiter, anoint the root and the lodestone with the Vervain oil. As you do so, use the passing of the power dua technique to infuse your desire into the this while reciting a basic chant. I use different renditions of:

"Money to the root,
Success through the stone,
Good Fortune comes to me and this home."

The chant can be that simple. In our experience, it is best to repeat the incantation over and over in a steady, rhythmic pattern as you build up your energy passing this to the root and stone. When ready place the lodestone and root in the center of the square of cloth. Then pull the corners of this

---

74. Patterson, Steve. *Cecil Williamson's Book of Witchcraft*. 2014.88

up creating a pouch. This is then tied shut with the yarn or twin. Be sure to leave enough twine at the end to make a loop in it. The entire pouch is then placed in the highest point of the home, or over the main entrance.

One could easily apply the same basic procedure to the sigils and seals discussed so far. Whether for protection, health, prosperity or any other general influence that the Witch is seeking, the simple act of gathering items which resonate with the goal, along with the intention put into the actual making of the amulet, can be highly effective.

Talismans

The talisman takes the object involved to a more powerful and direct level. Like the amulet, it too can and should be made of those items which resonate with the forces and intelligences one is seeking to work with. However, the talisman is meant to be specific and powerful usually functioning in a manner that is defined clearly by the forces invoked, as well as by the words and intent of the Witch. Where the amulet was general, the talisman is focused. Further, once the physical act of making the object is complete, a separate working is performed that opens the path between the being or force the talisman resonates with and this realm. In essence this rite causes the talisman to act as a conduit between worlds, linking the Witch to the otherworld force evoked.

As Francis King and Stephen Skinner state in their landmark work *Techniques of High Magic*, the talisman "should be constructed to attain a definite result". They go on to state "the talisman is ritually linked up with the planetary force concerned and also linked to the operator so that the magical energy is being continually channeled through to the objective, as more is attracted from the universe".[75] The following is a template we use for the activation of a planetary talisman.

---

75. King, Francis & Stephen Skinner. *Techniques of High Magic.* 1976.86-87.

Enchanting the Talisman

Looking to the list of qualities each planet corresponds to, choose the sigil, seal or marking that best relates to your goal. If this is one involving a specific spirit you will want to incorporate any instructions that are normally associated with the entity into this rite. The following can serve as an excellent foundational rite that has proven to be highly effective.

It is assumed that you have created the object to be enchanted in advance. If the item is a simple sigil that is to be traced on parchment you can opt to include the drawing of the talisman in the rite of enchantment itself. However, I find that sometimes things don't go as planned when drawing these. As such, I prefer to do this beforehand, and then have this ready for the enchantment itself.

Chose the appropriate tide of power. For any talisman meant to bring increase, the Waxing Moon is best. For those meant to release, disrupt or stop something, the Waning Moon is the tide to use. Then you will want to consider the day (or night) and hour governed by the planet. Note that if you are working with the Olympic spirits they prefer to be evoked at dawn on the day of the planet that they resonate with. I am also careful to consider the *Lady of the Moon* as described in *Horns of the Moon*, as this will give added power to the working.

Prepare your Roth Fail or working space as normal. This should include any opening evocations to your familiar, the spirits, as well as the Mistress and Master. You are going to want to have traced on the hearthstonè an equal sided Triangle of Art. Place the talisman inside this. Just behind this, but still inside the triangle, place a candle in the color of the planet involved. Preferably this would be a solid taper. If you do not have access to the appropriate color a plain white or a beeswax candle will work well. You will also want incense and oil that corresponds with the planet.[76]

---

76. See *The Willow Path* for a listing of incenses, herbs and oils related to the planets.

Planetary Correspondence					
Planet	Tone	Number on Material	Number in Abred	Color on Material	Color in Abred
Sun	G	1	6	Orange/ Gold	Yellow/ Gold
Moon	D	2	9	Green/ White	Violet
Mars	A	3	5	Red	Red
Mercury	E	4	8	Blue	Yellow
Jupiter	B	5	4	Purple/ Indigo	Blue
Venus	F	6	7	Green/ Pink or Red [77]	Green/ Aqua Marine
Saturn	C	7	3	All shades of grey up to and including Black	Black, Grey, Indigo

Place the stang behind the hearthstone ensuring that it is clearly displayed. If working with an actual hearth you may opt to use a smaller stang, approximately two feet tall that you can stand directly behind the furthest point of the triangle. The 'Hoodlamp' described earlier can take the place of the smaller stang. Either can be very effective in creating the link between worlds needed for this rite.

You will want to have the planetary incense burning from the beginning of the rite. Then anoint the candle with oil. While doing so use the dua to pass power into the candle, seeing the oil act as the agent that carries this. It should be

77. See *The Willow Path*, as there are several different colors used in practical magic in conjunction with Venus depending on the nature of the working.

noted that this does not have be an intense raising of energy at this point. Rather, you are simply seeking to further the link to the planetary force you are bringing through in the rite. This candle is then lit.

Next, with the Fe, just above the triangle, trace the outline of the Triangle of Art while envisioning this glowing with power. I prefer to see this as either an electric blue, or in the corresponding color of the planet I am working with.

Now, pick up the talisman and begin by first passing this through the smoke of the incense. As you do recite:

> "By the element of Air I conjure you, Spirit of (name of planet, or name of spirit)!
> That you may reside within this Talisman!"

Pass the talisman through the flame of the candle in the triangle and recite:

> "By the element of Fire I conjure you, Spirit of (name of planet, or name of spirit)!
> That you may reside within this Talisman!"

Sprinkle a small amount of water over the object:

> "By the element of Water I conjure you, Spirit of (name of planet, or name of spirit)!
> That you may reside within this Talisman!"

Sprinkle a small amount of salt over the object:

> "By the element of Earth I conjure you, Spirit of (name of planet, or name of spirit)!
>
> That you may reside within this Talisman!"

Now set the talisman in the triangle. With the Fe trace the invoking heptagram of the planet you are working with beginning at the point corresponding to the planet and following a deosil direction. This should be drawn in the air just above the triangle.

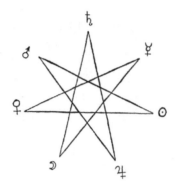

Planetary Heptagram

While tracing this chant:

"(Name of spirit, or "Spirits of ......") I conjure you,
By this sign of power I conjure you,
By this Ancient Art I conjure you,
By these words I conjure you,
That through this talisman I weave my fate!"

Replacing the Fe, take a moment to perform the Cloak but rather than envisioning the Moon (unless you are working with a lunar talisman), envision the light of the planet you are working with. Feel its energy flow into you, filling you. At the same time, envision the influence of the planet itself flowing through the stang that is set at the apex of the triangle. The stang, as the world tree, unites the different realms. Thus, it is the link between the Witch and the planetary force being sought.

When ready place your hands over the talisman forming a triangle by joining the thumbs and forefingers of your two hands. You should be able to see the talisman in the opening of the triangle between your hands. With both the hands allow the planetary energy to flow down through you into the talisman. At the same time you need to breathe energy through the opening into the talisman. Then, when ready, repeat:

"By my words, I conjure you,
By this breath of life, I conjure you,
By my will, I conjure you,
Spirits of (planet or the spirits name) I conjure you,
That through this talisman your power now flows!"

Now intone, hum, or if you are using a pitch pipe (which I often do), breathe the tone related to the planet involved. Let the tone fade. Then, when ready, in very clear and simple terms state the purpose of the talisman. Keep this short but ensure it is a goal that is within your realm of possibility. Don't place conditions on how or when the goal should manifest. Rather, be direct, respectful, clear and realistic. If possible, this should be done in a rhyming chant which you create for the purpose. But if you have trouble with rhyming don't stress over this. It is better to speak simply, clearly and with honesty. Also, this is not a prayer. You aren't asking, begging or cajoling. Rather you are stating a fact in honest and sincere terms. Remember that in magic words are reality. They are the vocal manifestation of the desire, passion and energy which you are now setting into motion.

At this point leave the talisman in the triangle, in front of the candle, to "cook". Often times I will also have a small food offering along with wine that I will give to the spirits involved, always partaking of these but leaving the largest portion for them.

The Roth Fail is then opened, without banishing. In fact, you should be certain not to do any closing or banishing over the talisman itself as you don't want to close the links you have formed. Once the candle has reached its 'burning time frame'[78] you may take up the talisman, carrying this. The food and wine should be taken into nature and either placed on the ground or buried.

As a side note, research is being done by some occultists into the sigils, spirits and seals of the outer most planets of Neptune, Uranus and Pluto. These are not normally used in Traditional Witchcraft. However, I feel that as an evolving and developing Art they should be. Essentially you will find that you can access these outer planets by seeing them as 'higher octaves' (not unlike tones) of certain other traditional planets. To use the influences of Neptune this can be reached through the days and hours of Jupiter. Uranus is accessed through Mercury, while Pluto is accessed through Mars.

If you are creating a talisman directly related to the zodiacal spirits the process is exactly the same. However, you will conduct the rite during the day and hour of the planet that traditionally governs the sign. Perhaps the following may be of help for those wishing to work with Zodiacal Spirits:

Zodiac Planetary Rulers		
Sign	**Planetary Ruler**	**Planetary Co-Ruler**
Aries	*Mars*	*Pluto*
Taurus	*Venus*	
Gemini	*Mercury*	
Cancer	*Moon*	
Leo	*Sun*	
Virgo	*Mercury*	
Libra	*Venus*	

---

78. See the chapter "Wax and Cord" for a clear description of the use of candles and their burning time frames.

Zodiac Planetary Rulers		
Scorpio	*Mars*	*Pluto*
Sagittarius	*Jupiter*	*Neptune*
Capricorn	*Saturn*	*Uranus*
Aquarius	*Saturn*	*Uranus*
Pisces	*Jupiter*	*Neptune*

Beyond planetary talismans there are a number of other sigils, seals and pentacles that form an important part of practical magic. While they are not specifically designed to bring through a particular spirit or force that resonates with the planets each of these do take advantage of specific tides of power. Here are some that I have found useful.

To Gain Friendship and Popularity

This particular talisman is used to bring popularity and friendship. It is best enchanted during the Waxing Moon on the day and hour of the Sun.

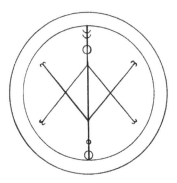

Seal of Friendship & Popularity

To activate this, follow the template given earlier, however you will want to change the wording to reflect your desire for this to be a talisman attracting friendship. This is especially so if you are looking to have this affect a specific person. For the sake of example, suppose you are creating this to gain the favor of a boss. When passing the talisman through the elements you may recite:

"The element of Air I conjure,
That the friendship of (name of person) increases toward me,
By this Talisman her/his favor I see!"

This would then be used with each passage, changing the element in the incantation. The tracing of the heptagram would be as it is for the Sun, as would the tone breathed in the enchantment. The further incantation could again be altered to reflect the goal:

"(Name of person) I conjure thee,
Your friendship and favor increase toward me!
By this sign of power I conjure it,
By this Ancient Art I conjure it,
By these words I conjure it,
Through this talisman your friendship grows toward me!"

Feel free to change the wording as needed to meet your goal, but follow the basic pattern of the template as it incorporates the underlying techniques proven to be effective in practical magic. Once the talisman is enchanted, carry this whenever you will be in the presence of the person.

Talisman of Knowledge
This seal is used to gain knowledge, assisting with memory and study. This is best created and enchanted during the Waxing Moon, on the day and hour of Mercury. As before the template given earlier works well, using the format for Mercury and adjusting the incantations to meet the needs of the goal.

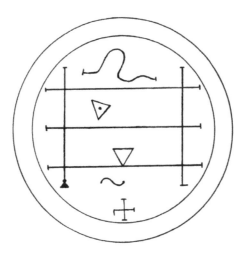

Seal of Knowledge

Talisman of Prosperity and Success

This would be enchanted during the Waxing Moon on the day and hour of Jupiter.

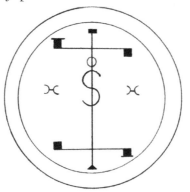

Seal of Prosperity

To Increase one's Second Sight

This particular seal is carried to increase one's ability to see the future. As such, it is excellent for seers and divination. This would be created during the Waxing Moon on the day and hour of Mercury.

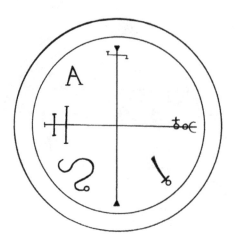

Seal of "Second Sight"

Talisman of Protection

The grimoires explain that this talisman ensures that "no one will have power against thee". This would be enchanted during the Waning Moon on the day and hour of Mars. Barring this Saturn could also work well.

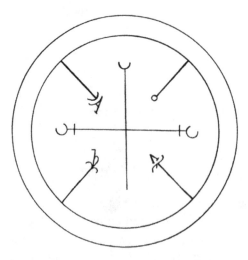

Seal of Protection

Love's Knot

This sigil is a traditional mark used to attract love. As a talisman it can be carried. If desired it can be combined with a Pentacle of Venus used also to attract love. On one side will be the knot, on the other the pentacle. These would be empowered during the Waxing Moon, day and hour of Venus.

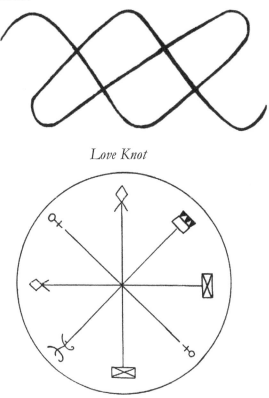

Love Knot

Venus Pentacle of Love

Talisman of Authority

This talisman is worn to enable one to be seen as an authority in whatever endeavor you may be involved. It also aids in directing others, including spirits. This is best enchanted during the Waxing Moon, on the day and hour of the Sun.

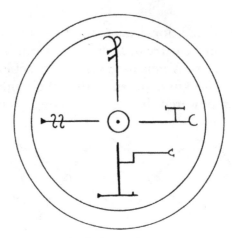

Seal of Authority

To Reverse Curses

This talisman is used to reflect and reverse curses back against those who cast these. This is best made during the Waning Moon on the day and hour of Saturn.

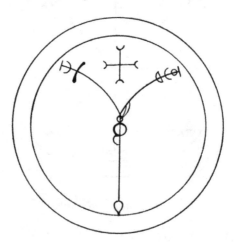

Seal to Reverse Curses

Chapter Seven

✥ THROUGH THE LOOKING GLASS ✥
MIRRORS IN TRADITIONAL MAGICAL ARTS

One of the most versatile, powerful and highly prized possessions of the Witch is the mirror. Whether these are nothing more than a carefully prepared drop of ink in which to gaze, to a handmade concave 'black' mirror, a well-crafted silvered mirror, or an actual crystal ball or 'show stone', mirrors can take on many forms and just as many uses. In the system of the Art that we practice, mirrors figure very highly. As such, I want to take the time to consider these carefully here.

Without a doubt, early humans first encountered mirrors in the reflective surfaces found in nature. The best example of this is the surface of bodies of water. In these, clear yet opposite images appear that have a subtle quality often drawing the viewer in. The more one looks the more deeply entranced one becomes.

In the Art we encounter an example of this in the creation of Moon Water.[79] In this, a natural spring, pond or well is sought in which one views the reflection of the Full Moon. Water, as a natural conductor of the Dragon's Breath, gathers astral energy easily. In starring at the reflection of the Moon on the water, one slips very easily into the state of becoming, merging with this energy.

Witches have learned how to gather this energy from the water. One of the most useful means for doing this is with

---

79. Complete instructions for the creation of Traditional Witches' Moon Water is given in *Horns of the Moon*.

the *Moon Rake*. This is a wooden staff approximately six feet long on which an old iron horseshoe is fixed to one end. The horseshoe is mounted with the horns facing to the side rather than straight up. This is then used to catch the power of the Moon by encircling its reflection inside the horseshoe on the surface of the water. As the energy collects, it is drawn in as the Witch pulls the rake back toward her. She then gathers this into herself in a similar fashion as she would when recalling the fetch.[80] From there it is only a matter of directing this into whatever object, tool, talisman, person, etc. that she enchanting.

Witches will also use silver bowls, or highly polished copper bowls, filling these with water. These are then set in such a way as to capture the reflection of the Full Moon. They can be used to collect the Moon's energy as well as a means of scrying. In some cases, an actual silver mirror can be placed in the bottom of the bowl. The Moon's reflection is then viewed through the water in the mirror below. This has a very unique effect in that two different reflections emerge at once and combine: that which forms on the surface of the water coupled with the image below. In doing so one is drawn into the images, immersing oneself in the power of the Moon while deepening the enchantment of the scrying that begins to take over.

The production and use of actual physical mirrors can be traced back at least to 6200 BCE, in Çatal Hüyük, near Konya, Turkey. There polished obsidian plates have been found. Çatal Hüyük was a sacred center with clear representations of Mother Goddess figures as well as horned bull forms. As such, the discovery of mirrors here almost certainly suggests a religious and possible magical purpose for these.

In Ancient Egypt polished Selenite mirrors, framed in wood, have been discovered dating to 4500 BCE, while in ancient Persia, now present-day Iran, copper mirrors from approximately 4000 BCE have been found.

---

80. See *Horns of the Moon* for detailed instructions on the fetch.

Some of the best examples of metal mirrors come from Egypt. The earliest of these begin to appear from approximately 2900 BCE. Like their Persian counterparts, the first of these were made of copper. However, the Egyptians quickly developed bronze, silver and gold mirrors.

To understand the magical significance of the mirror, some of the earliest references to this do, in fact, come from Egypt. In the inscriptions it is clear that the mirror was seen as sacred to the great Goddess Hathor. Texts frequently show handheld mirrors being offered to Her. For the Egyptians, the mirror represented the power of the Sun as "the Eye of Ra", a title for Hathor Herself. Thus, they were viewed as Hathor's power manifest on earth.

With Egyptian handheld mirrors the handle and cross bar at the base caused these to be seen as a form of the Ankh, a symbol of life. In Egyptian magic these were often used to see the actual life force, or 'Ka' energy of those people reflected in them. This was done by gazing at another person in the mirror in order to see their Ka, or spirit double. Offering mirrors at tombs was an extension of this function with the mirror becoming a means by which one could see the shades of the dead in the reflection.[81]

It may be important to know that Central American Aztecs used polished obsidian in very similar ways. The mirror was used to examine the reflection of a person, seeing their spirit self, in order to diagnosis illness and supernatural afflictions. The Aztecs also used these for divination and communication with the dead.

The earliest known glass mirrors appear to date to the third century CE. These were generally backed with lead or goldleaf. Around 500 CE the Chinese created the first known silver backed mirrors. In Europe though, glass mirrors really didn't begin to be produced much until the 11th century. However, these were both very

---

81.   https://www.nytimes.com/2003/08/03/books/chapters/mirror-mirror.html Last accessed 29/3/2022

expensive and rare. It wasn't until the 16th century that the technique of using a tin-mercury amalgam to coat the back of glass was applied to mirror making with the primary center of manufacture being Venice, Italy. There, larger mirrors began to be produced, with some being as much forty inches across.

In medieval Europe even a small glass mirror was highly prized. When a mirror broke the pieces would be saved. Often, they would be kept as smaller mirrors, with some being placed in wood frames formed around the jagged edge.

An alternative to the 'silver' mirror was the 'black' mirror. These were glass with their backs blackened rather than silvered. This was an easier process to produce, essentially by covering the backs with soot or black paint. Several examples of black mirrors exist, including in number of paintings related to the practice of the Art. For example, the 15th century painting of "The Annunciation", featured in the Fitzwilliam Museum is heavily laden with esoteric symbolism and shows a small round black mirror off to the side. A Flemish painting from the same century depicts a young Witch. Entitled "The Love Spell", this painting distinctly shows a round black mirror as being one of the many items she is using to weave her magic.

Despite the extensive versatility of mirrors and their use in the Art, their overall function falls within one of three categories: revealing, repelling, or enchanting. It is under these three classes that I want to discuss different workings and spells that mirrors are critical to.

Mirrors of Revealing
The Speculum
These are perhaps the most common uses of the magic mirror; that is for scrying, summoning and as gateways. In this capacity they can be thought of as passive in nature, creating points of focus which open as portals: passages through time as well as doorways between worlds.

A good example of this type of mirror is found in the simple employment of black ink. This can be used in and of itself as a small pool meant as a scrying mirror. Other than water itself, black ink would have been one of the most common forms of mirror scrying available to the country Witch as it was relatively inexpensive and very easy to hide.

A traditional ink that would have been very easy to make would have been *Lampblack*. Essentially this is made by blackening the back of a spoon with soot from a candle or oil lamp. The soot would be tapped off of this into a small bowl until there was enough to use. This was then mixed with a small amount of water to form a basic ink. This ink could then be thickened by adding any natural starch. In your own practice, rather than going through this process, a good quality black India Ink is perfect for scrying and is easy to obtain.

Beyond simply using a small pool of ink, other methods include mixing this into a goblet or bowl of water. The amount added depends entirely on the Witch herself. Some may find it useful to slowly pour small amounts in and allow the ink to form shapes and swirls that can then be 'read'. Others may find it helpful to mix this in a fairly uniform manner, allowing the water to take on different shades of gray and slowly merging into black, while gazing into the vessel.

Rites of scrying are best done at night, preferably on a Monday or Wednesday. You will want to be seated in a comfortable position where you can easily gaze into the goblet. Generally, it is best to be in a room lit only by firelight. Some find that it is best not to have any light reflecting on the surface of the scrying device as this can be distracting. In fact, many find it best to have a single candle off to the side and placed so that the flame isn't seen. For others though, where the candle is placed doesn't appear pose a problem at all, finding that they can scry well with candle light showing in the reflection. Each Witch needs to find what works for her.

Begin by using the Serpent, Cloak and Star techniques to prepare. Then call on the spirits, particularly your familiar, to be present and aid you. Let yourself relax as you slip into a light trance state and then pour a few drops dark Indian Ink into the water. Let this swirl in the goblet taking shape and form. Don't rush the process. Rather, take you time and watch the surface as you just let yourself go, allowing your intuition to see what it can.

With scrying the key, at least as I have come to understand it, is to remain completely relaxed and open, yet, maintain a 'gentle' focus as you allow the vision to take over. In my experience, I find that I do see forms in the item I am scrying yet these tend first appear as smokey, malleable figures. When scrying in a mirror it is very common for me to find that only my eyes remain visible with the rest of the mirror fogging over.

At this point, some people find that a point of light emerges from the mist, filling the scrying device and then changing to the visions desired. Others, such as myself, find that the mirrored object simply fades from awareness altogether as images and sensations take over. It is such an odd experience, for at once, I find that I am still aware of my physical surroundings but they seem to 'step back', becoming almost illusionary as the scrying images emerge in my consciousness, capturing my attention. In fact, when this happens the images tend to be very vivid and perhaps 'more real' than my material surroundings.

As with so much in the Art, much depends on your own intuitive abilities and how these manifest in you. Also, keep in mind that scrying takes time and a lot of practice. There will be sessions when you will stare at the mirror for what will seem like an eternity with no results at all. Generally though, with time most people are successful in varying degrees.

Another example of scrying can be found in the use of the Witch Ball. These are hollow glass balls that are often used in protective magic, however, in this setting they can also be used for scrying. In fact, their function in this regard extends back to at least the 16th century, presumably because access to an actual crystal ball or silvered mirror would have been very difficult.

One method that I am aware of is to fill a bowl with Mugwort and then place the Witch Ball in the center of this. The Witch then uses this as her scrying device in a similar manner to the way the goblet and ink had been used.

From the Witch Ball it is a small step to consider the use of actual glass or crystal balls, also known as *Show stones*. As rare as these were in earlier days we do have accounts of some country Witches who did use these in their practice. For example, accounts from the 1700's in Yorkshire, England speak of Betty Strother as a "White Witch" who employed both a "looking glass" and "crystal ball".[82]

If you can afford one, an actual clear quartz crystal ball is excellent for scrying and for spirit summoning. With quartz being so closely linked to the Moon and the Dragon's Breath, this is the perfect vehicle. In using these you will want to wash the ball in water in which an infusion of Wormwood and Vervain had been made. In addition, if you have made your own fluid condenser this should be applied after the crystal has dried.

The crystal ball is very unique in that, in many ways, it can step in as a substitute for skulls which are often used by some Traditional Witches. For them the skull acts as an oracle and vessel through which spirits can come through to our realm. We use the crystal ball in exactly the same way. An example of this was given in the rite of "Calling the Elders" as discussed in *Horns of the Moon*. Another use of the crystal or mirror is in the evocation of planetary and zodiacal spirits. If you are unable to obtain an actual quartz crystal ball, a good lead crystal or even quality glass crystal ball can work well.

---

82. Harley, Marie and Joan Ingilby. *Life and Tradition in The Moorlands of North-East Yorkshire.* 1972, 1990.123

Planetary Spirits in the Looking Glass
In this rite you will not only be scrying, as you seek to evoke planetary spirits in the speculum, you will then ask them to assist with the goal or spell at hand. For this you will need to draw the following sigil onto a quality paper or parchment in advance of your working.

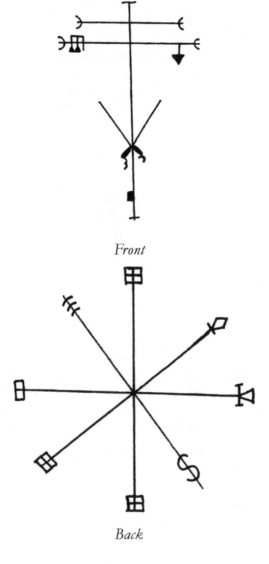

Front

Back

On the day and hour of the planet you are working with, prepare your Roth Fail or ritual space as normal. Then draw an equal sided triangle on the hearthstone/altar. This can be traced with herbs associated with the planet, or you may simply mark this with chalk or flour. We often use different colored cloths depending on the planet and force desired, and paint a triangle directly on this.

Place the sigil directly beneath the mirror or crystal. Then, in front of the mirror place another parchment with the sigil of the planetary or zodiacal spirit you are evoking. If you are simply calling on the spirits of a planet generally, as opposed to a specific otherworld being, then use the appropriate seal of the planet as shown in the previous chapter.

As always you will want to have entered into a state of becoming. You should have an incense burning that corresponds with the planet involved. In the case of working with the zodiacal spirits use an incense that resonates with the planet that governs the particular sign.

Proceed to trace over the triangle with your Fe, beginning at the apex and proceeding deosil. As you do, envision the Dragon's Breath flowing through you and out through the Fe vitalizing the triangle with energy. Then focus on the crystal or mirror as you chant:

> "I conjure you (name of the spirit, or if working the spirits of the planet generally, address these as "spirits of …"),
> By my breath I conjure you,
> By this smoke I conjure you,
> By these words of power I conjure you,
> Sator
> Azamor
> Spirit of (Name of spirit, or the particular planet),
> I conjure you,
> By this Art you do come,
> To aid me in this task!"

Chant this several times as you gaze into the crystal, allowing yourself to become aware of the spirits as they coalesce and emerge. When ready state your goal in clear terms. Don't dress this up in any way. Nor should you state how the goal is to come about. Magic follows the lines of least resistance and often times results come from avenues that one never would have imagined.

Once you have communicated the purpose of the spell, thank the spirits for their help, then give them a small offering of food and wine as appropriate to the planet. This is such a simple yet often overlooked step in the process. Offerings become links between the Witch and the spirits. Even the simplest of gestures help to create relationships with these otherworld beings. In doing so, channels open through which they can manifest in this realm.

Silver and Black Doors

As already mentioned, mirrors really are doorways to different worlds and realities. When gazed into, the simple surface of the mirror takes on real depth, revealing not just a reflection of the material realm, but also opening into worlds that reach far beyond. Whether one uses a silver or black mirror, they both are powerful.

In the Hermetic Order in which I did my training, one of the central items to our practice is the use of a full-length mirror that is taller than the average person and several feet wide. Referred to as the Speculum this is kept veiled in most rituals, yet, when opened, it literally acts as a portal linking us to any number of realms.

Of course, the country Witch from a few centuries ago wouldn't have been able to have such an expensive and luxurious item. However, she may have access to smaller silvered mirrors. Or, as shown in the painting of the Witch and "The Love Spell" described earlier, she may very well have had access to black mirrors. These would function in the same way. In fact, ceremonial magician Dion Fortune described in detail the use of black mirrors in her own form of Hermetic Arts.[83]

Whichever you chose, a quality mirror dedicated solely to your Art is well worth the investment. Ideally this should be new and relatively unused. Mirrors tend to gather and hold psychic energy (a factor that is important when we consider mirrors of enchantment). For the purposes of traveling in spirit to access different worlds you want to avoid using a mirror that may have acquired influences that are not desired.

The mirror should be prepared in much the same way as the showstone. That is, it should be washed in a Wormwood and Vervain infusion. If available, this should be followed by applying a very thin coat of the Witch's own fluid condenser to the surface of the mirror. Once this has been done the mirror can be used just as the crystal was, to summon spirits or for divination. However, the mirror has an additional advantage. The mirror can be 'tuned' (for lack of a better word) to resonate with very specific realms and dimensions. In doing so they then act as portals to those realms.

This is done during the actual ritual, on the planetary day and hour that resonates with the realm sought. Begin by taking an oil appropriate to the realm and tracing the *Sigil of Crossroads* on the surface:

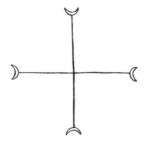

Sigil of the Crossroads

If you are seeking a realm that resonates with a planet, trace the appropriate sigil for this beneath the Crossroads

---

83. Fortune, Dion. *Moon Magic.* 1956 (edition referenced 1979).

sigil. This could even be something as simple as the normal glyph of the planet as used in Astrology.

The second part of this process is to 'load' the mirror with energy linked to the world one is seeking. In doing so, a resonance and linking between your working space and the realm is creating. This is done by drawing in the Dragon Breath and projecting this onto the surface of the mirror. For this use the formula of the dua, described earlier. Yet, while performing this, envision the energy flowing from yourself onto the mirror in the color, image or symbol that corresponds with the realm.

Feel free to engage the full complement of your imagination. Don't hold back in the least. Remember, 'force follows will', so use your imagination enthusiastically. You want to be able to 'see' in your mind the translucent veil between the worlds. If you were to reach out and touch the mirror, its surface should seem to be almost liquid in nature.

At this point you will want to employ a gesture that is only known to you or the group you are working with. This can be of your own design. Essentially this will be a hand gesture that designates opening or closing the veil between the worlds for you. Some will use a gesture in which they bring their hands together in front of the mirror as if holding the edges of a curtain. Then, when opening the mirror, they will pull their hands apart. After the working is complete the reverse gesture is used to close the veil. Along with this you may include a simple enchantment such as:

"The veil is drawn back,
The gate of (name of realm sought) opens to me!"

Like the hand gesture, the enchantment should be of your own making, keeping it simple and direct. You will use both in tandem whenever working with the mirror. This ensures that the mirror can only be used by you because it is linked through the gesture and incantation. Once this

The hearth prepared for Spirit Scrying

*Above: A Prosperity Spell with the Kamea of Jupiter set
before a candlewith fresh Vervain encircling this*

*Below: The hearth set with many of the tools of the Art including various
Fe's/wands, the wind roarer, black hilt knife, goblet, cauldron, small stang
and spirit gad, scrying "Witch Ball", pentacle, Alraun Root. To either side of
the hearth is the besom and stang. In front of the hearth is the eight spoked
spinning wheel*

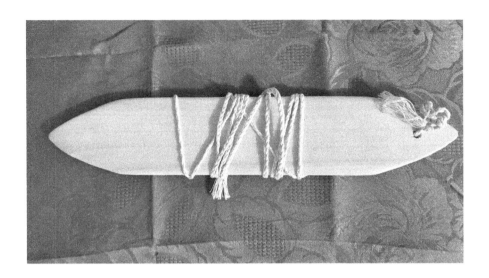

Top: Wind Roarer used to call spirits

Right: The Crystal Well prepared for the enchantment of the Serpent Fe

Left: Serpent Fe/wand set in the well as in the ritual of Enchantment

Below: Protection in magical affairs is critical. Rowan, Oak and Birch Bark all can be used to the construction of amulets and talismans

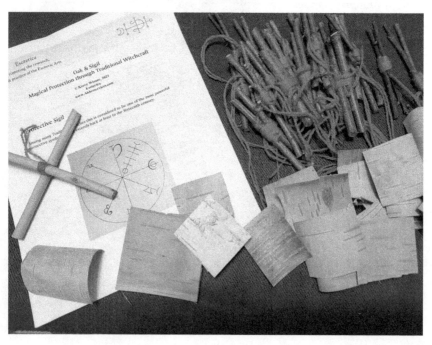

The hearth set for the festival of Samhain

The hearth set for the festival of Samhain

The hearth set for the festival of Samhain

Candle magic combined with planetary influences can be very effective. In these photos the "Solar Seal of Success" is engraved on brass and placed before a green candle. This is centered in a triangle of three orange candles.

Candle magic combined with planetary influences can be very effective. In these photos the "Solar Seal of Success" is engraved on brass and placed before a green candle. This is centered in a triangle of three orange candles.

The Serpent Fe/Wand

Left: The Serpent Fe/Wand

Below: A Jupiter spell of prosperity

Left & below: The hearth is set with a black candle, a sealed Mirror Box with a 'taglock' placed within. To the left is a hand mirror used only for spell casting. To the right is the black hilt knife. This is a classic setup for reversing curses

Left: The Lady's table set for ritual

Below: Placed directly in front of the 'smaller' stang, the flame of the candle acts as a portal and focal point between worlds that the Witch then accesses. Beeswax candles (as shown here) are some of the best for spell casting

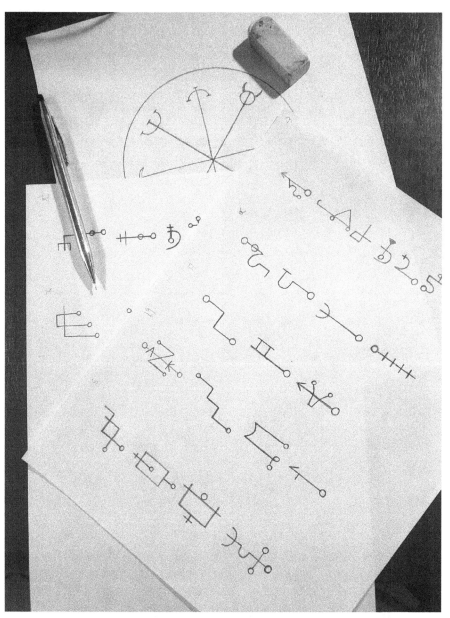

It is prudent to first trace sigils in pencil before the actual ritual to ensure accuracy.

In our system Ancient Egyptian magic also figures highly. This is a photo of the Goddess Hwt-Hrw (Hathor). Many Traditional Witches feel that Hwt-Hrw is one of the otherworld beings who guide this system of the Art.

In our system Ancient Egyptian magic also figures highly. This is a photo of the Goddess Hwt-Hrw (Hathor). Many Traditional Witches feel that Hwt-Hrw is one of the otherworld beings who guide this system of the Art.

is done it is only a matter of moving across the threshold, traveling in spirit.[1] Or, this would be the moment when the summoning of otherworld beings would be highly effective, allowing them to appear in the mirror or even cross through into our realm.

Mirrors of Repelling

From the receptive mirrors of scrying and doorways we move to the mirror as a defensive tool. Mirrors have long been prized in the Art for their ability to repel unwanted forces. This is particularly so when one suspects other people of directly sending malevolent forces and spirits in the form of a curse. A good example of this type of mirror is seen in the use of the Chinese Bagua Mirrors. These are hung at key points in the home or above one's exterior door to keep evil away.

Similarly, the Witch Ball noted earlier has been a very common protective mirror used for centuries. As a defensive tool these are set on a window sill. In some cases one may find one that is still inside a woven net, just as it would have been used by fishermen. These would be hung in the window. In either situation, the Witch Ball is meant to both fascinate spirits while reflecting any evil away from the home. Living in New England, we are lucky in that these can still be found in some local antique shops along the sea coast.

As a variant of the Witch Ball, the large Victorian Garden Gazing Balls have recently come back into favor. These function in a similar fashion, at once fascinating the spirits of the garden while repelling negativity.

In our system one of the most effective tools of protection is the 'Mirror Box'. This is a relatively simple object to make. It consists of six equal sized square reflective 'silvered' mirror tiles. These are used to form a box with the reflective sides facing in. It is probably best to have these line the interior

---

1. The complete technique for developing skill in Traveling in Spirit is given in detail in *Horns of the Moon*.

walls of a wooden box, however, in a pinch we have glued the tiles together directly. The top mirror is kept loose as a cover. The exterior of the box should be covered in black with no symbols at all placed on it. This maybe painted, or as we prefer, we cover these with black velvet.

Into this place a taglock of the person, or people, whom you suspect are behind any hexes or negativity being directed toward you. This can be something as simple as a photograph. However, I have found that the more personal the item the stronger the link is and the more effective the working.

Once this is placed in the box, the cover is set on top with the mirror facing in. At this point the person is surrounded by mirrors on all sides. The box is then placed on the hearthstone. Directly behind this place a black candle. Often times I will also use a handheld reflective mirror. In addition, I will have on hand the black hilt knife.

At this point the black candle is lit. Then pick up the handheld mirror and knife. With the knife in your dominate hand, and the mirror in the other, point the knife at the box while having the handheld mirror also facing the box. Then form the mental link with the person involved. See them clearly in your mind as you make that connection. Then begin a slow and steady chant:

> "Your curses and your sorcery,
> Are powerless to injure me.
> Reflect and return,
> Reflect and return,
> All you do reflects back on you!"

This or variation thereof are chanted over and over as you continue to point the mirror and knife at the box. Allow yourself to become completely consumed with the passion of your own ability to defend yourself. In your mind see any energy or spirits which the person may be sending being drawn to the candle and then into the box itself. Once there it has no place to go except into the taglock and, thus, back to the person who sent it. When finished let the candle burn itself out then put the box in a dark place in your home where it will remain undisturbed.

This is a highly effective means of self-defense which has the added benefit of having virtually no negative influence on the one who creates the box. For it only reflects what the person in the box is sending. If they aren't doing anything negative nothing will happen to them. However, if they are, the forces involved will rebound on to them and usually very quickly. The greater their anger, focus and power, the more swiftly and decisively the return to them will be. I have personally seen this happen on several occasions with surprising and very dramatic results. As an alternative chant to that given above the following is adapted from a hex removal spell of Sybil Leek's that she referred to as "The Witches' Formula":

"By the power of fire I conjure it,
By the power of earth I conjure it,
By the power of air I conjure it,
By the power of water I conjure it,
By the life in the blood I conjure it,
Be thou (name of person) stopped!
Your evil returns from whence it came,
Your sorcerous words return to thee,
As thou would have them be to me.
I banish you!"[2]

Sometimes it isn't practical to make a Mirror Box. They can be difficult to construct and are fragile. Also, they tend to naturally draw the attention of the curious who may stumble upon them in their resting place. As a substitute

---

2. Adapted from "The Witches Formula". Leek, Sybil. *The Sybil Leek Book of Curses*. 1975.32-33.

we have found that cheap, disposable compact mirrors are an excellent alternative. These can be purchased in most department stores and many have the added advantage of having two mirrors facing each other. Frequently one of these will be a magnifying mirror, which is so much the better when it comes to defensive workings. These can be used in exactly the same way as the Mirror Box. However, we have found that an effective final step in the spell is to seal the compact with black wax or even black waterproof tape and then bury this in a spot that the person in question has to cross over. Again, the effect can be quite dramatic and sudden.

Sometimes the Witch may find herself the subject of a blasting that may be coming from a coordinated group, an event that Julie referred to as a "drum roll". Or, you may not have a taglock on the individuals involved. It may be just a matter of some basic divination and a calculation of the tides that can give you a good idea of when the actual attack is likely to be generated. Of course, the Witch will want to have as many of the protections discussed previously in place. Nevertheless, a well-trained group of sorcerers placing a curse while in the correct tide can be quite formidable. Yet, even this can be repelled with the help of mirrors.

Once the probable time of the cursing is determined the Witch should retire to her Roth Fail and prepare this carefully. You will want to have with you all of your normal tools as well as a goblet of red wine, and four mirrors that can be set up easily to face outward at the circle's edge. At each quadrant you will place a tall solid black taper. You will also want only black candles on the hearthstone, however, if available, a single purple candle can also be placed in the center of the hearthstone. Be certain to have chosen a protective incense. This could be something as simple as a combination of dried Angelica Root, St. John's Wort and Pine needles.

As with all rituals you will call on the spirits and your familiar to assist with the rite. Then you will proceed as follows.

Standing at the hearthstone begin by dipping the tip
of the blade of the Black Hilt Knife into the goblet of
red wine, then pass this through the flame of the black
candles, smoke of the incense, then dip this into the salt
and then the water.

Beginning in the south, trace all three circles of the Roth
Fail with the Black Hilt Knife each in a tuathal direction
while chanting the following repeatedly until done:

"Elements come to my aid
Sun, Sky, Earth and Sea,
I am strong and unafraid,
Evil forces return and die!"

Returning to the south, point the Black Hilt Knife out
toward the direction. As you do recite the following:

"Your curses and your sorcery,
Are powerless to injure me!
With this mirror I give your curses back to thee!
Return, return, return, three times three!"

Do the same at each quarter moving in a tuathal direction.
Then return to the hearthstone. Take up the Stang holding
this in both hands as you state:

"By the Witch Queen Mistress,
By He who rides in the Night,
By the spirits of this coven
Gathering in the fire's light.
I am protected, in this compass of light.
Any evil spirit, thought or curse is banished!
Reflect and Return,
Reflect and Return,
Reflect and Return
From whence you came!
Sciath (Pronounced *SHKEEA*)!"

While intoning the final word envision a pure pulse of energy reverberating out in all directions from the Stang forcing all unwanted forces away. Then proceed to each of the quarters, again beginning in the south and moving tuathal. Hold the Stang aloft and intone the Word of Power:

"Sciath (Pronounced *SHKEEA)*!"

Remain in the Roth Fail for the remainder of the planetary hour, after which it is safe to leave. Leave the candles to burn out completely.

Mirrors of Enchantment

A unique quality of mirrors is their ability to absorb, retain and radiate psychic energies which they are exposed to. This appears to be due to the crystalline feature of glass combined with the reflective qualities they possess. This can have some important uses in the magical arts. For, essentially, a mirror can be loaded with a specific enchantment that is then meant to affect any viewer from there on.

A classic example is given in Charles Leland's *Gypsy Sorcery and Fortune Telling*, and later recounted in Paul Huson's *Mastering Witchcraft*. For this a new mirror is set to capture the image of two dogs copulating. While this is occurring a chant is said which identifies the enchanter with one dog and the person whom they desire with the other. The mirror is then wrapped in cloth until such time as the Witch is with the other person. At some point during this meeting the Witch contrives a way to unveil the mirror and have the person look into this which, in turn, releases the spell causing the person to desire them.

While this was a crude example, the principals involved remain essentially the same when enchanting a mirror. And, of course, a mirror can be enchanted for almost any purpose so long as the ultimate goal is to influence the gazer. Ideally the mirror should be new. Barring that, this should be cleansed in advance. Probably the best method for clearing a used mirror would be through an adaptation of the tool cleansing given in the first book.

Then a tide of power needs to be chosen that clearly resonates with the desired goal. The stronger the alignment the more energy there will be to charge the mirror. Look to the planetary functions as well as the *Ladies of the Moon* to assist you here. If possible, the closer to the Full Moon the better as the Dragon's Breath is strongest then. If you can tie the goal directly to those things normally governed by the Moon, so much the better as mirrors naturally have a strong lunar quality to them. In the rite of loading the mirror, be sure to do this in a darkened place with only the light of candles related by color to the tide you are using present.

Think of the mirror as being similar to old plate glass film photographs from the early 20th century. Like these you want to expose the mirror to the exact influence that will be imbedded in this going forward. The greater the power and emotional intensity, combined with a strong focus of intent, will determine the vividness and strength of the enchantment.

At the appropriate tide, with those items that most strongly resonate with the forces to be evoked begin by clearing your mind and gently performing the Serpent, Cloak and Star. Then vividly envision the scene or goal that is to be placed into the mirror. Once again, use your imagination to the fullest. Don't hold back at all. Let the image build in your mind and, more importantly, in your emotions. The image forms the structure of the goal, but the emotions generate the power that will take shape in the mirror itself.

A solid, well thought out chant that evokes both the forces within the tide along with the clear verbal image of the goal as manifest *in the present* will aid dramatically. As the image, emotions and chant build, raise your palms toward the mirror and perform the dua, as you envision the force of your desire flowing into the mirror itself. See the glass as being a liquid pool that eagerly receives the energy, the two merging as the image you have generated spreads across its surface, permeating its depths. Spend some time on building this image up. How long depends on the strength of the emotion and your clarity. Once the emotion reaches a distinct peak, let that be the final push flowing into the mirror.

At this point lower the hands, and relax for a moment. If you were using a planetary force or specific spirit, seal the mirror by tracing the appropriate sigil associated with the force. You may also intone the force's name or use a specific Word of Power.[3] Then cover the mirror with a new cloth and put the mirror away until such time as you can arrange to have the person to be enchanted look into this.

For added strength this procedure can be done several times, or in a series of workings over a distinct period of time. Because mirrors are so prone to absorbing, retaining and then radiating energy back, the more the mirror is exposed to the same force the greater it will function. The concern is that you must be careful to use the same imagery, emotion and goal in each loading for this to be effective. If anything is different in the other sessions it will have a similar effect to a photograph that is 'double exposed' presenting a confusing and blurred response.

Obviously, like so much in the Art strong ethical repercussions need to be considered when enchanting a mirror. Be certain of the goal. What consequences, both intended and unintended, may result from enchanting a person with the desire that will be given? Also, often there is a side effect of enchanting a mirror that is seldom considered. That is the very real possibility that the mirror will be looked upon by others who are not the intended target. In the case of the Romany seduction mirror, what happens when someone other than the hoped for lover picks up the mirror and gazes into it? One may have suitors that one never expected or wanted. So, think very carefully before using the enchanted

---

3. See the listing of Words of Power which we frequently use further in this book.

mirror. Still, they can be wonderful tools. A mirror that is regularly loaded with the intention of bringing harmony and happiness to a home and is then hung in a hallway where guests glance into as they enter, can be a tremendous aid to domestic stability and peace. The key lies in the intention and emotional maturity of the Witch herself.

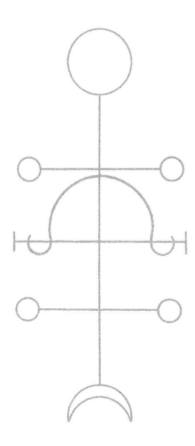

Chapter Eight

✤ MIST AND GLAMOUR ✤
THE SECOND SKIN AND THE ART OF
FASCINATION

When looking through old legends surrounding Witches, a frequent theme involves the placing of a 'glamour' on people, places or objects. In fact, there is real truth in these accounts. The art of fascination and the glamour form an important part of Traditional Witchcraft. At its most fundamental a glamour is exactly as the legends describe: a series of occult techniques that cause others to see and react to a person, object or place in a specific manner that may not normally be consistent with how these were perceived before. This includes a glamour that is placed causing a person or object that previously had been seen as 'plain' or 'unnoticed' to now become utterly hypnotic, capturing the attention of those around them.

The techniques used to create this condition vary greatly, yet at their heart they involve the same basic elements: the ability of the Witch to alter and project the second skin or etheric substance that is the cloak. This second skin can be compared to the auric double which surrounds each of us. This is highly malleable and with practice can be made to change in form, shape and color. And, as was shown in the discussion surrounding the fetch, this same substance can be projected away from the body and then modeled as needed. In either case, this is done through will and desire.

Perhaps the following can serve as a very simple example. Early in my training I was working with a number mental exercises and breathing techniques that were meant to energize the aura, the second skin. I had practiced with these daily drawing in energy through a technique that was very similar to the Serpent's Breath. At the time I was without transportation and walked home from work each evening. On one particular night, as I was making my usual journey, I decided to use the techniques. As I walked, I began the breathing pattern accompanied by the visualizations, drawing in the Dragon's Breath and then using this to strengthen my aura. In doing so I decided to place a real effort on changing the color of the second skin to a brilliant fiery orange. I did this with sole objective of seeing if I could get the attention of the different auto drivers who were passing by. I didn't make any effort to flag any vehicle down. Rather I just kept walking as normal, with the added process of using my own visualization to project the energy to the aura and see this in my mind as a flaming radiant orange.

Within minutes a car going the opposite direction pulled over. A woman rolled down her window and asked if I need a lift. She stated that it was cold and wanted to help. I was somewhat surprised, but thanked her for her offer, explaining that I was only a couple blocks from my destination.

One could easily state that this was pure coincidence. Yet, this had never happened before despite walking this road several times. However, in the very moment that I was practicing the glamour a total stranger's attention was grabbed to the point that she felt compelled to stop. This was just a simple example, yet the principals involved are essentially the same. Over the years I have used this technique in business meetings, social gatherings, as well as when confronted by individuals who were clearly attempting to threaten me. In each case it was a matter of focusing the will through desire and intent, accompanied by careful breathing, to project a specific appearance or persona in order to change how others perceived me. That is the very definition of a glamour.

While this can be, and in many cases is, brought on through ritual procedures it doesn't have to be. In fact, the very nature of fascination is organic, often occurring in the moment. Whether it be the looked-for glance across the room, the customary handshake, a brief hug in a social gathering, or the unexpected brush of a person's body in a crowded room, each can be used in the placing of a glamour.

I know this sounds terribly manipulative, and it is. Yet, don't we do the same when dressing and preparing to go out in public? We pick out specific clothing, fix our hair in a desired style, all for the sole purpose of causing others to see and react to us as we desire. Fascination takes this a step further using one's natural occult abilities to strengthen and project the image.

When it comes to the Art all practical magic, more or less, is an attempt to gain some measure of control over a situation or person. Magic is the art of creating change in accord with the will through occult means. Why should fascination be shunned or somehow seen as less than moral? It is here, once again, that the Counsels of the Wise need to be considered. Emotional maturity, wisdom and a solid consideration of the ramifications of one's actions always need to be a part of the Witch's calculus before performing any magic. Yet, we wouldn't have this ability if it wasn't meant to be used. This applies to the glamour in all its forms.

Perhaps the real advantage of fascination is that it doesn't require specific spells and incantations. These can be used, but they don't have to be. Rather fascination is a simple matter of drawing in and then projecting the Dragon's Breath through the natural channels inherent in one's own body. Paul Huson points out that energy tends to gather and be projected most readily through one's eyes, hands and genitals.[4] To this list I would also add, a person's hair and most importantly their breath.

One of the most potent ways to regulate and project this energy is through the use of one's breathing. As noted

---

4. Huson, Paul. *Mastering Witchcraft*. 1970.

elsewhere steady, rhythmic breathing coupled with simple visualization helps to build up energy relatively quickly in the body and more importantly in the second skin. Regular work with the Serpent, Cloak and Star methods will go a long way in giving you access to this energy. This can then be easily projected through the breath. As we have already seen, there are many spells which require one to breathe life into an object, be it a poppet, talisman or amulet of some sort. This same technique is used by some Traditional Witches and Hermetic Orders during initiation rites. Often calling this the 'charged breath', I would like to present the technique here.

The Charged Breath
Begin by calming the mind and gently regulating your breathing, moving through the visualizations involved in the Serpent, Cloak and Star. Then focus your attention on your solar plexus as you envision energy centering there as light, or force. In visualizing this choose a color that best matches the intention. Coupled with this 'light' keep a clear, focused image of the desire you seek. Allow yourself to fantasize in detail about the goal, letting this become emotionally charged in every way possible. Remember that while will and visualization form the structure through which a goal manifests, it is emotion that powers this. The greater the desire the greater the energy, and the more powerfully the goal will come into reality. This is particularly so when seeking to influence another person.

Then, when you feel the energy is at a peak you will want to close your mouth, take in a deep breath through the nose and briefly hold this. Then open the mouth near to but not touching the area of the person's body or the item to receive the charge. Exhale through the mouth letting the energy ride your breath. This needs to be done slowly and carefully so as not to appear awkward when doing this directly to another. Rather, gently exhale while visualizing the full force of your emotion and will passing into the person or object to be affected.

Naturally if you are seeking to influence someone without their knowledge this act needs to be done in a manner that appears natural and spontaneous, perhaps as part of a conversation. Of course, when used in initiation rites this precaution isn't needed. But in the art of fascination discretion is a powerful tool. Rather it is best to proceed in gentle but steady steps that build.

Touch in the Art
In traditional magical arts the use of one's hands to pass power is very potent. Examples of this have already been discussed when looking to energizing talisman's, Moon Water and more. The same holds true when it comes to how the Witch touches another person. There is a long practice of healing among Cornish Witches involving touching and stroking the afflicted part of a client's body. Sometimes this may also involve the use of prepared lotions or oils. At other times it simply consists of the Witch herself using her natural ability to transfer healing through touch. This form of magic is considered to be so powerful that artificial replicas of different parts of the body are sometimes used by the Witch for those clients who can't be physically present for the 'stroking'.[5]

It was on a similar concept that the 18th century physician, Franz Mesmer, developed his practices of passing his hands over clients in an effort to change the 'magnetic fluid' that he felt surrounded them. Despite the criticism he faced, he managed to achieve some surprising results. This developed into 'Mesmerism' and out of this the modern science of hypnosis was born. Eventually, hypnosis became its own separate area of study relying less on the passing of the hands to move the etheric or magnetic 'fluid', and instead focusing on the use of suggestion coupled with eye fixation.

The interesting thing about is hypnosis is that in many cases it can be used to manipulate the same energies

5. Gary, Gemma. *Traditional Witchcraft: A Cornish Book of Ways.* 2008.

employed in fascination. Many trained hypnotherapists have experienced times in private sessions when the room begins to fill with a faint mist or fog that emanates from the client. The deeper into hypnosis the client goes the more this tends to manifest. As a trained hypnotist myself, I have experienced this. However, this isn't necessarily a physical substance but rather my own ability to see certain phenomena that transcend this material realm. I know that others who are not trained in the Art and aren't as sensitive to psychic influences may not experience this. Nevertheless, I have personally seen this on several occasions.

In my opinion what is happening during these sessions is that as the person relaxes, moving into deeper levels of consciousness, their cloak begins to 'loosen'. The Dragon's Breath within them begins to expand beyond its normal boundaries, away from the normal mental construct of the self that shapes this.

This is one of the reasons why trance forms such an important part of shamanic practices, including Traditional Witchcraft. For once the cloak loosens and this energy expands, the Witch can manipulate this energy easily. It is in such states that Witches can use 'stroking' to literally control and change the flow of this energy, using visualization to see the person as whole.

Of course, this same touch can be used in any act of fascination. One Witch whom I trained with was a very spontaneous and outgoing, frequently managing to casually 'touch' people in a carefree manner that appeared harmless and even welcoming. It was normal for her to walk up to people she had recently met and hug them. During my time with her she explained that this was largely a calculated move on her part to put herself close enough to both breathe on the person near the nape of their neck while also placing her palms directly over their spine. Then in a single act of emotional will she would project her intention directly into them without them having the slightest idea of what was just done. In addition, this put her in a perfect position to pick a hair, or some other simple taglock, without them being aware that it was taken.

Like the Charged Breath, the touch is delivered with the same disciplined emotional power. Desire, intention and energy is visualized in the solar plexus or chest and then sent through the arms and hands. If one can manage to place one's hands directly on or near the areas of the body which this energy normally passes so much the better. As such, it just comes naturally for lovers to hold hands. For through the palms their personal magnetism flows and mingles easily.

I don't want to leave the subject of touch in relation to fascination without addressing sexuality. As pointed out, the genitals are also a center in which the Dragon's Breath pools and through which this power can be transmitted. This isn't the place to begin to go into sex magic as it is such a vast subject. However, there are historical references that may help to explain how sexuality has been used in the art of fascination over time.

In Ancient Egypt it was customary for women and sometimes men to expose themselves during some rituals and celebrations. This was seen as an act of bringing happiness, life and joy to the moment. It was also used to drive evil away. Essentially, as the genitals are the means by which all life comes into being, for the Egyptians they represented the very force of creativity and joy. This custom carried on well into European lore with engravings showing women lifting their skirts to drive the devil away.[6] It was from the expression of the life-giving power of sex that amulets shaped as both the phallus and vulva became popular. Both objects were worn as symbols of luck, joy, fertility and protection. The use of cowrie shells as amulets in necklaces and belts around the waist by women are clear examples of this.

---

6. An example is the "La Fontaine plate" illustrated by Charles Eisen in 1762.

This leads to the use of jewelry in general as tools of fascination. For anything that will catch the eye of the person can be filled with the intention of the Witch. Prepared ahead of time and worn at an occasion that the other person will be present, the jewelry becomes a talisman in itself capturing, even if briefly, their attention. It is in that moment that the Witch can release her force on a subtle level.

Another historical example of the use of the genitals in fascination is the 17th century custom of making 'cockle bread'.[7] In this a woman seeking to gain the love of a potential suitor would knead bread dough, pressing this against her vulva making an impression. The dough was then baked. This was then given, as part of a meal, to the person desired. While this was a not-so-subtle act of fascination, the concepts were essentially the same. That is the building up of desire and intention in one of the centers of the body that easily transmits the Dragon energy. Then transferring this to an object that can then be used to influence others, in this case taken directly by the person in a meal.

Please know that I am not advocating exposing yourself as noted in the Egyptian examples. Nor am I suggesting that you prepare food in any ... unconventional manner. Rather, I present these to help exemplify the fact that the Witch's power can and does reside in this center, that this is accessible and, with some thought, can be used as needed. Take from these examples what you will.

Overlooking

The old sayings of "if looks could kill" and "the evil eye" have their roots in very ancient practices. Known as 'overlooking', the use of one's gaze to project the Dragon's Breath is very powerful and not to be discounted. However, among contemporary occultists overlooking is all but forgotten. Perhaps that is for the best. Yet, in Traditional

---

7. Baker, Jim. *The Cunning Man's Handbook*. 2013.302.

Witchcraft the practice is very much alive, for the eyes are very powerful, being a liminal point of transition between the outer world and that which resides within.

In Ancient Egypt the eyes were considered sacred. The "Eye of Horus" was a prevalent amulet of protection denoting all that was good and healthy, while the "Eye of Ra" was seen as the raw power of Hathor as the divine feminine in Her aspect of protector and avenger. In Hermetic practices the eye became a symbol of the all-seeing presence of the divine, power and wisdom combined.

For the Witch her eyes are yet another vehicle for the Serpent Breath to pass from her into the person she seeks to influence. The most opportune moment for this transfer is when she and her intended target first lock eyes, particularly in what may seem to the other person as a 'lingering glance'. Such moments always cause one to stop and take notice, if only for a moment. It is in this second of time that the Witch can deliver her intention on a subtle yet very real level. This is more than a keen awareness of body language. Rather, in that moment the Witch can focus the power of her desire directly into the other quickly and decisively.

Please don't think that this has to be accompanied by some odd staring 'look' that would simply be seen as 'weird'. In my experience such suggestions should be avoided completely. Now you are going to find that some of the older traditions do make use of specific gestures, such as standing on one's left foot while pointing with the left hand and starring at the person with one's left eye. From a symbology point of view this makes sense but it draws way too much attention to one and the theatrics will almost certainly ruin the intent and concentration needed to really deliver a powerful spell.

Rather, you want to keep your appearance as natural and subtle as possible while also clearly delivering the full impact of the desire through the flow of natural Dragon Force from within. This all takes practice and concentration. Yet it can work quite well. A simple exercise to show the effectiveness of overlooking is to focus your gaze on the back of the head or neck of a stranger while gently but firmly sending the idea that they must turn to look. You will be surprised that, with some practice, this can be highly effective. From there it is only a matter moving on to more potent suggestions.

As with all else in the Art what type of influence you wish to deliver depends entirely on your own motives. Overlooking is not relegated to vengeful attacks or "the evil eye". Virtually any desired result can be delivered in this manner: sending strength, health, happiness, good fortune as well as the more obvious uses of love and seduction. Again, think carefully before using the glance, but use it. This is a natural ability that can and should be developed.

A Glamour on the Land

I have spent some time discussing fascination and glamour as it relates to the person. There is also the glamour that is cast over a place. We've all experienced this, perhaps walking in an old forest and feeling the presence and power that resides there or, visiting an ancient archeological site that was used in ritual for thousands of years. The atmosphere in such places is thick and charged with power. Rather than relying on the second skin of a person, such places pull directly from the Dragon Force inherent in the land itself.

This type of effect is usually built up over time. When it comes to human made constructs, particularly those which are ancient sacred sites, a combination of factors contribute to the glamour that surrounds them. In many cases the sites were chosen carefully, usually in a place where the Serpent Breath emanates freely. The structure itself is then aligned to collect this force so that it can be housed within while also being accessible to those who have the skill. The final step though involves the esoteric intent of those who commissioned and used the site thereafter.

In other words, once the site is set, aligning with the natural flow of the Dragon Force, those of the Art mold this energy. This is done through the trained use of imagination, concentration and emotion, coupled with ritual. The goal is to build up the glamour on the Abred, the astral, linking this directly to the place. By using the natural abundance of Dragon Force found in the place, the astral images are then constantly fed by this energy, giving the glamour life and substance. The ancient Egyptians were masters at this, carefully tying their temples to the natural forces in nature, using ritual to shape that energy and leaving an astral legacy which continues to captivate us thousands of years later. We see similar structures around the world, from Asia to Europe and well into North and South America.

When it comes to the Witch's place of working, a measure of the same process can and should be applied. This is particularly so if you are seeking to create a sacred space in nature. In such instances you want to find a place that resonates well with you. Somewhere that at once is liminal, yet has a sense of both peace and power. The Witch is normally drawn to such places easily. Follow your instincts as they will be your best guide.

Assuming this is on your own private property you can then begin to carefully mark out the spot, usually in the form of the Mill or Roth Fail. If, one the other hand, this isn't private to you, rather it is someplace that is accessible to the public, once again discretion is key. Without a doubt, on those occasions when Witches met in nature, these were in predesignated areas. Most groups almost certainly had more than one location, with names or simple code phrases used to designate which would be used on a given night.

The locations themselves would have been kept as natural as possible with very few markings or structures present to indicate their use. People in the British Isles and portions of Europe were lucky as there are many ancient circles and standing stones scattered across the region that did serve as different gathering sites. But these weren't always used. And, in fact, more often than not 'lonely downs' or clearings in forests would have been employed. It is interesting that in the New Forest of England very old Witch Marks have been found carved into some of the oldest trees dating back as far as five-hundreds years.[8] The New Forest is recognized for its long association with Witchcraft. It is tempting to see these markings as one of the ways that members would designate different gathering sites.

At such places, over the steady practice of ritual, those involved would manipulate the Dragon Force in the location giving it structure on various levels of the Abred, including the astral. Yet on the physical level any sign of the site as sacred would have been kept minimal. One might find a small stand of stones that served as a table, or an odd carving in a tree. The remains of any fires from ritual would be buried or carried away in a cauldron. In such places the glamour comes through the conscious building of the forms on Abred.

The repeated setting of the Roth Fail in a specific location does begin to create a change in the psychic atmosphere of location. However, this is just a start. To create a full glamour you are going to want to purposely create the forms and images on the Abred through careful creative visualization. This requires that you choose specific tides of power in which the Dragon Force is flowing strongly. Again, those dates closest to the Full Moon will serve this purpose well. Also, early to midspring is a very powerful time as the natural force within the land is awakening and rising. Both tides will bring a tremendous amount of etheric energy to the site which you can use freely.

---

8. See Smithsonian article https://www.smithsonianmag.com/smart-news/witches-marks-and-other-tree-etchings-offer-window-english-past-180976003/
Last accessed 24/4/2022
What is intriguing to me is the fact that these markings are in many cases the same as those found in homes at the time. This would potentially throw into doubt the current academic view that such markings were created and used by "Christians to keep evil from the home". Why are they found deep in obscure portions of the forest? Again, it would seem plausible to me that these markings have other, deeper esoteric meaning and could have been placed in such a manner to mark specific points of power or places of gathering.

The process of visualization itself should begin even as you prepare the site for ritual. This should be done in a state of active imagination, clearly seeing the images and symbols you want associated with the site in your mind's eye. Let yourself enjoy this process. Picture the site as you feel it should be on an astral level. Keep this simple yet clear and well defined. It is going to be vitally important that you recall these images and symbols in detail as you will want to employee them repeatedly and over different times. As such you may want to write down a basic outline that you can refer to each time, listing the features and symbols you will be incorporating. Throughout all of this, spirits, particularly your familiar, need to be invited as they will act as participants in the process.

Begin the rite with the actual setting of the Roth Fail. However, take extra care in all of the visualizations that accompany each step. Use your imagination to the fullest. Let the astral forms build, taking on life. Yet, keep the images tied to your physical actions, in this way anchoring the forms in the Abred to the location. Some Traditional Witches will even go to the point of driving an iron stake or nail into the center of the circle to form this link between worlds.

Once the Roth Fail is set, evoke the primary otherworld being or beings whom you normally work with. This can be through the tracing of their sigil, the careful visualization of their form, the incantation of their name, as well as an actual evocation you may use when calling on these beings. You want the place to have a distinct link to the forces you work with.

Of course, many places in nature have their own spirits who emerge from the land. These should be honored and invited to be part of this construct as well. They can and should form an important aspect of the glamour you are setting. In fact, long before you have decided to create the glamour for the location you should have already begun the process of contacting and engaging with the local spirits.[9]

---

9. The process for doing this is covered in detail in *Horns of the Moon*.

How you visualize your glamour is entirely up to you. However, it is important to use established symbols and imagery that resonate with the system of magic you are performing, with the otherworld beings you work with, and to the very nature of the land itself. Further, the actual process works best when conducted with one's magical partner. The combined will of two workers of the Art carefully envisioning the same esoteric landscape can be very effective. In such a case both partners will vocally recite a narrative of what it is they are projecting.

The following may serve as a possible example of a ritual with visualizations that you may want to pattern your glamour on. As you read this bear in mind that the description I am about to give includes both physical ritual actions *as well as images and scenes that one will need to visualize*. In doing so allow as much creative emotion and feeling to be evoked as possible. The occult axiom of 'enflame thyself with prayer' has merit. For while this isn't worship, it is an act in which you want to let the passion of your creative will take hold in clear imagery and ritual actions. In this way the forms begin to mold and form on the Abred.

Ritual of a Glamour on the Land

On the night of a Full Moon, preferably in the spring or midsummer, have prepared your normal ritual items. With these be sure to have an iron stake or nail and a simple offering of food and wine. These will be carried with you. As you walk the path to the site become acutely aware of the ground beneath your feet, feeling the life in the land as it pulses and flows. The Dragon's Breath is rising, moving up through the trees of the forest as you wind your way steadily toward the clearing where the Roth Fail will be set. As this power rises up through the branches, reaching toward the sky, the stars overhead appear bright against the deep azure backdrop of space. Through it all the Moon's light illumines the forest as the spirits in nature come alive, emerging from the hollows in rock and cliff, the spaces within the tress and the mists of the glens. You feel alive as the pulse of the Dragon rises up through you, while the warmth of stars and Moon shower down over you.

As you walk, the path begins to ascend. In doing so envision nine natural stone steps carved into the landscape. With each step you steadily climb upward through the forest, as if you are rising with the Serpent Power toward the Moon itself. Upon reaching the ninth step you see that the path continues into the forest, yet just up ahead a stag stands proudly as if waiting. Even in the glow of the moonlight his tawny skin and full antlers show magnificently against the tress. On his brow the distinct image of a white crescent emerges, almost hypnotically calling you on. You walk toward him. Yet he suddenly turns and darts down the path disappearing in the distance. Let yourself continue to follow the path, leading on through the trees.

Soon you emerge from the forest, stepping into a clearing that opens to the sky. The Full Moon is shining brightly as its form is clearly visible. The stag is standing here, next to a circle made of stones. These are stacked upon each other, like an ancient fence only a few feet high. As you approach you realize that the stones themselves are glowing in the iridescent illumination of the Moon. Yet, the circle is also an extension of the land, and within it the gathering essence of the Dragon's Breath begins to swirl around the circle in the glow of the Moon's light.

Here, earth and sky merge, the ring of stones focusing and coalescing as the living essence the flows through the worlds. Looking to the stag you see that he is beckoning you on, welcoming you to the Roth Fail, the circle of light. Next to him an opening in the circle can be seen, a passage in the stone wall that you now step through.

A single stone threshold marks the boundary on which the engraving of a sword and a besom, crossing each other can be seen. Stepping over this you feel a shift, as if moving through a veil, and then you emerge inside the circle. Once inside the energy continues to gather, swirling gently in a soft spiral of power. The stone wall of the Roth Fail glows brighter, and looking up, the stars and Moon have come closer filling the sky with a transcendent luminosity that pervades the entire clearing.

In the north a series of stones support a single slab of quartz, the hearthstone. Envision this as glowing with a light from deep within: white and silver, merging in hues of violet and green. The colors seem to change and flow in the moonlight. Walking to the north edge of the Roth Fail place the Stang in its stand, a series of rocks are set to hold this. Then set a single candle between the horns of the Stang and light this.

Now, begin the ritual of setting the Roth Fail as you normally would. In each portion of setting this hold the image of the stone circle in the clearing firmly in your mind, letting this build.

Once the Roth Fail is set, take the iron stake and move to the center of the circle. Facing the Moon hold the stake high, drawing the Moon's power down into this. See the stake glow with power. Then drive this into the ground. While doing this incant:

"Anál nathrach   (onal NathRack
Bandia Gelach   Banjeeah Geloch
Draiocht dénmha"   Dray-aht de-N-may)

This roughly translates to:

"Serpent's Breath
Mistress Moon
This Enchantment I make!"

As you do, allow the current flowing from the Moon to merge with the pulse of the land becoming one force that radiates from the center of the Roth Fail outward. The energy flows as silvery white light that causes the stone walls of the circle to glow even brighter under the Full Moon glow.

Turn to face the hearthstone. With your Fe trace the sigil of the Transformative Power of the Moon. See this as a brilliant electric blue hovering in the air.

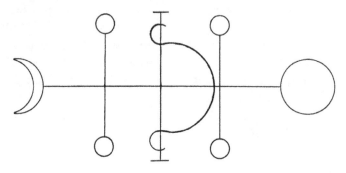

In this situation this is the sigil we use to resonate with and evoke the Mistress, the Great Queen. Once this is traced, use the charged breath to breathe life into this. At this point I will also use the following Ancient Egyptian incantation, thus tying the three systems of the Art which we draw from to the glamour. This is an ancient invocation of the Great Goddess Hathor, given in a transliterated form, from the temple of Dendera:

Ind.hrt Hwt-Hrw nbt 'Iwnt.
'Irt-Ra, 'It mt
Sat Itmw, hnwt-wrt, asat Khprw.
Ankh ntrw n dgt.s
Nbt rnw m-kht tawy N Rkh tw ssm.s nfrt hr shbt.
Mh ib n Ra m wbn.f Wrt mrwt hmwt,
Nfrt hr m hnk swt.
Tpyt pw nt Hwt-Hrw
Sawy imytw Saw-n-Sn ant nfrt an.tw maa.s

The Egyptian invocation is optional. If you don't find yourself drawn to the Egyptian Mysteries please don't feel obligated to use this. For our part we find it to be highly effective in helping to tie this stream of wisdom to our practices.

Whether you use the Egyptian invocation or not, you will now want to continue with the invocations of the Mistress and Master:

"Silver circle and crystal well,
She who rides in the night,
Witch Queen & Mistress
Bandia Gelach, Bandia Gelach,
Bandia Gelach, Bandia Gelach,
Dragon's power in Full Moon's light."

This can be followed by the invocation of the Master:

"Master of the Wild Wood,
Horned One in the night,
Janicot, Janicot,
Janicot, Janicot.
Serpent Power and Dragon's Breath,
Arise, awake this Full Moon night."

At this point take some time to let yourself become aware of the forces and beings drawn to the circle. It is highly likely that you will become acutely aware of the Mistress and Master. Let this unfold, for the barriers between the physical and the Abred fall away and you will find that you can become aware of both realms at once.

A key component of this process is to envision the light of the stars and Moon flowing down into the entire scene, giving this life and power. With this the Dragon Energy inherent in the land rises up, giving form to these images on the Abred. Together these are the Geassa, the living consciousness of nature merged into the glamour of this place.

When ready, offer food and wine to Mistress and Master, the spirits and all those who may be present. Don't be surprised if you find that you also become aware of figures, usually robed and hooded, standing at the outer edge of the Roth Fail watching. You will find that they often can be perceived in rituals of the Willow Path. These are the elders of the tradition. Those beings who teach and guide. Hermetic Orders often refer to similar beings as the "inner world contacts". Many ceremonial magicians find that reaching a point where beings such as these appear is rare and highly important. However, I have found that in Traditional Witchcraft it is fairly common for them to come through. Be sure to acknowledge their presence, thanking them for their guidance and be sure to toast them as well.

Once the food and wine have been shared, the initial work of setting the glamour in place is finished. The more times that you do this the stronger the forms become on the Abred. As these gain in strength you will find that the psychic atmosphere of the place itself becomes more perceptible to others. You will also find that with each working the site itself becomes more powerful until just stepping into the physical space brings the Witch into direct contact with these other realms.

The above was meant to serve as a possible example. Within this we incorporated imagery from Traditional Witchcraft, Hermetics and Ancient Egyptian magic while tying this directly to the sacred space we have created on the little mountain in New England we call home. This then brings these systems to a focus here.

Ideally you will want to do something similar with the space you have available. Even if this is a spare room in an apartment, you can still use your will, imagination, the different tides of power and symbols to create this glamour. Once this astral setting is created it literally gives you a starting point already set in the Abred that you can then work from. In such settings you will find that your magic tends to work faster and is more powerful than it had been before.

On a completely different level, you can use a similar technique to change how people feel about perfectly mundane settings. From your home to a business, the art of placing a glamour can be applied easily. Essentially, it is the same process. At a time when the Dragon Force is strong, on a planetary day related to the impression you want others to have, you would use your creative will and imagination to define exactly what that glamour would be.

You will want to have this written out clearly in advance. Then set a small hearthstone up somewhere in the structure and have on this items related exactly to the image. If you have tied this to a specific planetary resonance, have the appropriate sigils and seals for the spirits involved set for the spell. Then take your time to go through the visualization slowly, carefully and completely while evoking as much emotional enthusiasm as possible. This could easily be coupled with some of the prosperity techniques which will be discussed later.

Personal Appearance, 'Shape-Shifting' and Fascination
I began this chapter with a brief description of the time I drew attention from a driver by manipulating my second skin. This was a very rudimentary form of applying the glamour to my appearance. We all hold in our mind a mental image of what we think we look like. More often than not we allow the conditioning brought by society and the comments of others to form this image, rather than taking the time to decide this for ourselves. However, it is possible to change how others perceive us and, in turn, react to us. This is done by clearly defining the image in specific terms ourselves and then carefully envisioning this.

Of course, this doesn't physically alter the body itself . . . at least not initially. But what does happen is that as we create the mental image of how we want to be perceived, projecting this as the appearance of our second-skin or aura, others will react to this on a subconscious level seeing this as reality, just as the woman had felt compelled to pull over and offer assistance when I changed the aura.

This is very similar to the discussion had regarding the magical personality in *The Willow Path* except this was meant as a vehicle for one's higher spiritual aspirations. What I am speaking of here is much more mundane, being used to directly influence how others interact with you in immediate situations. But, as with the placing of a glamour on a place, this requires a very sharp image and the discipline to hold this in the mind while also using the breath and active imagination to see this as an absolute reality. If you can do this it can be a highly effective tool in any setting when dealing with others. Of course, a good psychic or those well trained in the Art will probably be able to see through the mental construct, however the vast majority of people won't. And, for them, this image will affect them on a subliminal level.

As with other glamours, the more often you project the image into the second skin the more lasting it will become. In addition, over time the astral image may very well manifest as changes in the physical body. Keep in mind that oftentimes what is created on the astral eventually appears on the material. This is one of the key elements of practical magic. So, it stands to reason that how you picture yourself mentally may very well become a physical reality providing the material circumstances are such to allow this.

It is in this vein that skin walkers and legends of shape-shifting came into being. This was discussed at length in my previous writing when considering the bodies and the projection of the fetch. As such there is no need to discuss the technique further here. However, I wanted to bring it up as the use of fascination and glamour are yet another way that this phenomenon can occur.

'Invisibility' - to Move Unseen

Perhaps the opposite of fascination is the ability to use magic to go unnoticed, or what the ancients would term becoming 'invisible'. Beyond certain nefarious purposes that some may think of, there are times when the Witch may simply desire to not be noticed. I can see that there would have been real advantage to this ability during the persecutions, when making one's way to and from nighttime gatherings, or to escape prying eyes when practicing the Art. Now I don't for a second think that there are actual methods by which the physical body disappears or becomes transparent. However, to move unnoticed is very common.

Using the techniques described thus far, the method is essentially the same except that instead of creating an image that changes form and attracts attention, the Witch dons the cloak of her aura while simply willing herself to blend in, becoming hidden in the shadows. In addition to using the second skin, there are certain potions and herbs that are very useful for exactly this purpose. Perhaps the one that is the most widely celebrated is the use of spores from the Male Ferns. However, these must be gathered on Midsummer Eve Night. Once gathered they can be carried on one when wishing to be invisible. They can also be used as a powder scattering this around objects that you wish to keep concealed. I will often mix this with dried Solomon Seal root, grinding this into a fine powder and then sprinkling this over objects, or at the entrance to property which I want to keep hidden. This has proven to be an effective recipe.

'Four Thieves Vinegar' is also highly valued for this purpose. This is made by infusing Garlic, Rosemary, Wormwood and Juniper in Apple Cider Vinegar for eight days. This is then strained and vinegar store for future use. This is employed simply by wearing this as one would a cologne or perfume.

Chapter Nine

❖ CANDLE AND CORD ❖

Of all the teachings that Julie passed to me perhaps the most important was that, if nothing else, Witchcraft is practical. Unlike much of ritual magic that requires elaborate preparation and exotic ingredients, almost always Witchcraft is straightforward. It boils magic down to its most fundamental forms. Again, it is important to remember that this is the magic of the common people using those things that were readily available and part of everyday life. From an iron cooking pot or cauldron, to a pitchfork or staff, a simple knife to wooden sticks carefully crafted as wands, from rain water to the use of various stones found in nature and herbs growing wild. It was out of this simplistic approach that the use of wax and cords in the Art came about, as both were easily obtained.

Wax, in various forms, has been a part of the Art from the beginning of recorded history. Temple inscriptions from Egypt describe the burning of red candles to statues of the lioness Goddess Sekhmet. Wicked candles dating to at least 3000 BCE were use in Egypt. There, temple candles tended to be made from beeswax as they burn cleaner with less smoke. Yet records also show the use of candles made from hollow reeds into which animal fat was poured.

Ritual texts from the Osirian temple of Abydos in Egypt give an important spell that is part of a larger ritual. Yet this simple version can be used as a cleansing ritual in one's working space. The text explains that a red candle is placed at each of the four cardinal points. These are lit while a specific chant is repeated. The following is a simplified version which we use:

"The candle has come!
The Eye of Heru has come, shining brilliantly in this place!
The Eye of Heru is your protection,
It spreads protection over this place,
It drives away all evil!
Pure is the beautiful one,
It has come, the Eye of Heru, the beautiful one.
It has come, the proclaimer,
The candle shining brilliantly in this place!"[10]

Throughout Europe the use of tallow, candles made from animal fat, was very common among rural people as it was readily available. Living close to the land nothing was wasted. However, there were many people who did keep bees. According to Sybil Leek this was particularly true of Witches.[11] Both the wax and honey would have been valuable for mundane purposes *and* for their applications in the Art. Sybil points out that during the persecutions talismans and amulets were often made of beeswax. Beeswax amulets were easily constructed and could be carried without notice because they could be quickly destroyed should one be in danger of being discovered. Yet, the wax would be retained to be used again. In the British Museum a pentacle made by the

---

10. See Dr. Alsion Roberts *My Heart My Mother: Death and Rebirth in Ancient Egypt*. 2000.87. The text she gives reads: "The candle has come... There has come one who proclaims night after day. The Eye of Horus comes, shining gloriously in this sanctuary...The Eye of Horus is your protection, it spreads protection over you and overthrows your enemies. Pure, pure is the beautiful one. It has come, the Eye of Horus, the beautiful one, it has come, the proclaimer, the candle of new fat"
11. Leek, Sybil. *The Complete Art of Witchcraft*. 1970.

famous renaissance magician Dr. John Dee is carved from solid beeswax.

This same method can be applied today. In doing so one would choose the appropriate lunar phase, as well as planetary day and hour. The wax would then be melted and poured into a disc mold. If desired, herbs or essential oils corresponding to the work at hand can be added. Once the wax cools the Witch begins the work of carving the design into this. While doing so she may chant the spell while infusing the wax with her intent. Depending on the work at hand this may be all the preparation needed. Or, on the other hand, the talisman can then be further empowered through rites similar to those given when we examined talismans.

Another source of wax is Bayberry. The wax from this is very difficult to harvest, but the quality of the wax is considered to be superior to that of beeswax. A folk saying used in New England states:

> "A Bayberry candle burnt to the socket,
> Will bring good fortune to the larder,
> And gold to the pocket."

Wax derived from the boiling of Cinnamon became available in Europe as imports from India began. Then in the 1850s paraffin, which is a petroleum product, became the primary source of wax, remaining so to this day. Most recently the use of soy wax began in the 1990s.

In my opinion beeswax and Bayberry are probably the best to use for magical practice because they come directly from the natural environment. Yet paraffin is a good substitute that is much less expensive and far more accessible. I have used paraffin quite successfully in spell crafting.

Poppets

Wax has some unique qualities. The most notable is that when warm it becomes very malleable and easy to shape. This gives it the ability to readily absorb the Witch's intention, emotion and the Serpent's Breath while working this. As such, wax is excellent to use when creating poppets, also known as mawkins. Essentially a poppet is a doll, an effigy of a person of the person the Witch choses to work their magic on. Immediately, most people think of curses whenever poppets are involved. But in reality, these can be very versatile tools. I have seen these used in spells for friendship, bindings, protection spells, of course, the proverbial love and seduction spell, but more importantly they can be highly effective in healing spells. They can be made from any number of items. I have known Witches who would obtain unwashed clothing that the person wore and sew this into a mawkin. Clay is also a common substance that is used. But wax is probably the easiest and most accessible, again holding the unique property of being able to absorb intention and thought as it warms and is molded.

Added to this is the fact that the poppet can be made from wax in the color that best resonates with the goal of the spell. So, one might choose pink wax for friendship, green for healing, blue for tranquility, etc. See the table in this chapter that lists the basic magical uses of colored candles to help you decide which to use for your poppet.

You are going to want to choose the correct tide of power to prepare this. Again, much depends on the exact purpose of the spell. From there the simplest way to proceed is to then ensure you are in a quiet place where you have access to a means of melting the wax. You want to be certain that you are alone and free from disturbances. Of course, you will need the colored wax itself. But most importantly you will need some type of taglock. Hair, fingernail parings, a spot of blood or other bodily fluid, something that is directly tied to the other person. I should note that sexual fluids from the person are considered to resonate best, as these link specifically with their will. As such, if you use these fluids keep in mind that you are directly affecting how this person functions and makes choices. Be very careful as this carries with it a heavy responsibility that may result in consequences that you hadn't foreseen.

At the appointed time sit quietly and begin the merging, as described in *Horns of the Moon*, with the person. No matter how distant they maybe, when done properly the link will form. It is then that you begin the processes of making the poppet. As you do, take your time to gently and methodically form the wax into the shape of a person. Be certain to work the taglock *into* the poppet itself, all the while maintaining the mental link with them. It is also advisable to have written out a simple enchantment describing the intended goal of the subject. Keep this very basic, preferably in a rhyming chant that you can easily remember. Repeat this over and over while you pour your intention and power into the effigy. Once the poppet is created set it aside for the moment.

What happens next depends entirely on the purpose of the spell. For the sake of example, we will assume that a poppet was made with the purpose of healing someone who has been ill. The poppet would have been made of green wax during a Waxing Moon on one of the days related to a "Lady of the Moon" associated with healing. Barring this, the day and hour of Mercury would be an excellent tide given his association with health. After that either the day and hour of the Sun or those of the Moon would also be highly effective.

Once the effigy is finished the Witch would take this to their place of working, whether this be the hearth, Roth Fail, or a place in nature that one uses for the Art. Like the timing of the making of the poppet, this next step should occur in one of the tides just mentioned. In your place of working you will want to set an equal sided triangle. As with the others this can be traced with herbs related to healing, flour, chalk, or even in a permanent triangle stitched on a cloth used solely for magic. At the three corners, either white or green tapers should be placed. The poppet is then set directly in the center of the triangle.

Prepare the ritual space as you normally would, being certain that you call on the spirits whom you normally work with to be present. In particular, if you have formed a relationship with a familiar, it is vital that she or he is present and their aid is sought for this operation. Then light the three tapers at the corners of the triangle. You will then need to once again form the link with the person, merging through mind and magic. Once this has been established, pick the poppet up and pass it through the four elements as you do so recite the following:

"By the element of air, I conjure it,
That you are (name of person),
Healthy, well and full of life."

Of course, the element named in the chant will change depending on the one you are passing the effigy through. When you pass this through the flame of a candle be careful as, being made of wax, this can melt or catch fire. Rather, it is perfectly acceptable to pass this near the flame without exposing this directly to it.

Replace the poppet in the triangle. You will then need to anoint this with an herbal oil directly related to the goal at hand. There are any number of essential oils one could turn to. Again, if you are uncertain which oil to use, Vervain is a good all-purpose magical substance.

As you do this you will want to envision the person as vital, well and healthy in every way. Engage all of your senses in this image. See them as strong and alert, hear their voice, clear and robust; smell the distinct scent that they may have. As you rub the oil onto the poppet feel the warmth of their body and the smooth, healthy touch of their skin. In your mind hold the clear image of them fully recovered.

As with the making of the poppet, you will want to have a simple chant that encapsulates the essence of the working itself. Keep it simple, clear and don't place any conditions on how it will manifest. Again, I cannot stress too much that magic follows the lines of least resistance. Let it manifest as best it can. Simply hold firm to the intention of the person healthy, vital and happy.

After anointing the poppet, take a moment to once again draw in the power, the Serpent's Breath, feeling this well up inside and through you. Let this build until you feel as if the force is ready to spill out through you. Then, using the passing of the power technique, allow this energy to flow into the effigy through the palms of your hands. See the poppet as filling with power. Then finish with the Charged Breath, breathing life directly into and over the mawkin.

At this point, you may want to step back, pick up your Fe and trace an appropriate sigil or seal related to the working directly over the mawkin. However, this isn't essential and if you don't have one that relates to your working that is fine. Simply proceed to then point the Fe at the poppet and, once again, begin the chant while focusing the healing Serpent's Breath through the Fe into the triangle. Again, see the person as whole, healthy and happy, not in some distant future, but now, today, in the moment! Let yourself become totally immersed in the chant and with it the power you are generating. This should build in intensity until the power simply can't hold back. Then in a final burst of power let this completely merge with the poppet.

You will probably feel somewhat exhausted for a few moments. Replace the Fe. Thank the spirits. Then take some time to step away from the working, leaving the candles to burn. The length of time will depend on the color involved. For green candles this is either four hours or until the candles have completely gone out, whichever comes first. Once the time period is over, return to the space then carefully wrap the poppet in cloth, preferably in the same color as the image itself.

There are a few options as to what to do with the poppet. You can either place this is safe, clean space keeping it available to continue to work with at later times to strengthen the spell in the months to come. Or you can place this somewhere near to the person themselves without their knowledge. I would not give it to the person directly. I know that this is a favorite way of instilling fear in those that one may curse. My feeling is that, if you really understand the Art there is no need to use such theatrics in your practice. Further, in the case of the healing poppet, I would be concerned that the person might remove or alter the energy through their own handling of the image while in distressed state. Rather, the preferred option is to place the effigy in a place very near to, or in a room frequently occupied by the person, unbeknownst to them. It should be some place secret, safe, clean and dry where it won't be disturbed by animals, children, or anything else.

This little example should serve as a practical template that you can use in your workings. Again, this can be altered to meet most needs. As with all magic, you need to consider the full consequences when working with poppets as they can be very powerful.

Before leaving this subject, I feel it is important to address how to reverse the effects of poppet magic. What do you do if you find that you are the subject of an unasked for and unwanted mawkin, for whatever purpose? Whether it be a classic doll curse, seduction spell, of even a healing from someone whom you don't want ties with, the process of neutralizing these is essentially the same.

When found, place the poppet in a triangle of Art. At each point of the triangle light a white candle. As always call on the spirits of the tradition to aid with the work. Then with the Fe trace over the triangle envisioning this as glowing in power. Next, pick up the poppet. Holding this in your left hand, pick up your Black Hilt Knife in the right. Then, with all of your will, envision the blade as being alive with power and red hot as you pass this over and around the entire poppet. Pay special attention to the solar plexus region of the doll. In making these passes, in your mind, see the link that the original sorcerer formed with the doll as being completely cut away. Take your time with this but continue the passes until you feel the distinct moment when the link is severed. It can help to see this almost as a silvery cord cut and falling away, flying off into the distance. As you do so chant the following:

"Your curses and your sorcery,
Are powerless to injure me.
Your sorcerous words return to thee,
As thou would have them be to me."

Place the poppet back in the triangle. Now scatter salt over the poppet as you continue the chant. After a few moments begin removing any taglocks that you may be able to get to. Also remove any pins, nails, or other objects that the person may have stuck into this. Leave the taglocks in the triangle, but place the remains of the poppet in a bowl filled with fresh water that you have added salt to. The bowl is then taken to a place where there is clear running water. The ocean is perfect for this. But even the kitchen sink with fresh tap water will do. With the water running, remove the effigy from the bowl and proceed to wash the negative energy out of this, again repeating the chant. Leave the remains of the effigy to dry. While this is happening return to the triangle. There, retrieve the taglocks. Then take these and the effigy outdoors, assuming you have not been performing this outside in the first place.

Now build a small fire around which you have made a circle of salt. When the fire is going very well, place the place the remains of the poppet in the fire. Let this burn completely. Then place the taglocks on the fire doing the same. All the while you will continue the chant. When these too are burnt recite the word of power:

"Deoraidhin"   (pronounced JER-rid-hin)

Let the fire burn itself out. At this point collect the ashes and take these to some natural running water and dispose of them. Barring that, you can bury the ashes in the ground and scatter salt over the surface. Then walk away and don't look back. Simply let it go, knowing that you have destroyed the link and removed any negative energy and spirits from the doll.

Candle Magic

Fire has always been held in extreme awe by humans. Without it, civilization would not have advanced in any measurable fashion. In fact, one could easily argue that fire is the single force that enabled us as a species to develop, giving us the means to exist anywhere on the planet. It was through its agency that we were able to explore the deep regions of caves and caverns, or survive the harshness of winter. And it was around firelight that some of the first magical workings were discovered.

Fire really is a point of transition, a merging of all of the elements in a single moment bringing light and heat. As Julie had pointed out so long ago, whether it is through the use of a candle, an oil lamp or the wood on the hearth, all four elements join together in one moment bringing about an alchemical act of transformation. But beyond the physical aspects, in the Art fire is much more. For the Witch fire is a living entity. It becomes a point of merging, a portal or 'pinch point' enabling energies to flow between worlds, realms and dimensions. It is because of this that spirits and a variety of otherworld entities are drawn to fire. And it is through fire that energies that have been collected and held within can be released into these different realms. It is because of these qualities that candle magic works so well.

As noted, wax has the unique property of being able to absorb and contain the Dragon's Breath. The flame of the candle then releases this as it burns. While colored candles have been used for thousands of years, in medieval and colonial times most candles would have been an off white, with some being purposely colored black by mixing soot in with the tallow. As such, many in Traditional Witchcraft will use primarily either white or black candles depending on the work at hand: white for increase and positive working, black for decrease and negative spells. Rather than using colored candles these Witches will practice the old custom of inserting a pin into the candle that has a colored glass head. The various colors correspond to the type of goal sought. As the candle burns down the pin, along with the energy of the intention of the Witch[12] is released from the wax. The challenge is in pushing the pin into the candle during the spell. I have found this takes patience and practice, usually heating the pin up before inserting it. Again, many people enjoy this technique and, by all means, if this appeals to you then you should certainly use this.

Once colored candles became more accessible and easier to make, many Witches were quick to adopt these, following the color correspondence related to the different energies that had been in use for thousands of years. I will say that all of my teachers did prefer to use different colored candles in their workings, with one in particular stating that "a Witch knows the ways and means of her time". As such, my teaching too embraces this practice.

Keep in mind though, that candles are not essential to spell casting. Far from it. There are many works that do not involve the use of candles at all. Rather, the candle is but another tool that the Witch can and should use when the occasion calls for it. In using these it is common to manually imbue the primary working candle with power. The working candle generally is that which is meant to embody the goal at hand. The most common method for doing this is through the process of anointing the candle with oil. Oil, like wax, has the ability absorb, concentrate and then release psychic energy. The act of ritually anointing an object, person or candle with oil has long been understood to be representative of imparting energy

---

12. Gary, Gemma. *Traditional Witchcraft: A Cornish Book of Ways.* 2008.

to the object. As such, while one can pass objects through the four elements, it is the final act of anointment that represents the element of spirit.

How one anoints the candle depends on what school of thought you follow. I have seen many contemporary Wiccans and occultists insist that this must be done by starting at the middle of the candle and rubbing the oil into the candle working upward. Then start at the middle and work downward. Others will simply rub liberal amounts of oil onto the candle with little regard to the direction or starting point. Sybil Leek, on the other hand, makes clear that in her system all that was needed was to place a spot of oil on the forefinger of the dominant hand and dab this on the candle.[13]

In my experience it doesn't really matter. I don't adhere to the 'more is better' camp that enthusiastically drenches the candle in oil. However, the goal is to allow your power, your desire, to merge with the candle. The techniques regarding passing the power discussed elsewhere in this book would certainly apply here.

The following table is meant to be a reference that you can use, indicating the different colors and uses of candles, including the minimum length of time that these should burn to be effective. This is far from conclusive. Rather, is meant to be a starting point from which you can build.

---

13. Leek, Sybil. *Sybil Leek's Book of Curses.* 1975.

Candles in Practical Magic		
Color	**Uses**	**Minimum Burning Time**
Red	Passion, power, sexual desire, love on a passionate and sexual level, life, regeneration. Red Dragon power in the land. Gives energy and vitality. Can cause anger, destruction and chaos. Red always works very quickly but its effects often don't last.	One Hour
Pink	Love, friendship, happiness	Two Hours
Orange	Similar to red but not as forceful. Used to bring passion, desire, quick action and results. Excellent for success in legal matters	Two Hours
Gold	Material wealth, prosperity, success, encourages intuition, also resonates with the realm of Gwynfyd.	Three Hours
Yellow	Stimulates intuitive ability, aids with communication, brings joy, enhances the memory and aids with all intellectual pursuits. Good for business success.	Three Hours

Candles in Practical Magic		
Green	Life, restoration, growth, healing, abundance, prosperity, fertility, love and harmony. Attracts money. Aids with stability, bringing happiness & joy. Takes time to manifest but the effects are long lasting. Corresponds to the lush fields of the Annwn.	Four Hours
Blue	For the Egyptians this resonated with life, rebirth, fertility, the heavens, prosperity. Stimulates the intellect. Brings peace and protection. Enhances one's second sight. Aids with calming, concentration and trance. Resonates with the Abred.	Three Hours
Light Blue	Life, the sky, regeneration, air and intellect. Aids with love.	Three Hours
Dark Blue	Very spiritual. Corresponds to the deep Annwn and Caer Wydyr. Used to gain knowledge and wisdom. Increase psychic perception.	Two Hours

Candles in Practical Magic		
Purple	Power, energy, brings grace, expansion and can be used for prosperity, as well as spiritual knowledge. Very powerful but can be difficult to control. Reverses curses. Used to banish illness.	One Hour
Brown	Brings help when in dire financial crisis. Brings stability.	Four Hours
White	Purity & cleanliness, joy, potential. The White Dragon force of the Moon and Mistress. Union of Earth and Sky. Can be used as a substitute for any other color except black.	Depends on use
Black	Attracts and absorbs energy which can be redirected. Negates other forces. Can be used for rites of rebirth, regeneration. Conversely, it is also used to summon spirits and give access to the underworld. Can be used in works of cursing, blasting and causing of discord.	One Hour or until completely burned out

When using candles to directly affect other people, it is helpful to learn their zodiacal sign. Once this is obtained one can use a colored candle corresponding to their sign. I honestly don't know how 'traditional' this actually is. I have found records of this reaching back to the late 1800's, but beyond that I am not certain. From personal experience I can say that this can be very potent. I have used this technique repeatedly for decades with excellent results. The color scheme which I follow is that which is recommended by Sybil Leek. As I mentioned in *The Willow Path*, her arrangement matches very closely to those colors attributed to the signs in many contemporary Astrological texts, which makes sense given Ms. Leek's passion for this science.

Zodiacal Colors		
Sign	Primary	Secondary
Aries	Red	-
Taurus	Orange	Yellow
Gemini	Yellow	Clear Blue
Cancer	Pink	Green
Leo	Gold	Orange
Libra	Lavender	Light Blue
Scorpio	Dark Red	-
Sagittarius	Green	Indigo
Capricorn	Brown	Dove Grey, Black
Aquarius	Electric Blue	-
Pisces	Purple	-

There are some additional points to consider when using candles. First, always use new candles or those that you have stored away solely for spell working. Ideally these should be solid in color all the way through. If you can make your own, so much the better. Never use a candle for a new spell that had been partially used in a different spell. Having said this, you may use the same candle if this is a repeat of the same spell, i.e., a 'drumroll' spell. The only exception that I am aware of was a practice followed by the coven I was initiated into following Julie's passing. In this the candles used at initiation were given to the new member afterward with the instructions that these could be used in spells but only when in dire need. I held onto mine for many years, using them very sparingly.

I try very hard to avoid working with scented candles. In most cases the scent is too overpowering. Oftentimes I don't know what was used to give the candle its scent. Frequently the scent does not resonate with the spell itself which, in turn, defeats the purpose of the candle in the first place. Rather, I prefer to leave any scents used in ritual to incense and oils.

I also do not use candles that have objects melted into the wax. It is very common today to find different shops that have added minerals, crystals and herbs to candles. Again, this tends to distract from the work at hand and often the objects may be resonating with entirely different forces than those I am seeking to call one. The only time I have made an exception for this was when I personally crafted a solid beeswax candle that I then used in an Egyptian rite to the Goddess Hathor. For this I did add specific herbs which directly related to this wonderful being. But as a general rule, I only use solid colored, unscented, new or personally made candles.

Candle holders should also be kept solely for use in the Art. I have even kept separate ones for different purposes. For example, some are used solely for defensive magic while others are for prosperity, others for healing, and so on. In this way they tend to build up a 'natural' resonance and energy that links them to the goals being sought. There are some Witches who do have a single candle holder that they use for most of their workings. I briefly discussed these when considering the hearth, specifically when looking at the

Cornish use of the 'Hood Lamp'. You will also find some spells that require specific holders which are prepared solely for that working. These tend to be more for the evocation of specific otherworld beings.

An additional feature that I like to include when working candle magic is the placement of herbs and the taglock. In many spells, I will sprinkle a small amount of a dried herb that relates directly to the work at hand directly into the candle holder socket. With this I will sometimes place a taglock of the person as well. In doing so I have found that, as the candle burns down, releasing the energy within, it finishes with a direct link to the person while delivering a final boost of power. This can be highly effective. If, however, you don't want to have the taglock burnt with the candle (perhaps because it is your only taglock to the person) this can be placed either directly underneath the candle holder itself or in front of this.

Lastly, like all spells, the timing is critical. All normal rules for following tides of power should be followed. Having said this, it is important to note that some Traditional Witches feel that candle spells work best when done at midnight.[14] In fact, Sybil Leek often wrote that her group usually did most of their magic during the Witching Hour. I consider this to be more of a suggestion than a requirement for success as I have worked magic, including candle spells, at a variety of times with success. Nevertheless, I wanted to include this here as you may want to experiment with midnight spells.

Candle Reading and Wax Divination

Sybil Leek devotes a major section in her work on divination to scrying through the use of candles and melted wax. Like the medieval practice of pouring molten lead into water, Sybil would pour hot wax into water and then divine the answer to questions from the shapes formed. These will often form initials, recognizable shapes including outlines of seacoasts

---

14. Leek, Sybil. *The Sybil Leek Book of Fortune Telling.* 1969.121

and more. Sybil explained that the key to interpreting these images lay in the intuitive ability of the reader herself. Still, Sybil went on describe the basic meaning of certain symbols that she found to reoccur when reading wax:

Arrow – unpleasant news can be expected in a letter.
Bird – news from a distance.
Crescent – an increase in prosperity.
Cross – a certain indication of trouble.
Snake – depending on the question, an indication that a friend may not be entirely friendly.
Square – trouble or a blocking of ambition.
Sword/knife – beware of scandal.
Tree – prosperity; a group of trees mean that prosperity will extend to the whole family.
Triangle – good luck.
Wagon (or other vehicle) – stop and think carefully before pursuing a current ambition or project.
Wheel – unexpected gift or a successful new idea.[15]

Because of wax's susceptibility to magical and psychic influence, it is also possible to 'read' candles themselves to determine what type of influence is present. This is especially important when looking to the candles that are present in ritual. You are going to find that candles and their flames show the first signs of spirit or otherworld beings present. This is particularly true of those set at the edge of the circle. Often the flame of one or more will begin to burn brighter, perhaps becoming taller. Sometimes the flame may split in two, or it will change color. There will also be times when the flame may bend as if in a draft when none is present. The Witch needs to be aware of any or all of these for they each can represent some form of occult

_____

15. These definitions and additional comments by Ms. Leek on this form of divination can be found in the collection of her writings: Leek, Sybil. *The Best of Sybil Leek*. 1974.

presence or interference. How a candle drips will have equal meaning. Candles that are psychically hit will often burn faster than the rest.

In reading candles, look to the direction that the candle is stationed at in the circle. An irregularly burning taper set at the circle's edge corresponding to one of the Wards will tell you where the interference is coming from. If only one Ward candle is 'hit' then the influence is coming from that direction. However, suppose two different candles are dripping excessively, perhaps the south candle and the east. This would indicate that the interference originates in the southeast. If on the other hand three or all four candles at the edge are burning erratically there are a couple different possible reasons. You could be the subject of a drumroll working in which several people from a variety of places are trying to influence you. Another possibility is that the space you are working in has spirits or forces that are moving around the circle and are present in the general vicinity.

As general rule of thumb, if only the outer Ward candles are burning oddly but those on the hearthstone/altar are not, the influence is considered to be fairly mild. If, however, candles on the hearthstone are also burning oddly then this would be considered a 'direct hit'. That is, it would indicate that either someone is purposely working magic on you, or that a very powerful otherworld being is present and very much aware of you. It doesn't necessarily mean that your Roth Fail has been compromised. Rather, think of the candles as acting in a similar way to a thermometer. They are tools that the Witch uses to gauge what types of influences are present and how strong those may be.

Just because a candle shows that some form of psychic interference is present, it doesn't necessarily mean that this is harmful. Energy is energy. Some clues to the nature of the influence may be found when looking to the flame and tip of the candle. When these are subject to influence, it isn't uncommon for either to change color, even if for a few moments. The colors will often reveal the intent of the force. To determine the type of influence, look to the chart of color correspondence given earlier to get at least a quick understanding of the influences present. From there it is a matter of using any number of divination techniques to get to the finer details.

Some further notes on reading candles. Generally, I have found that when performing candle magic and using a single working candle, how this burns will often speak to the effectiveness of the spell overall. I find that, when the candle burns quickly with little or no dripping, this indicates that the spell was strong and probably hitting its intended target easily. If, on the other hand, it is dripping or has difficulty staying lit, something is off. Either one's concentration during the spell wasn't focused, or there was some interference blocking the spell. If this happens give the spell some time to work. The minimum time is one lunar cycle. If at the end of that time there was no discernable effect, you may want to reexamine whether this was the correct goal to reach toward, or decide if this was even within your realm of possibility. If yes to both, then by all means attempt the spell again. If need be, you may want to use a different spell altogether that will achieve success.

Cloth, Weaving and Cord Magic

The distaff and spinning wheel have very deep associations with Traditional Witchcraft. Before the Industrial era a large part of many women's time was spent spinning wool and other fibers into different thread or twine, and then weaving these into cloth. This then would be sown into garments. The methodical process of spinning, weaving and sewing lend themselves perfectly to entering meditative or altered states of consciousness, that is, to moving into the 'becoming'. Perhaps more importantly though is that once in the becoming, there is a point of merging with the fabric and with this the very real ability to infuse this with one's intent. This is the essence of Cord Magic.

Today very few of us spin yarn or make clothes. For those who do I have the utmost respect. You have a real advantage in that you can enchant the garment being made. This can be done through the simple use of a basic rhythmic chant that captures the essence of what you would like the wearer to experience or feel. For those of us who lack the skill to spin, weave and sew, there are simpler tasks that can be performed. Perhaps the easiest is the act of braiding and knotting string, yarn and cords.

Cords have been a part of the magical arts for centuries. I discussed their symbolism in relation to binding the Witch to the Geassa and her system of the Art earlier in this series. However, cords have a very real place in practical magic as well. For Witches and cunning folk of the 1800s it was very common to wear a plain length of cord around the waist. In Cornwall this was often called a "balsh". These almost always had loop on one end.[16] Their primary function appears to be the containing and controlling of spirits. The legends speak of cunning folk encircling spirits and leading them away from houses which they haunted. Interestingly, the cord also acted as a protective shield around which a spirit could not be harmed by malevolent entities that may have been tormenting it.

This bears a striking similarity to the use of cords in some Hermetic Orders and, by Traditional Witches today. This was shown in the techniques surrounding the formation of the fetch. It is also common to use the cord as a focal point in which one may evoke otherworld beings.[17] When worn the cord acts very similarly to the Roth Fail or Maze. That is, it becomes both a protective circle around one, while ensuring that the Witch is in her own personal point of power wherever she may be.

---

16. Bottrell, William and Joseph Blight. *Stories and Folklore of West Cornwall* (1880). 29.1880

17. This is discussed in the previous book in this series *Horns of the Moon.*

In preparing your own cord you may choose to braid this yourself, using three strands of natural fiber cloth, cording or rope. As you braid these, enter the becoming and use a simple chant to infuse this with your power, making this unique to you. The chant could be something as simple as:

"Hands weave, power now bound
Braid together, this cord is wound!"

Like the Cornish do with their balsh, we too tie one end into a loop, through which the other end will be inserted when worn. These represent the female and male energies joined. When not inserted, the loop has a similar look, meaning and function as the Ancient Egyptian Tyet, also known as the "buckle of Isis". As you can see the cord then is a very personal tool carrying the energy and intent of the person within.

Cords, string and twine have long been used as personal taglocks. This is usually done by 'taking the measure of a person'. There are several different methods for doing this depending on the situation and purpose. In Traditional Witchcraft initiation ceremonies the Mistress will frequently take the new initiate's measure. Some groups do this by taking yarn and cutting this to the exact height of the person. However, in the system in which I was trained, the measure was taken using a natural yarn that was first drawn around the circumference of the initiate's head. Then from this point in the string the measure around the person's chest was taken. Holding this point in the yarn she would then measure around their hips, followed by the knees and lastly around the ankles as the person stood with the feet together. Thus, five points representing the five elements of the initiate were stored within this single strand of yarn.

Yet there are other ways to take a measure, and many other reasons for doing so. Jake Richards explains that in Appalachian folk magic it is common to take the measure of different parts of the body in order to directly affect these.

For example, if someone has chills and a cough, a length of red yarn is measured around their chest. This is then taken to a tree. A knot for each day that the person has been sick is tied into the yarn. The yarn is then wrapped around the tree, tied and left. He explains that, if done correctly, the sickness will leave the person within the same number of days as are present in the knot.[18]

You will find that, beyond the cord itself, the use of knots forms a vital part of many forms of cord magic. The reason is simply that knots are seen as the way in which power is bound to the string. Sometimes the knots are left in the cord causing the entire piece to become a talisman of sorts harnessing the force to aid the Witch. The number of knots used will vary depending largely on numerological considerations and how these resonate with the force being bound. To understand the basic premise of knot magic, the following quote from Sybil Leek may be of help:

> *"Even a piece of string, certainly less glamorous than jewels and metals, can be charged to receive and expel powerful vibrations. Take a piece of string and concentrate on your need for protection with all the thought forces which you can command. Picture the power streaming down through your body until it reaches the fingers holding the string. Then tie a knot, pulling it with a strong jerk. Some of the power within you will enter knot. Do this seven times, always waiting to feel a special surge of power within yourself before tying the knot and you have a simple, homemade, very personal talisman."*[19]

Sometimes though the knots are made with the sole purpose of tying a force to the cord so that it can be unleashed later when needed. Excellent examples of this include the accounts of Witches binding the wind to a piece

18. Richards, Jake. *Backwoods Witchcraft : Conjure & Folk Magic From Appalachia*. 2019.79
19. Leek, Sybil. *The Sybil Leek Book of Curses*. 1975.135

of rope, using three knots. These were then sold to sailors who would then call the wind while at sea. The manner in which a force is bound to a knot is essentially the same no matter the spirit evoked.

The Moon Cord

For this you will want to braid a cord to a length of three feet. Traditionally this would have been of plain beige cord. However, today most people have access to a variety of colors. For the Moon Cord this should be either plain/natural, white or green. This spell itself is performed on the night of the Full Moon when one is outside and able to see the Moon clearly.

Holding the cord in your hands, begin to chant the following repeatedly in a slow and steady pattern as you allow yourself to slip into a state of becoming. Let the light of the Full Moon engulf you, rising in power within. This chant, in fact, is one which can be used for many different occasions as it evokes both the Serpent's Breath and the essence of the Mistress as the Moon, inviting them to merge within one:[20]

> "Serpent's Breath
> Mistress Moon
> This Enchantment I make!"

As the power rises, keep looking at the Full Moon. Let the chant flow in a rhythmic repetition as you gather the power that rises. Then, when you feel the energy is strongest, tie your first knot in the middle of the cord. Some witches

---

20. We use this frequently, often as Words of Power in Gaelic, finding it to be quite effective. The Gaelic words and pronunciation are presented elsewhere in this book. As an alternative to this you may choose to simply chant the name of a specific lunar Goddess. Julie was fond of working with Diana. As such, I could easily see the Witch using this name in place of the chant shown here.

will hold the cord up and look at the Moon with their left eye through the hole the knot makes just as they tighten this. Whichever you choose, feel the Moon's essence flow through your arms and down through your hands becoming part of the cord itself as you tie the knot. Then take a moment to let the power well up within again, all the while continuing the chant. Now tie a second knot to the left of the first. Then proceed with a third knot to the right of the center. The fourth knot is then tied to the left further up the cord, alternating to the right on the next, and so on until there are a total of nine knots in the cord.

The cord can then be used in one of two ways. It can be kept as a talisman of the moon. This can be placed in the home, or in you place of magical working, drawing the power of the Dragon and Lady to your work. Alternatively, one may use the cord in ritual when added power is needed. To do this untie a single knot releasing the power. In such cases the Witch would work backwards untying the ninth knot first. All that would be needed is to undo one knot for a single working, saving the rest for other occasions.

You will find in cord magic that many times spells will call for different objects to be incorporated into the knots themselves. These can be anything from hagstones, bones and feathers, to shells and glass beads. It is in this vein that the much celebrated 'Witches Ladder' as well as the 'Wytcha' used in spirit travel are created. While the Witches Ladder has been written of extensively by many other authorities, perhaps it would be helpful to describe the Wytcha here.

The Wythca
This is a device meant to be used to help enhance one's ability to travel in spirit. As such, it can be employed in any of the techniques I had described for this purpose in *Horns of the Moon*. Essentially, it is talismanic in nature, created in such a way as to resonate to the process of leaving and re-entering one's body. To my knowledge this

was first described in the writings of Andrew Chumbley, from his work *What is Traditional Craft?* This is our method for making this tool.

Start by obtaining a length of leather lacing, no longer than two feet. It can be shorter. However, you want this to fit loosely around your wrist when tied, leaving enough slack to place a hagstone to which the thong is secured, in the palm of your hand. On the night of the Full Moon take the leather and slip one end through the hole of the hagstone. As you do envision yourself moving through the opening in the stone, slipping out of your body and into the different realms of spirit. Let the cord become immersed in the intention that it is the 'second road' of spirit and faery on which you will travel. While you are not, at this point, actually projecting your fetch through the opening, you are engaging your will and imagination so that this becomes the sole purpose of the Wythca.

If desired, by all means feel free to use the incantation employed in the making of the Moon Cord to help call the forces and to help you slip into a state of becoming. As you do, tie seven individual knots in the cord. Then tie the two ends together. Finally, finish by setting the Wythca on the hearth and then, using the middle finger of your left hand, trace the *Crossroads Sigil* in the air above the talisman. In doing so see the sigil glow an electric blue with power. Then, with the charged breath, exhale the energy you have been collecting through your chant directly onto the hagstone.

To use the Wythca, slip the leather cord around your less dominant wrist. Keep this loose enough that the hagstone can rest comfortably in you palm. You can then proceed with your chosen technique for traveling in spirit. Conversely, many Witches will wear the Wythca around their wrist when retiring to bed. This is done with the intention that it will help them to travel to the realm of the Elders and what some see as the 'Witches' Sabbat', in their sleep.

This was but an all too short examination of Cord Magic. Yet the essential elements presented here should give the apprentice the means to explore this subject with confidence. As with so much in the Art, each technique requires practice. Cord Magic is a very traditional means of causing change in accordance with one's will.

Chapter Ten

✤ FOOTSTEPS IN THE NIGHT ✤
SUMMONING THE DEAD

It was still dark, well before sunrise, as I sat in the small kitchenette on the second floor of the old house on King Street, drinking coffee as I prepared for work. The house was old, going back at least to the 1800s. Three stories tall with a series of staircases, long halls and side rooms, the house was truly unique. Perhaps its most unusual feature was the top floor. This was two large rooms that had been finished. Curiously one of the rooms had a floor that was painted jet black while the walls were a dark blue. There was an otherworldly presence to the chamber. As Witches we found the room to be perfect for ritual, setting up our Roth Fail in this space.

On this particular night though I was focused on the day ahead. I had dressed and was about to leave for my job as a laborer at a local boat manufacturer. As I was relaxing over breakfast I heard the distinct sound of footsteps coming up the stairs from the first floor and walk down the hall. I assumed they were those of the woman I shared the house with. "It looks like another beautiful day ahead," I said as the steps grew louder. Then I heard the bathroom door at the end of the hall close. That was odd, I thought, as there was one on the first floor. After several minutes passed and no sound from the hall or bathroom could be heard, I decided to check on her. The door was shut but there was light showing underneath. I knocked on the door. "Are you ok?" No sound came from inside. I slowly opened the door. The light was on, the same light I had shut off earlier, but no one was there. Later when I mentioned this to my companion, she insisted that she had been sleeping, never coming up the stairs.

About a week later she and I were sitting in a small room off the kitchenette, again on the second floor. It was early evening and we were enjoying dinner while going over coven activities. When suddenly, just above us on the third floor, there was the distinct sound of furniture being moved, legs of tables or chairs scraping on the floors, banging sounds that went on for several moments. These were clear and very loud. I bolted out of my chair and ran up the stairs to see who or what was there. Bursting onto the third floor and flipping on the lights I saw ... nothing. Nothing had been moved. Everything was exactly where we had left it. I searched the entire floor but there was nothing out of place. Yet both of us clearly heard the disturbance. These were just a few of the phenomena that occurred.

There is nothing quite so fascinating and yet, for some, unnerving as living in a haunted house. Over the months that we rented the house there were many such incidents, some being even more dramatic than these. For me, the most intriguing aspect was the fact that when these happened they were impossible to deny. The phenomena were very real, occurring on a frequent basis and always when least expected. These weren't looked for events. Rather they were spontaneous and, in many cases, involved material objects being directly influenced without any physical explanation. In some cases, multiple witnesses were present during the phenomenon.

In the Art we recognize that the material realm is not as structured and concrete as most people like to believe. Rather, it is quite porous. The world we live in is but a thin threshold between the two greater realms of the Annwn and the Abred. As such, the Witch recognizes that otherworld beings can and do cross through, influencing our world in very real ways. This includes the spirits of the dead. As Witches, we can reach across these realms to directly contact the deceased.

The methods for doing so are varied. I already spoke of household spirits and the means for communicating and appeasing these earlier. In this chapter I would like to explore different techniques for summoning the dead. This can range from very simple procedures, such as the use of spirit boards, candle divination and scrying, to séances and ritual necromancy.

Spirit Boards & Séances
Spirit boards and their equivalent have been around for a very long time. Perhaps the simplest versions of these are the placing of a series of cards or pieces of paper with letters and numbers on them in a circle around a smooth topped table. A wine glass is then set in the center upside down. Everyone present places their fingers lightly on the glass. Questions are then asked. Like the classic spirit board or Ouija board the glass frequently begins sliding to the various letters as it spells out messages.

Spirit boards differ from the wine glass technique in that they replace the table with a wooden board on which letters and numbers have been embossed. With this the sitters place their fingers lightly on a planchette which then moves. Over the years a tremendous amount of mystique has built up around these tools reaching a point that many people are afraid to use them out of fear that they will invite negative or 'evil' spirits into one's life.

My view toward spirit boards is that, in and of themselves, they are completely neutral, just as neutral as a phone, or computer. Yet, like any tool used in the magical arts, the energies and intention that the individual board was used for in the past will influence how it functions in the future. It is quite possible for entities to become attached to individual spirit boards, essentially haunting these. Additionally, any emotional energies that may have been projected into the board previously by sitters, whether wittingly or unwittingly, can linger causing the board to be tainted. In such cases, these different forces are likely to come through to those in the group who are most sensitive.

Yet, spirit boards can be an effective tool for communication provided precautions are taken. Perhaps the most universally recognized, and that which the Mistress here prefers, is to sprinkle a light circle of salt around the area that you will be working and only invite those forces that mean no harm. Also use only boards which you know the history of. I would recommend boards you purchased new or have made yourself. You may also find that those that have been used successfully in the past and have been handed down through your family or coven are safe and effective.

I would like to note that Sybil Leek did not advocate the use of Ouija Boards. She was clear that she felt these were more or less crutches that weren't needed. In her opinion the messages that often came through were frequently influenced by the sitters' own subconscious. Or, at the least, the subconscious of those involved interfered with any real phenomena that any spirits might be trying to communicate. She went on to state that if her students insisted on using these, she would ask the sitters to be blindfolded and the board turned the opposite direction. Then an observer who was not participating could record the figures and letters that the planchette spelled out.[21]

Rather, Sybil preferred to use the classic séance as an effective means of communicating with the dead. She did this in order to help her students learn how to slip into trance. She, herself, was a trance medium, working extensively with parapsychologists in this capacity. A close read of her many books reveals that trance also figured highly in Sybil's ritual practices. She makes this point very clear in her pivotal book *The Complete Art of Witchcraft* where she discusses trance work and astral projection as a normal part of coven meetings.

---

21. Leek, Sybil. *ESP: The Magic Within You.* 1971.77

In regards to communicating with spirits, Sybil described her technique for teaching this to students quite clearly in her writing. Her goal in doing this was to develop their abilities while they directly experienced otherworld beings for themselves. However, at the same time she gave very clear instructions strongly advising against techniques that could be misconstrued as fraud. Having been the subject of a number of investigations herself, she was highly concerned about maintaining integrity.

The method she used is very traditional, reaching back to nineteenth century séances and earlier. Yet, they proved very effective for her.[22]

> *"I like to use a very heavy old table for séances, preferably one that cannot be easily moved by a single person. Let everyone examine it for creaks and make sure it is firmly set on the floor. A round table is best because the round shape itself has a special esoteric force about it. It is one of the earliest known shapes. I like to have the sexes alternate in position around the table, seated on comfortable armless chairs. All hands should be placed on the table but without exerting pressure on it. Nearly always some student will insist that all fingers should touch each other to make a chain around the edge of the table, but this has never been proved to my satisfaction. The link, I think, must come from the thoughts within the sitters, and physical contact may thus be quite unnecessary."*

Sybil goes on to explain that some may prefer subdued lighting. While this may be conducive to creating the

---

22. It is important to note that Sybil grew up at a time when Spiritualism was very active, as was psychical research into séances and different forms of mediumship. Sybil's family was well connected in different occult circles at the time, both in England and in Europe. As such, she would have been exposed to these techniques at a very young age. She describes some of the experiments her father performed with her own abilities as a child in several of her books.

'mood' and helping to alter the state of consciousness, she makes it clear that this isn't necessary and, in fact, she had conducted séances in all types of light including sunlight and under the glare of television camera light. She also advises that, when working with new students, it is best not to have anyone who is overtly skeptical of the experiment to be at the table. Rather, she recommends having sitters who can harmoniously tune their minds as they function as an organic unit. However, she went on to say that if one is an experienced medium, there is no concern in having a skeptical person present, but for best results all should be open to the potential process.

In addition, Sybil liked to have some members remain away from the table as observers and independent witnesses. These folks should record the events. Ideally this could be with recording equipment as well as their own personal notes. She explains that the time, date, the number of people and their names as well as the temperature of the room or area should be noted. She explains "the latter is important, for when messages come through, there is always a drop in the room temperature. This can be quite dramatic." She goes on to suggest:

> *"The second student should record all the actual messages, at what time they come and through whom, or if the message comes through the more usual way, by the table rapping or use of the alphabet, that also should be set down."*

She goes on to state:

> *"The sitters at the table should leave the recording and interpretation to those designated to do it because sometimes, if there are strong forces around, it is not unusual for the alphabet of a foreign language to be spelled out and this can only be identified and translated after the session."*

Sybil explains that early sessions often result in the table moving, rapping on the floor. She states that this can be quite extensive with the table moving well beyond what any one person could control.

> *"But once a group has been established over a period of time, with consistent séances attended by the same group week after week, a strange thing becomes apparent. The table ceases to throw itself around and becomes secondary to the people sitting around it. Now messages begin to come through the sitters, and it is noticeable that many of them will fall into light trance states, recognized by an appearance of near-sleepiness, coming when the personality no longer matters and the entire person is devoted to responding to the forces of energy that are capable of transmitting messages."*

Eventually, she explains, many people will get to a point when it is no longer necessary to sit around a table. Rather they become used to slipping into trance and allowing the forces involved to move through them.[23]

Beyond spirit boards and séances, there are number of other techniques that one can use to summon the dead. In Traditional Witchcraft these can range from simple spells to specific rituals. I would like to present two different techniques that we are familiar with. However, before doing so, there is some basic preparation that one will want to do in advance of the summoning. This should begin with creating a necromantic incense, as well as Graveyard Dirt, followed by the creation of the Seal of the Spirits.

Spirit Summoning Incenses and 'Graveyard Dirt'
There are any number of incenses that the Witch can use to aid in spirit evocation. As explained in *Horns of the Moon*, the traditional three parts Wormwood to one part Vervain incense is very good for this purpose, as is the *Wormwood and Vervain*

---

23. Leek, Sybil. *ESP: The Magic Within You.* 1971.77-79.

Compound also discussed in that volume. Dittany of Crete can be added to these as it has long been used to evoke spirits. If this isn't available, one can substitute this with Marjoram.

'Simple' Strega Spirit Summoning Incense

A very old, traditional means of summoning spirits is to place a few drops of your own fresh blood on Laurel Bay leaves. These are then burned as incense whenever summoning spirits of the deceased.

Graveyard Smoke

Another very simple but highly effective necromancy incense that can be used is Graveyard Smoke. On a Saturday nearest to the Full Moon, in the hour of Saturn, mix equal portions of dried and powdered Valerian Root, Mullein leaves and either Mugwort or Wormwood. If desired, you can also add Patchouli as this is frequently used in spirit communication. As with the other incenses, this is burned on hot coals.

Graveyard Dirt

In addition to incense, you will want to make Graveyard Dirt. This has a long history in rural magical practices going back centuries. Rather than being burned this is a powder used to attract spirits to your working. To make this, you will need the same three ingredients as you gathered for the Graveyard Smoke; Valerian root, Mullein and Mugwort or Wormwood. In addition, you will need to visit a cemetery. Ideally this should be during the Waning to Dark Moon. There you will gather soil. If possible, this should be from a freshly dug grave. Though, if this isn't available soil from the cemetery grounds will do. You want enough to equal the volume of herbs you will be using.

Once home let the soil dry completely. Then sift this using the fine dirt that comes through. Then on the day and hour of Saturn nearest the Full Moon, mix this with the powdered herbs. Once done, bottle this, labeling it carefully and set it aside until the time of the working.

Seal of the Spirits

Along with an incense and Graveyard Dirt, to work the following rites of necromancy it is best to create a talisman which we call the *Seal of the Spirits*. This is derived from two different magical texts reaching back hundreds of years. This talisman is worn by the Witch giving her the power to summon spirits while also protecting her from malevolent forces. For this you will want to have assembled your necromantic incense, a quality pen and ink used solely for ritual purposes, and a good quality paper or parchment on which to draw the following seals. One should be drawn on one side of the paper, with the other on the reverse. When worn, it doesn't matter which is facing out.

This should be done during the Waxing Moon during the day and hour of Saturn. Essentially follow the ritual outlined in Chapter Five for enchanting talismans. In this case you will want to follow the instructions using the planetary correspondence of Saturn. Ideally, for this operation the Triangle of Art may be traced with Graveyard Dirt.

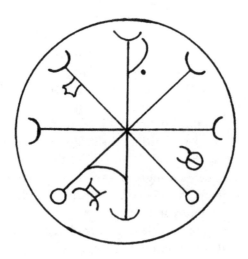

Front

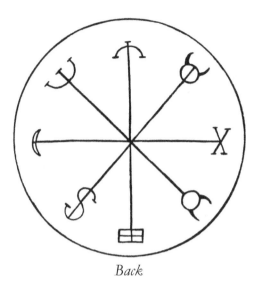

Back

Once enchanted, this can be strung with black twine or ribbon so that it can be worn during ritual around the neck.

Spirit Scrying
Spirit Scrying really is a form of divination in that the Witch uses a crystal, or some other scrying device to communicate with the spirits and ask questions of them. As such, think carefully about what you want to ask before embarking on this exercise. Having said this, you certainly can use this technique to simply open the veil between realms and start a dialog through the images that come through. In either case take some time to think through some basic goals and questions for the ritual.

This is best performed during the day and hour of Saturn or the Moon, preferably on one of the nights that correspond to any of the *Ladies of the Moon* that relate to spirit communication. Barring this, chose a Saturday or Monday that falls closest to the Full Moon.
Whether working indoors or outside, you will need to trace a Triangle of Art using the Graveyard Dirt. The apex should be pointing north. At each point of the triangle, set a black

candle. In the center of the triangle place the device you will be using in your scrying. This can be anything from a crystal, a showstone, a silvered or black mirror, the goblet of inked water, the Mugwort and Witch ball, whatever means you are most comfortable employing in your scrying. Inside the triangle, at the apex, place a bone. At the base of the triangle mark the sigil of spirit evocation.

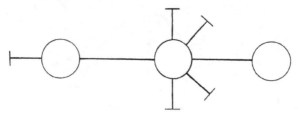

Lunar Sigil used in Necromatic Spirit Evocation

You will need to be wearing the *Seal of the Spirits*. To the left side of the triangle place a goblet red wine and mead. Also place a small plate of sweet cakes near this. To the right set a thurible or small fire cauldron in which hot coals are burning. To this add a handful of necromancy incense.

The rite itself should be done in the Roth Fail, which will be carefully crafted allowing the Witch to move between worlds while also protecting her should any malicious spirits manifest. Once the Roth Fail is completed, the Stang should be set in the north. If working at your hearth, place the Stang to the right of this, while the besom is placed to the left.

With the Fe, trace the triangle, imbuing this with power. This is done by starting at the apex and moving in a deosil manner. Add more Graveyard Smoke, or other spirit summoning incense to the coals and then, while holding the Fe, incant:

"I conjure you spirits of this place,
By my will I conjure you,
By my breath I conjure you,

By fire and smoke I conjure you,
By these words of power I conjure you,
Neamhshaolta, Neamhshaolta, Neamhshaolta
(pronounced *Nav-healta*)
See the meal I bring to you,
Come spirits, this offering of food is for you!
Visions and words of truth are what I seek from you!
I conjure you, I conjure you, I conjure you!
Come, arise and let me see!"

Repeat the incantation three times, then replenish the incense as you clearly state your question. At this point sit comfortably in front of the triangle and begin scrying just as discussed earlier. Take your time with this as you relax and let yourself simply experience the flow of images or impressions that come through. It may be important to note that, in the earlier stages of using rituals such as these, you may not consciously be aware of messages or the presence of spirits. Nevertheless, continue the rite. Patience and persistence are important in necromancy. Also, you are very likely to find that the ritual may act as a catalyst, opening your deeper senses.

When finished, thank the spirits for their presence. This should include specifically offering the food and drink to them. In this, ask that there be peace between you and that they may aid you again when you invite them in the future. The Roth Fail is then cleared. If working outdoors the food and wine can be poured on the ground, or buried if you don't wish others to find these later. If the rite was held in your private ritual chamber you may want to leave the offerings on the hearthstone until morning and then take these outside and pour them on the ground.

Spirit Mist – The Summoning
In the rite of spirit scrying the Witch invited entities to move through a crystal stationed inside the Roth Fail. In this rite however, the Witch draws the spirits of a place to

239

the outer edge of the Roth Fail rings. I find this is excellent for becoming aware of the spirits who may be lingering or haunting a place. I have also used variations of this to connect with specific spirits. The fundamental technique is essentially the same.

As with the spirit scrying you will need the *Seal of the Spirits*, a suitable incense and the Graveyard Dirt. Also have a small quantity of Pine and Silver Sage available. If you can't get Silver Sage, the Pine alone will be sufficient. Have present all normal tools to set the Roth Fail. In addition, you will need some way of intoning specific musical tones. As mentioned earlier, I frequently use a standard pitch pipe to ensure the tone I vocalize is accurate. Whatever way you chose to create this, keep it simple and accurate. Be sure to test it in advance of the actual ritual, as there is nothing more distracting than fumbling to find the right tone when conducting an evocation.

This ritual is best performed any time between the Summer Solstice to the Winter Solstice as this cycle lends itself well to the materialization of entities. As with the scrying, this should also be done as near to the Full Moon as possible, ideally on a Saturday or Monday evening. Again, try to choose a date that corresponds to one of the *Ladies of the Moon* that resonates with spirit communication. These could include the seventh, thirteenth, fourteenth, fifteenth days of the lunar month which are probably some of the best.[24]

Lay the Roth Fail as normal. Trace the Sigil of Spirit Evocation on the hearthstone with the Graveyard Dirt. Then, with the bone in hand, go to the north quarter and sound the musical note of "D". Ideally, if you can find a hollowed bone, use this as a type of horn through which you send the Charged Breath in the musical tone. In doing so, envision the silvery-gray mists of the Serpent Breath

---

24. See chapter fourteen of *Horns of the Moon* for a complete description of the twenty-eight Ladies of the Moon.

gathering in the north. Then in a tuathal (widdershins) manner move to the west and tone the note of "D", seeing the mists form, moving in like a fog that rolls in off the sea. Now proceed to the south and summon the mists here using the bone and musical note. Do the same in the east taking care to visualize the entire area around the circle as filling with the mists of the Dragon's Breath.

Return to the hearthstone replacing the bone. Replenish the incense. Standing before the hearthstone begin to enchant the *Stirring of the Spirit Mist*:

"Anál nathrach   (onal nathrack)
Taibhse brádán   (tie-bsha bardan)"

If room permits, feel free to circumambulate around the Roth Fail in a tuathal direction as you continue the chant. In either case, let the evocation flow from your lips as you envision the spirit mist begin to swirl and billow, gathering in thickness. Take as much time as you need to gather the Nephesh substance that is inherent in the Abred, coalescing into shapes at the edge of the circle.

Returning once again to the hearthstone, pick up the Fe and trace over the *Sigil of Spirit Evocation* seeing this blaze with power. Then holding the Fe enchant:

"I conjure you, I conjure you, Spirits of this place.
By my will I conjure you,
By my breath I conjure you,
By my word I conjure you,
By fire and smoke I conjure you.
Come spirits, the Way is open!"

Place more incense on the coals and continue the incantation:

"By these words of power I conjure you,
Neamhshaolta Taibhse   (Nav-healta tie-bsha)

241

Neamhshaolta Taibhse   (Nav-healta tie-bsha)
Neamhshaolta Taibhse   (Nav-healta tie-bsha)
I conjure you, I conjure you, I conjure you
Come and appear spirits of this place!"

Take up the bone and intone the note of "D" as you continue to envision the mists swirl, taking shape. Replace the bone. Holding the Fe complete the final portion of the evocation:

"From Tír Na Marbh I conjure you,
From Rostau you do come.
Spirits of this place,
Taibhse, Ka and Ba.
Neamhshaolta Taibhse   (Nav-healta tie-bsha)
I conjure you, I conjure you, I conjure you
Your presence here this night!"

Then chant the *Stirring of the Spirit Mist* repeatedly as needed:

"Anál nathrach   (onal nathrack)
Taibhse brádán   (tie-bsha bardan)"

    Let yourself open and become aware of the energies and presences in the area. Those with trance and mediumistic abilities will likely feel the spirits' influence first. As with the Spirit Scrying, the more you do this ritual the more effective it will become. It isn't unusual to have the candles react to the evocation, indicating the presence of otherworld entities. Too, you are very likely to become acutely aware of forms standing or moving around the circle. This is exactly what you are striving for. Once this happens feel free to ask your question. In this setting, within the Roth Fail, you may choose to use a spirit board or some other form of divination to help facilitate the communication. If a member of the group is prone to mediumistic abilities, she may well be encouraged to slip into trance in order to bring any messages through. When ready to finish the ritual stand before the hearthstone and enchant:

"Spirits of this place I thank you for your presence.
The Geassa is made, the Bond is set.
Return now to Tir Na Marbh,
Return now to Rostau!"

Sprinkle the Pine and Silver Sage on the coals and carry this around the Roth Fail deosil. Returning to the hearthstone recite the following:

"I/we thank you for your presence spirits in this place.
In peace return, by my word, this word of power,
Return in peace to your realm.
Deoraidhim   (JER-rid-hin)
Deoraidhim   (JER-rid-hin)
Deoraidhim   (JER-rid-hin)
Until such time as we seek to meet again!"

The Roth Fail is then cleared as normal.

Chapter Eleven

✤ SALT AND IRON ✤

Salt and iron are two of the most frequent elements used in Traditional Witchcraft. Highly versatile when applied to practical magic, both come with a certain amount of controversy. This appears to stem from both minerals' ability to repel otherworldly forces while also being able to contain these. Because of these qualities, there are many Witches who will not use either it ritual. In my training though I have seen that both can and should be part of the Witch's practice provided she understands how these can best be applied, as well as when to avoid using these.

To understand this perhaps we need to think in terms of these as holding inherent qualities that the Witch can manipulate to bring her intentions to fruition. At first this may seem difficult to understand. However, by way of example, think of a copper wire. It has the ability to conduct electricity. Yet in and of itself it doesn't do so unless it is hooked to a source of power. Even when the copper is connected and sending electric current, it is up to the person manipulating the wire to decide how this will be used. On the one hand, it can be hooked to a lightbulb, or one could use it to send an electric shock to repel or harm others. Thus, the wire is the means that allows the person to create the effect, but it is the person themself who *decides* how that energy is going to be applied. In my opinion the same concept applies when looking to salt and iron.

Always keep in mind that the Art is a type of 'technology' - a science, in that it uses various procedures to get results.

The ingredients and elements used in these techniques need to conform to certain fundamental standards, but the 'art' of manipulating those elements remain completely in the hands of the Witch.

Salt in the Art

In many places in these books, I have demonstrated several of the ways we use salt in magic, from cleansing tools to removing negative forces and spirits, purifying oneself and a space, to certain occasions when we have marked our compass with this. All of these are valid, yet there is so much more.

The use of salt in ritual can be traced back at least to the Ancient Egyptians. There, a naturally occurring combination of salt and sodium bicarbonate (baking soda) was found in many of the oases. Known as natron, the Egyptians used this in ritual bathing as well as in the cleansing of ritual chambers prior to magical practices. In such cases, some natron was dissolved in water, which was then sprinkled through the room. Similarly, a small amount of natron was crushed fine and sprinkled. Natron was so highly regarded that a small bowl of the mineral was then presented to spirits and the Neteru (Egyptian Gods and Goddesses) during temple rites of evocation.

This would seem to be in direct conflict with certain folkloric customs which strongly advise against using salt in ritual as it was said that spirits can't abide this. Yet, many of these same sources of lore contain many spells which directly call for the use of salt for several different purposes. In our practice, we have come to see the use of salt as being dependent on the context in which it is employed. In fact, I personally knew Welch traditionalists Witches who conducted the majority of their rituals in a series of three circles, one of which was salt.

I can say from firsthand experience that when a salt circle is employed the goal is to set a very clear boundary separating the mundane world from the ritual space. In such rites the objective is to contain and focus the energy being evoked in very powerful and direct ways. These rituals tend to be very intense, oftentimes carrying those involved to an awareness of realms not easily accessed through other means. I feel this was achieved specifically because we employed the salt both in its ability to repel that which we did not want, while containing the forces we were calling on.

However, in our practices today, the use of a salt circle is occasional. It is only brought to bear when great amounts of energy are needed or when we are seeking to tap directly into realms well beyond the threshold of the Abred *without* using techniques related to projection of the second skin. For all other situations we trace the three circles with blade, Stang and Fe.

Like the Egyptians, we oftentimes, though not always, will have a small amount of salt present on the hearth and will mix some salt with water. Salt is life. Without this mineral our bodies can't function. Saline is in our blood. Lightly salted water present in ritual is a recognition to all life's dependance on the oceans. As for the folkloric direction that "Earth spirits can't endure the Sea, nor anything that comes there from, and above all they abhor salt; so brine or sea-water"[25], it would seem from this that the beings referred to represent a specific class of spirit. I can say that in my experience over a very long career in the Art that I and those whom I have worked with have had great success in ritual whether salt was present or not. Again, much depends on exactly how this mineral is used. And so, we find that salt can be very versatile in the Art. To demonstrate this, it is appropriate to present some of the many other ways that salt can be used in magic.

Prosperity Powder
This is used to secure steady employment. Mix equal

---

25. Bottrell, William. *Traditions and Hearthside Stories of West Cornwall.* 1873.

portions of Benzion, Gravel Root and Sea Salt. Place some of this in a small bag that will be carried while applying to jobs. This same mixture can be used as an incense when working spells for employment. Keep the ashes, as these too can be carried while looking for work. An infusion of these can be made in warm Olive Oil or Mineral Oil. This is then dabbed on one's palms before going to an interview. It can also be applied to taglocks related to the job one is seeking.

Luck Bag

In this Italian spell salt is used as a key ingredient to bring one luck. Place a small sprig of Rue, a morsel of bread, a pinch of coarse salt and a few Cumin seeds into a small bag. Sew this with red thread while chanting:

> "This bag I sew, luck to me,
> And also, to my family.
> That it may keep by night and day,
> Troubles and illness far away!"

Harmony Powders

To bring peace and harmony to one's home combine an equal part of Cumin Seed with that of salt. This is scattered around the home in a deosil circle. A similar powder to help maintain control and peace in a home is to mix Dragon's Blood resin, salt and sugar together. Place this is a small box or envelope and hide this in the home where others won't find it.

Protective Powders

As a protection from malicious spirits, combine Dill Seed with salt. This can be carried in the Nata Bag to ward off evil. It can also be scattered throughout the home to disperse negative forces. Another salt powder for protection involves boiling a dried Beth Root (Trillium, Low John Root), making an infusion in water. This is allowed to cool. Then pour some of this over the salt, being careful to use just enough to moisten the salt but not melt it. Let this dry and then scatter it through the home. This has the additional advantage of helping to draw good fortune.

On many occasions I have combined salt and powdered Vervain, sprinkling this around rooms and across thresholds. This is done as part of an overall regiment to prevent negative forces or people from entering the space. Similarly, a mix of mustard seed and salt can be used in the same way, creating a barrier that spirits can't cross.

A more complex formula involves mixing equal parts of Dragon's Blood resin or dried Bloodroot, Sandalwood and salt together. This can be burned as incense or sprinkled as a protective powder.

Salt Sweep

For this tie fresh sprigs of Hyssop and Vervain together forming a small hand broom. Pour salt into white vinegar. Dip the end of the broom in the vinegar and use this to sweep the area, removing any malicious influences. If desired, Rue can be added to the broom for additional cleansing power. In fact, some Witches will dip Rue into salt water and sprinkle this in the home for protection and to drive away evil.

Fiery Wall of Protection Oil

While not a Traditional Witchcraft formula, this is a famous Hoodoo recipe that is renowned for its effectiveness. Grind into powder equal parts of sea salt, Dragon's Blood, Frankincense and Myrrh. Add this to a small amount of Castor Oil. This is then mixed with Mineral Oil to help thin this so that it flows better. This is then dabbed on oneself, as well as on doors and window sills for protection.

Banishing Powder

This is used specifically to ward off, or banish, entities that drain life from one: i.e., vampiric beings. Grind dried

Hawthorn leaves, Rowan leaves and Garlic. Mix this with an equal portion of salt. This is then sprinkled around the boundaries of the home and can be carried in a pouch.

Hot Foot Powder

This is used to cause one to leave you alone. Likewise, it can be used to cause the person to leave the place altogether. For this combine dried and powdered spiders (please only those found dead, as there is no need to kill these wonderful creatures for this spell). With this add salt and pepper. This is then sprinkled in the form of an "X" on the ground where the person must walk.

Black Salt

This is an important and often used ingredient in a number of Traditional Witchcraft spells, from protection to banishing, from hexing to removing curses. It is a very versatile substance that many turn to. I have seen several versions of this. However, there are always two essential ingredients: salt and the black iron seasoned scraping from one's cauldron. Ideally this is made by pouring salt into a well-seasoned, lovingly used Witch's cauldron. The salt is stirred and ground in the cauldron using a pestle-like object, all while chanting a basic incantation. As you do this, the blackened iron of the cauldron will begin to color the salt, turning it darker. Some Witches will burn specific herbs as well as parchments with sigils related to the planet that resonates with the energy they are seeking to infuse the salt, in the cauldron. This ensures a fresh layer of residue in the cauldron to help color the salt. Oftentimes Witches will grind charcoal into the salt to blacken this as well. The unique thing about black salt is that it combines the power of iron with its own, both of which are in many cases so closely aligned.

Iron in the Art

In the first book I briefly discussed the Irish legend of Owen Boyle in which he used an iron bladed black hilt knife to protect himself and his new bride from otherworld beings. Iron has long been seen as a protective mineral used in many spells and ritual work. We see this in everything from the iron and steel pins placed in a Witch's Bottle to the blade of the ceremonial magician's sword on which he binds spirits. Interestingly, it is because of this martial quality, and this mineral's ability to repel spirits that some are reluctant to use this in ritual. As such, it must be stated that repeated experience in practical magic has shown time and again that iron in and of itself can be a powerful agent in turning back negative entities. However, in our practice we find that, like salt, much depends on the context that one is using this in and how one is directing the inherent potential of the iron in ritual. For example, the traditional Witch's cauldron is most often made from solid cast iron.[26] Yet for many, it is a vital part of most ceremonies. So, too, the chimney hook in a traditional hearth is made of iron, yet it is the embodiment and home to the house spirit.

Iron is a martial metal, bringing energy and vitality to anything that it is involved with. In Ancient Egypt this was known as Bia-en-pet, the "Metal of Heaven" or "Metal of the Sky". For them iron was seen as sacred and as having divine origin largely because, until the late period, the only source of iron to the Egyptians was from meteorites. As such, when it was available, iron was used to make sacred objects. A foot long, double-edged iron bladed knife was found among the many ritual objects in the tomb of King Tutankhamun. Pyramid texts often speak of the doors of the sky (other realms) being made of iron. None of this negates the overall occult properties of iron to energize and repel. And what it does show is that, at least for the Egyptians, iron was not forbidden in ritual.

---

26. Though bronze and copper cauldrons have been used was well.

In rural folkloric magical systems throughout Europe iron was used magically to repel unwanted or evil forces. Hence the use of the black handled iron or steel knife. Iron nails are often driven into doors, window sills or bed posts to keep evil away. When this was done, it was frequently in series of three or five. Both numbers having a direct resonance with the planet Mars.

An iron or steel knife or a pair of scissors placed under the doormat is an old custom for keeping evil from entering the home. Driving three new nails into the threshold of the home of a person whom you suspect of cursing you will help to reduce their power. Carrying nails on oneself has long been thought to help protect against hostile otherworld beings, while providing one with strength and vitality.

Horseshoes
This, of course, leads us to the mystery of the horseshoe. Made of iron, this would seem to be an unlikely symbol of luck, and yet it is one of the most potent images of sudden prosperity and fulfilment in western culture. We encountered this in the making of the Moonrake earlier in this book. In my opinion, the reality behind the use of iron is that it is active and potent, bringing power to anything it touches. As such, it can be used to collect and retain, as well as to repel.

When this is combined with the long history of the horse in human culture, we find a resonance that links it directly to many of the various lunar otherworld beings, primarily different Moon Goddesses who also have the horse as their image. The horseshoe itself is obviously lunar in form. This carries with it the links to fertility and abundance, the natural ability of the feminine to bring life from her body. So, in the Moonrake we see a direct correlation in using iron, in the shape of a crescent to collect and retain the energy radiated by the Moon.

Horseshoes themselves are also hung over doors to both protect the place (the martial repelling quality of iron), while attracting and retaining prosperity and luck (the lunar qualities of abundance coupled with iron's ability to retain). In these cases, usually the horns of the shoe are placed facing upward to catch good fortune and bring it to the home.

Often times straw is tied to horseshoes. As Sybil Leek explains, straw also draws luck. To help improve the enchantment qualities of Rowan, it is common to bury an old used horseshoe nearby, thus ensuring that the Moon brings Her blessings to the trees.

America Appalachian folk magic calls for wrapping an iron horseshoe in red cloth on a Wednesday, Thursday or Friday and hanging this with the points facing down to drive evil spirits away. An iron horseshoe can be placed in the hearth or woodstove with a handful of salt scattered on top of this. Then, as long as the horseshoe is kept warm it will drive evil away.[27]

The Witch's Nowl

In some forms of Traditional Witchcraft a large iron nail, known as the Nowl,[28] is used. I introduced this tool earlier in the book when discussing enchanting a place. The qualities of potency and power are tied directly to this tool. It is used in a number of different ways, again, depending on the working at hand. Some will drive this into the ground at the center of the working Compass / Roth Fail. This, at once, awakens the power in the land itself, helping to give the Witch access to this, while also linking this to the energies from the heavens, thus harkening back to the Egyptian "metal of heaven". So, we can see in this simple ritual act a bringing together of the microcosm and macrocosm, placed at the center of the circle. The Roth Fail then, for this one moment in time and space, becomes the center of all that is, and with it the Witch can engage with the very fabric of reality.

---

27. Richards, Jake. *Backwoods Witchcraft : Conjure & Folk Magic From Appalachia.* 2019

28. Gary, Gemma. *The Devil's Dozen.* 2014-2015

The Nowl can also be employed in necromantic rites "to listen to the dead". In these instances the Nowl is pushed or driven into the ground of graveyards or suspected haunted places. It then acts to 'awaken' and 'energize' the spirits present. This also becomes the link between the otherworld and the Witch herself.

Success & Prosperity

This is an interesting spell that uses the power of iron to attract and retain prosperity. During the Waxing Moon take a head of garlic and stick a brass nail in one side. In the other push an iron nail. Then push nine iron or steel pins into the garlic from different angles. Next, using green and red thread tie a kernel of grain to the brass nail. Then wind the two colored threads around the nine pins, eventually tying these off at the iron nail. This is then soaked overnight is Olive Oil with an infusion of Vervain, Juniper and if available Bayberry. The next day remove this from the oil, allowing any excess to drip away. Then hang this over the door. Each week anoint the garlic with the oil. If the Garlic begins to rot replace this, performing the spell again.

A very simple custom that is said to ensure that one always has money in their wallet or purse is to burn the natural paper found on the exterior of onions in an iron container. This can be a frying pan, cauldron, or we even use our iron woodstove.

Water of Mars

This is a very old recipe that uses iron to harness the power of Mars. This, in turn, can be used for anything related to martial activities. Some traditional uses include both placing and removing curses.

During a fierce thunderstorm collect rain water. To this add iron nails or filings and sulfur.[29] This can be stored until

---

29. Some older recipes also ask that you add your own urine to this. This is extremely reminiscent of the Witch Bottle meant to reverse curses back on the sender. As such, I would only use urine if this is the intent of making this water.

needed. However, do not use this if mold develops. If this happens the entire potion needs to be discarded and you will need to start over.

Another version of this is to use the slag water from an iron black smithing process. Essentially, this is the water used to cool down red hot iron. In the process fine particles of iron will dissolve in the water. It can be poured over objects, used to anoint doorways, windows, etc. Either version is used to bring the raw power of Mars, embodied in the iron, to bear on any working that the Witch desires. I could see this applied not only to removal of hexes, but also in bringing life and vitality in healing rituals, or even as a stimulus in arousing the passions of a potential lover.

The key to understanding the use of different objects, plants, minerals or even sigils and words in Witchcraft, is that each holds within it the potential for a set of reactions depending on the forces it resonates with. Yet, it is the intention of the Witch that directs this. All is consciousness. Directing and resonating your will with the force inherent in the items of a spell will determine how they react. You still need to have a very clear understanding of the power that is inherent in each. Further, every object holds within itself its own unique properties. As with so much in the Willow Path form of Witchcraft, much depends on getting to know those properties, engaging with the spirit of the object, and partnering with this to enable its potential to merge with your will manifesting in the goal desired.

Chapter Twelve

❖ HORN AND STONE ❖
THE MAGIC OF PROSPERITY

It always surprises me when I read different occult authors who state that the Art shouldn't be used for personal gain. Many refuse to give techniques for prosperity magic. It is certainly true that beyond having enough to survive and thrive comfortably, most Witches really don't have much concern for obtaining wealth. However, there is nothing in the Art that says you can't. Afterall, Witchcraft has its roots in the daily struggle to meet one's needs. In ancient times this would have been ensuring that the crops grew and all supplies were in before winter. Today, however, survival is concerned almost exclusively with safeguarding one's financial welfare. The two are essentially the same.

Please know that the Willow Path as we practice it is a way of life, a way of being, a way of relating to and experiencing other realms and the beings who live there. If your sole reason for practicing the Art is to become rich, I can think of far easier career choices that will get you there quicker. Still, magic can and should be used to turn the currents of prosperity toward helping the Witch when she needs this. Always remember though that no amount of magic is likely to work unless the goal sought is within one's realm of availability. You can cast all the spells you want, but unless you are also applying yourself in the material world it is highly unlikely that your crafting will manifest in the funds desired. You need to create the means on a material level through which the astral currents can manifest.

Magic is like water. It follows the lines of least resistance. While you may be looking for money to come through a very specific venue, the fact is that your spells could manifest this through completely different sources. You have to create outlets on the material level for these currents to come through. You can't expect to get a new job unless you create a resume and start applying to different companies. You can't expect your business to thrive if you don't advertise. You need to allow the magic to bring the prosperity to you by allowing opportunities to exist that are within your realm of possibility.

You will find that, unless the spell is designed to influence a specific person or group of people, it is best not to state how or where the money will come from. Rather, it is much more effective to put the image and desire out on the Abred in clear and uncomplicated terms. Then let go. Walk away from the desire for a few days or weeks and let the currents in the astral carry the image through to completion in the manner that is easiest for it to manifest.

Beyond this I am firmly convinced that, when it comes to prosperity magic, the Witch needs to create an overall environment that invites money and success to come. This is done through simple, general spell work. This can be anything from growing certain herbs near the home, placing general talismans and charms throughout the house, to carrying different items that traditionally resonate with the currents that bring money.

In several places in this book, I have touched on different techniques to draw luck and money. We saw this in the deposits placed in the home foundations, the loadstone hung in the highest portion of the house, the *Horseshoe of Luck* and the nine pin garlic spell for success. Perhaps though it is prudent to present a few more techniques that have proven effective.

To create the circumstances which help to turn the currents of prosperity toward yourself and your home, you should first ensure that the place is cleansed and protected beforehand. I am assuming that you have already done so using the techniques described earlier. To my mind this is an essential first step as it clears the area and sets the slate clean, ensuring that no interference is present preventing prosperity. If you haven't already begun to employ the Nata Bag now is the time. There are several different botanicals that you may want to carry that act to draw luck and good fortune. Here are a few:

- Bergamot is used to attract money while ensuring that any spent will return to one. Traditionally a small amount is carried in one's wallet or purse.
- Cedar has a long history of helping to draw money and success.
- Goldenseal similarly aids with attracting money when carried.
- Juniper Berries resonate with the benefic power of Jupiter and are excellent ingredients in Mojo, Nata or Medicine Bags.
- Vervain is used by placing leaves from this herb in the wallet or purse to ensure that money is always present.
- Ginger powder carried in a small bag is used to draw money.
- Bayberry leaves and the berries themselves are very good for this purpose.
- Bay Laurel leaves can be placed in a Nata Bag, purse or wallet attracting money.
- Allspice also has a long history of being used to draw good fortune.
- Cornsilk is an American folk ingredient in money spells and is considered to be very powerful for attracting success, money, good fortune and love when carried in a handbag or wallet.
- Horseradish has been used to draw money and to help ensure one doesn't run out of this.

• Periwinkle, also known as the Sorcerer's Violet, is also carried to attracted money.
• Poplar leaves have long been used in folk magic, and can be carried for prosperity.
• Blackberry leaves are also carried to draw money.
• Sarsaparilla, which is part of the Ginseng family, is very powerful. This is a common plant found here in New England. The dried root lends itself well to being carried in a Nata Bag while aiding in bringing financial success.

To draw good fortune to the home, there are a number of plants that can be grown in or near the house that set up a natural resonance for this.

• Elder helps to draw prosperity.
• Goldenrod planted near the house attracts success.
• Vervain grown in the garden aids in bringing money to the home.
• Ginger is another plant that when grown near the house is said to increase money and good fortune.
• Marigolds, with their strong association to the Sun, also act to draw a measure of success when planted nearby.
• Geraniums are interesting. When grown outdoors they are considered excellent for drawing prosperity. However, one teacher of mine was adamant that these should never be brought into the house as, once inside, they will have the opposite effect.
• Basil is one of the most sought-after herbs for drawing money. This can be grown near the home, carried in one's wallet or handbag, or even placed in sachets near the hearth.

There are so many other herbs that can be employed in this manner. I suggest experimenting with those given here as a start.

Potions of Prosperity
Beyond growing and carrying different botanicals, there are certain potions that can be easily employed. In these cases, the potions are meant to be used as washes, applied to objects or documents, or sprinkled throughout a room or building to attract success.

Basil Money Potion
During the Waxing Moon, on either a Sunday or Thursday, chop two cups of fresh Basil. Place this in a pot and cover this with spring water. Bring the mixture to a boil, then turn the heat down to a simmer for twenty minutes with the top on. After twenty minutes have passed remove this from the heat and let it cool. Strain the liquid. If available add four drops of your Fluid Condenser to this.[30]

This potion can be used in any number of ways. It can be sprinkled on the floors to draw money to the home. It can be rubbed on the threshold of doors, on window sills, even on the door handles. One could also sprinkle this on the walkway leading to the front door or over the house mailbox.

Red Clover Potion
Clover in all of its forms has always been seen as indicative of luck and prosperity. A very simple potion for bring luck is derived from red clover. Gather three cups of dried blossoms. From these make an infusion by steeping these in boiling water. Then remove this from the heat and allow the potion to cool naturally. Strain the blossoms from the water. Like the Basil potion, this can be employed many ways. For example, if you are going to an important appointment such as a job interview or some other business gathering, add some of the potion to your bath beforehand. Or, like Basil, this can be applied to the doors, window sills, sprinkled on the floors of the home, or anywhere else where you would like to have your luck improved.

---

30. See *Horns of the Moon* for instructions on making the fluid condenser.

Beth Root Potion

As noted elsewhere, the Beth Root is also known as Trillium, or Low John. It carries many of the magical properties of High John Root and is far more accessible to those of us living in New England where it grows wild. On the first day of the crescent Waxing Moon, place nine dried roots in half a pint of quality grain alcohol. Some sources suggest Whiskey though I feel Vodka is better as it has less of a scent. Whichever you choose, allow this to steep until the Full Moon. Then strain this and use this to anoint objects, doors, contracts, even dabbing some on oneself to draw success and money.

Incenses & Oils of Success

Incenses and oils have been employed effectively in the Art for attracting success, prosperity and money for thousands of years. Whether as an adjunct to spell casting, or as a means to permeate the home with a general resonance for prosperity, these can be used well in either situation. The following are a few that I use.

   • Pine Gum, the hardened resin found on Pine trees, is an excellent incense. It corresponds to the planet Jupiter. As such, it helps to bring through the prosperous nature and qualities of this planet.

   • Cinnamon. While this is not native to Europe or the Americas, with the spice trade routes that occurred over centuries, this was available at least in some regions, off and on, for several centuries. For the Egyptians this was one of the base ingredients in many of their solar incenses. As such, this is very effective when burned during money spells, success, and personal attraction rites. This is best used during a Waxing Moon on a Sunday. Cinnamon oil also has a long history in the Art and is used to anoint talismans, candles and other objects meant to attract attention, success and good fortune. Be careful though as the essential oil can be an irritant to the skin.

• Juniper Berries, dried and mixed with Rosemary, form a wonderful prosperity incense.
• Vervain, once again, comes to bear here. Sybil Leek recommended Vervain oil to bring success in business and to attract money.

• Nutmeg is also considered lucky. Like Cinnamon, Nutmeg was not an indigenous plant for European Witches. However, with the spice trade it would have been available in a very limited supply. This has been used as an incense in money spells.

The following are more complex recipes for incenses and oils, combining a number of ingredients specifically to draw good fortune and prosperity.

Gold of the Sun Incense

During the Waxing Moon, on the day and hour of the Sun, mix the following:

- Two Parts Cinnamon
- One Part Rosemary
- One Part Frankincense

Powder these and burn on incense charcoal or embers from a wood fire.

Crown of Venus Prosperity Incense

On a Friday evening, in the hour of Venus and during the Waxing Moon, mix equal parts of the following:

- Dried Lemon Balm or Lemon Verbena
- Cinnamon
- Nutmeg
- Cloves

These should be ground into a powder and sprinkled on coals.

Jupiter's Reward Incense
While the Moon is Waxing on a Thursday, during the hour of Jupiter, mix equal parts of:

• Juniper Berries
• Allspice

Red Luck Oil
This is one of the most renown practical magic oils, sometimes referred to as 'Fast Luck'. It is primarily used in businesses but can easily be adapted to personal success as well. It is termed 'Red Luck Oil' as the color red resonates with action, swiftness and in many occult systems with attracting luck. During the Waxing Moon, on the day of Jupiter blend equal parts of the following:

• Cinnamon Oil
• Wintergreen Oil
• Vanilla extract

To this add enough red food coloring to give this a nice scarlet tone. One could easily use the red juice from a Blood Root in place of food coloring giving it the added martial power of this plant to bring quick results. The mixture can be cut with olive or mineral oil to extend the ingredients. This oil is used to anoint anything associated with drawing money to one's business. It is used to bring success to one's business quickly.

Money Attraction Powder & Incense
This has the unique quality of being able to be used both as an incense and as a powder. Powders act in a similar way to the potions in that they are intended to linger in the place that they are sprinkled drawing the goal for which they were enchanted, in this case financial success. When using this as

a powder, sprinkle this very lightly. More is not necessarily better. Rather, you want to ensure that the herb's essence is gently infused throughout the room or area without it being overtly noticeable to others. Mix equal portions of the following in dried, powdered forms:

- Sarsaparilla Root
- Cinnamon
- Dried Basil

During the Waxing Moon, on either a Wednesday (if a business) or Thursday, sprinkle this through the building to draw money. If used as an incense, carry the burner through the building letting the smoke lightly scent the atmosphere.

Sigils, Seals & Talismans for Success
Once the general home environment has been set to begin drawing prosperity, it then may be prudent to begin using specific talismanic forms to help focus the currents more acutely to one's needs. Two of the most important that we have come to use are the Seals of the Sun and Moon.

Sun and Moon Seals of Success
You may recall seeing these in the first book of this series. However, no real explanation was given as to their function. We use these extensively. They are seals of the Sun and the Moon. When used together they help to bring success to whatever goal is being sought. As such, during most rituals, we will place these on either side of the hearthstone, the solar seal to the right and the lunar on the left. After all, no matter the ritual, we are seeking a successful outcome.

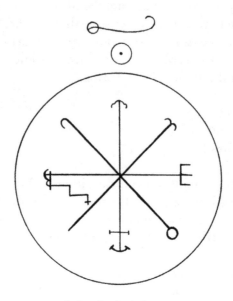

Solar Seal of Success

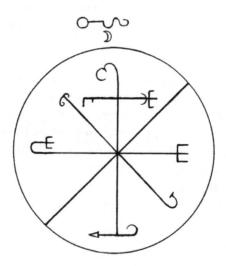

Lunar Seal of Success

These can easily be incorporated into a talisman that one could wear helping to bring success in daily activities. Beyond their use together though, they can be used separately with very good results. Obviously, the solar seal is used in any rites resonating with Sun workings, while the lunar seal resonates to those of the Moon.

I have made the *Seal of the Sun* from a variety of materials. Like the others, it can be traced onto a quality paper, parchment or birch bark and carried. I have painted this on small canvas squares to be placed on the hearthstone during ritual. Another excellent way to use this is to trace this onto a small piece of brass sheeting approximately three inches square. This can then be placed either in front of, or directly underneath candles. In our experience this has proven to be a powerful means of drawing attention and bringing success to the goals sought.

The *Seal of the Moon* is more subtle in its influence, and yet in practical application it has proven to be equally powerful as that of the Sun. In my experience this seal tends to draw success from unlooked for or previously unknown sources. As with the Seal of the Sun, this can be traced on paper, parchment and canvas. If applying this to a metal I would suggest silver, though this can be costly.

Sigils of Luck

These particular formulas derive from very old traditions in the Art. The first is meant to resonate with the planet Jupiter, drawing prosperity and luck through its influence. Not only is this meant to bring general prosperity, this was often used to help bring success through gambling and lotteries. I can't confirm its success with the latter two. However, in keeping with the strategy of drawing luck through any means that is within the realm of possibility, it can be a solid talisman for overall success.

During the Waxing Moon, on a Thursday evening during the hour of Jupiter, draw the following symbol on parchment, birch bark, a quality paper or engrave this on a small piece of tin. As you do this chant the following Word of Power: "Phetomeus"

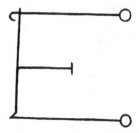

This is then carried as a personal talisman. If the goal is to draw success to a business or home, it can be hung over the main entrance. Interestingly, this same talisman also is said to aid in "keeping one from the violence of other and from condemnation by the law." This is certainly a talisman worth experimenting with.

This second talisman is more aligned to the forces inherent in the planet Mercury. It is meant to bring success through business, and to help obtain the favors of those in authority, including success in court.

On a Wednesday, in the hour of Mercury, and during the Waxing Moon, draw the following image. As with the others this can be on a quality paper, parchment, or Birch Bark. If a metal talisman is desired, I prefer to use Aluminum, though this would not have been available to the original creator of this spell in the era it was devised.

While tracing this intone the Word of Power: "Yparon". This can then be carried or set in the place of business to draw Mercury's benefits.

The Key of Acbalaz
This is adapted from a spell found in the rare 17th century manuscript now referred to as "The Book of Magical Charms". This is meant to enable the Witch to "prevail and fulfill one's will". It uses a combination of items and techniques, from sigils and talismanic objects, to directly appealing to specific spirits to enchant an item.

For this you will need an iron skeleton key with a place on this large enough to paint the symbol shown below. Skeleton keys are still somewhat accessible through antique stores and secondhand shops. They are often used in folk magic for luck and to create opportunities. I try to pick these up whenever possible.

You will also need a fine paint brush and red paint. To the paint add a small pinch of dried Vervain and either Dragon's Blood resin or Bloodroot. In addition, you will need to prepare a small meal. This will be offered to the spirits evoked in the rite. This meal needs to have as the main ingredient cooked chicken.

The spell itself is performed during the Waxing Moon, on the day and hour of Venus. Place both the key and the food on the hearthstone. Then, over these recite:

"O Spirits,
Haylon and Acbalaz,
Receive this meal prepared by my hand.
I offer this to you, this food from the land.
That no creature, no person, no spirit or spell, can raise against me.
This key is my will!
For where this key is put,
Before whatever bars my way,
Forever it be turned about,

My will fulfilled; I prevail this day!"

With the brush and paint, trace the sigil on the key while repeating the following enchantment:

"Haylon, Acbalaz,
I prevail, my will fulfilled!"

Sigil of Acbalaz

Once the sigil is painted hold the plate of food up, again addressing the spirits thanking them for their assistance. Leave the key on the hearth and retire away from the place of working to enjoy the food you had prepared. The key itself is then left for three days and nights. On the third night retrieve the key before sunrise. This is then carried as a talisman. The cunning book that describes this spell explains that beyond attracting success, when faced with a situation with which you need assistance, turn the key as if opening a lock. I suggest also reciting the names of the two spirits while doing this.

Lasting Prosperity Spell
This spell is meant to ensure prosperity over a long period of time. How long really depends on one's circumstances. However, the entire rite involves the use of items that resonate with bringing in and sustaining success in a steady progressive way. This draws from traditional sources across the three related disciplines that I work with: Traditional

Witchcraft, Hermetics and Ancient Egyptian words of magic. Yet, as with everything that I have presented, the goal is to keep it simple and direct. In practical application you will find that this spell tends to take time to manifest, yet the results are long lasting.

You will notice that this uses the same seal and Words of Power as we saw in the *Home Prosperity Deposit* spell when discussing house spirits earlier. This is intentional, as I have found the seal and words to be quite effective. In using these here, the apprentice will see the versatility of how different formulae can be applied in a variety of ways and for different, but related purposes.

For this you will want to assemble a green cloth to place over the hearthstone. In the center of this demark an equal sided Triangle of Art using dried Vervain. If available include with this Juniper Berries. You will also want to use a money drawing incense as described earlier.

In the center of the triangle place either a beeswax candle, a Bayberry candle or a tall green candle. Any of these will do well. Ideally you will also have Vervain oil, or barring that, Olive oil. In front of the candle, you will need to have a drawing for the Jupiter pentacle of wealth, on parchment, quality paper, Birch Bark, or canvas. Or, this could also be engraved in tin if so desired. You will recognize the design from the chapter on house spirits.

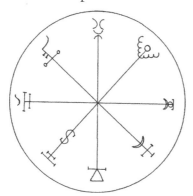

Seal of Sustained Wealth

This is performed during the Waxing Moon, on a Thursday evening during the hour of Jupiter (the third hour after sunset). As with all other rituals in this system it is best to begin by performing the Dragon, Cloak and Star techniques. Call on the spirits, including your familiar if you have one. Place incense on the coals. Beginning at the apex of the triangle, trace over this using the Fe. In doing so, pass power into this, seeing it spring to life with light and energy.

Next anoint the candle with the oil. In doing so use the technique of the dua, the passing of power, into the candle while clearly envisioning success and money. Take your time with this process, letting all of your senses actively engage with the image of success. See this as alive and real, flowing to you in tangible ways. Then, when ready, place the candle in its holder. You may want to then use the charged breath to gently breathe life into the intention that the candle now manifests.

Light the candle and slowly, gently begin to chant the following as you immerse yourself in the image and experience of the success you are drawing to you.

"baH HAw, baH HAw,
Prosperity and Success come to me now!
baH HAw, baH HAw,
Money and Good Fortune flow to me now!
baH HAw, baH HAw,
Joy and Happiness come to me now!"

This is simple, direct, with no definition or distinction of how or where success will come. Rather, it is meant to increase the flow of prosperity, allowing this to manifest through whatever means it can the easiest. In chanting this, let it start slowly and evenly. Yet, as you become more involved in the mental and emotional vision of success, let the chant increase in intensity until it reaches a climax merging with the power you are focusing. Then in one final release, let the energy and chant go. Just let yourself be silent in the moment. Yet with the totality of your creative will, envision energy in the form of a brilliant white light that then merges with a rich green with flashes of gold, flow from the Abred into your image of success and manifesting in the triangle concentrating on the candle and pentacle.

Now leave the candle to burn completely. Once this is out return to the place of working and gather the Vervain, Juniper and Bayberry from the triangle and sprinkle this around the home, or place the herbs in a Nata Bag and carry this with you.

I should note that "baH HAw", is the pronunciation of Ancient Egyptian words meaning "wealth in abundance". The capital letters are meant to indicate which sounds should be emphasized when spoken. In the context of this spell, they are being used as Words of Power. For the Egyptians, spoken words in ritual were seen as being the actual embodiment of the thoughts and energies being evoked, becoming real. As such, you have no doubt noticed that in the form of magic we practice, we place a strong use on Words of Power, drawing from Celtic, Egyptian and Basque sources.

While this spell was designed to bring general prosperity, with a few minor changes it can be used to bring specific results when needed. Suppose you have applied to and been interviewed for a job that you sincerely want. Or perhaps you have submitted a proposal to a business, an art project to a dealer. Whatever your situation, it is in such cases that this spell can help push your offer to the forefront and gain the attention of the person making the decision.

In such instances you would use the same setting, the same ritual objects, and the same time frame. The only difference is that, for this, place a solid orange candle at each point of the triangle, three in total. Instead of the pentacle of Jupiter though you will replace this with the Kamea of Jupiter (shown earlier). You will also need a taglock, some kind of link to the business itself, but more specifically to the person making the decision. Obviously the more personal the better, preferably something that has been in close contact with the person. I like to use a person's signature. But this isn't always possible. Fortunately, in this day of the internet and social media, photographs are almost always available. These can work well, though again, I prefer something that has come into direct contact with the person.

If you simply can't get a solid taglock, at the least you should get one on the business itself. Most companies today will have an individual logo purposely designed to reflect who they are and to make themselves easily identifiable to the public. It is their own corporate sigil. These will work very well in this ritual.

Follow the ritual exactly as you had before. However, there is an extra step. While you are in the state of merging, yet before passing the power to the green candle, gently turn your imagination to the person who will be making the decision. Let yourself recall anything you can about them: how they sound, how they look, any personal mannerisms, anything at all that will allow you to connect with them on an occult level. I spoke of this technique at length in *Horns of the Moon*. In this spell you will be applying this talent. The more you can engage all of your senses in this reverie the greater the connection will be. Remember, all is consciousness. In this spell you are changing your state of consciousness to align with that of the other person. Once this connection is made it is just a matter of planting the seed of your spell in their mind.

In those cases when you don't have a link to the person, or you don't know who will be making the decision, you will use the taglock to the company itself. For this it is best to get familiar with the company. If it has a physical location become very familiar with the appearance. If you can personally visit the location without causing any suspicion, by all means do so. If not, check on-line as many companies post photographs of their facilities. Then, in the spell you will need to place yourself mentally in the company itself.

See the logo in your mind, imagine yourself entering the front door and being welcomed, hear the voices in the halls, the sound of your footsteps walking through the building. And above all else know that you or your proposal have been accepted, welcomed, and even eagerly anticipated by the company. Take as long as you need to form this image. Have fun with the creation of this.

It is then that you will anoint the green candle, passing the power and resonating with Jupiter energies to bring this into reality. Light the green candle and then the three orange candles. The orange candles are used as they help to bring attention to any goal, add energy to the task and almost always act quickly to bring the subject into manifestation. In the case of a proposal, this is exactly what is needed: quick decisive action before some other person or project comes along to replace yours.

The chant is going to need to be individual to you and your needs. You want this to be decisive. Keep it simple, clear, direct. It doesn't matter if it rhymes or not. But don't be verbose. If you are placing the thought into the decision maker's mind, phrase the chant as if you were speaking directly to them. If you are using a corporate taglock or logo with no real knowledge of who is deciding, then the chant needs to revolve around placing yourself in the business itself.

The chant should contain three key elements. First, it needs to address the person or group being influenced. Use their name, because names have power. Let them know that you are there as an important member of their business plan. Second, you will need to tie the chant directly to the forces of Jupiter, prosperity and abundance. In doing so you are pulling these forces into the spell and creating a link between these, yourself and the goal at hand. Then finish with a strong recognition that this is real and will manifest. Be sure of your wording. The example of the Mercury spell I used on my boss, discussed in the first chapter is a good example, except that rather than stating exactly what the goal was I, instead, appealed to a quality he admired. That was fine, except that it was open ended which led to the unintended consequences that followed.

As for a traditional Witchcraft chant to help with this, any number of those given in this series would be useful. But the chant you use yourself will be best if it is drawn from your own desire. Again, simple, direct with no conditions of when or how it will happen should be applied. Rather, keep it to the fact that they need you or your proposal and that it will be a reality. When chosen properly the use of Words of Power can be a tremendous aid in any spell, hence our use of the Egyptian "baH HAw, baH HAw".

Once the rite is finished it is always helpful to scatter the remaining herbs from the triangle in a place that the people making the decision must cross. Of course, this isn't always possible. If it is the case that you can't, the herbs can be scattered around your own residence, or around the means by which the news informing you of the decision will come, mailbox, computer, etc.

I have used these spells successfully many times. The results have always depended on how strongly the goal lay within the realm of possibility for me, the strength of the taglock I had, as well as the connection made to the person or group during the ritual, the clarity of the chant itself, including tying this to the resonating influence of the planet involved (Jupiter), the intensity of emotional energy and the engagement of my total self in the rite, and finally, my ability let go once the spell was cast.

There is one final step that the Witch can take before finishing that is very powerful and quite traditional. For those of us who work with familiars, once the energy is spent and the Witch is about to leave the candle to burn, speak directly to your familiar. Ask it to visit the person or place you are looking to influence. Instruct the familiar to convince the person that the proposal you are presenting is not only the right decision, it is also something that they absolutely need for their own success. In my case, my familiar works through an Alrune Root.[31] As such, I will physically show the familiar the taglock, and whisper to her, asking her to visit the person. I then will leave the root near the triangle, taglock and candles so that she can go to the person, deliver the spell and then return to the root when done. When compared to those times when I have not followed this last step, the use of the familiar has proven to enhance the effectiveness of my magic dramatically.

In your spell casting, whenever you work with spirits and otherworld beings of any kind, always remember to finish the rite by thanking them. You want them to know you appreciate their presence and assistance. Again, unlike ceremonial magicians that seek to command spirits, the Witch partners with them, becomes familiar with them and enjoys their company. This is such a vital aspect of Traditional Witchcraft that is so often overlooked by those involved in more contemporary versions of the Craft. For my part, after any rite in which I directly appeal to my familiar I always give her a small portion of red wine, often bathing the root in this.

Lastly, when working spells, any spell, don't be afraid to become totally immersed in the experience. This is especially so when working alone. Let yourself experience the flow of the words, act on the images evoked, let your movements in ritual be full and real. Don't hold back. You are using three key factors in spell casting: a disciplined will focusing on the goal through the prescribed techniques of the Art, a rich imagination using all of the senses to create the goal on the Abred, and above all else your passion! By letting go and being in the moment, you allow your emotions rise with the spell. Let yourself move to the rhythm of the chant, feel free to use hand gestures, let your voice rise in passion or drop to a whisper. As long as you are lost in the intensity of the moment, feeling the power move through

---

31. The process for evoking this is discussed at length in *The Willow Path*.

you, letting it form the image of your goal as deeply and vividly as you possibly can, this all adds to the success of your enchantment.

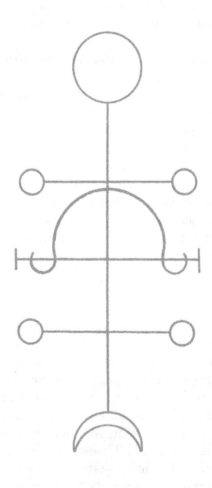

Chapter Thirteen

✤ FULL MOON RITUAL ✤

In many forms of Traditional Witchcraft the Full Moon holds immense importance, from Sybil's coven drawing power directly from this orb, to Julie's family singing the ancient Moon Goddess name of 'Diana'. In our practice as well, the Full Moon is absolutely vital. Even as a child, long before meeting Julie or reading Sybil's books, my experiences under the Full Moon were at once subtle, unprompted and natural, while being deeply profound to the point of affecting the entire course of my life.

In our experience, the Full Moon is one of the many ways in which the Lady manifests in our realm. Every culture has known Her, giving different names and images. Ancient Egyptian inscriptions from the temple of Dendera refer to the Goddess Hathor as having "numerous manifestations" with "many names as you cross the breadth of the land". Each of the 'names' are unique and individual in their own right, yet behind this lies a deeper mystery. Beyond the simple attempts of the human mind to comprehend these forces and beings, dressing them in the symbols and language of local culture, there rests a deeper reality. It is in this more sublime essence that the rich beauty of the Lady comes through. In Traditional Witchcraft She is often referred to as the Mistress, the Dame, the Queen of Elphame, the Witch Queen and by many other titles. Different groups will use different names, many drawn from myth, while others use secret names known only to initiates in their particular coven, clan or system.

277

No matter the name or form, the essence of this incredible intelligence remains. She is the conceiver, creator, mother, lover, daughter and wise one, at once caring and nurturing, as well as sexual, independent, strong and erotic. Yet She is also the spinner and weaver of fate, the seer, as well as the death crone. In Her we also find the protector and warrior who, when brought to this point, has a passion and fury that is unmatched by any male counterpart. All comes from Her and to Her all returns. She is the spiritual source, the center and the hidden essence found in nature. Whether in ocean depths, forest deep, caverns and caves, the budding of life in spring, as well as in the night sky and Full Moon's light, the Witch Queen, the Lady is there waiting.

This doesn't imply that the Master is any less important in our practices. On the contrary, He is also vital as we will see in the discussion on the fire festivals. However, it is the interplay between these two otherworld beings that compose the essence of much of nature. Still, in our system of the Art, we never forget that the Lady is the source behind and within all, and it is during the monthly Full Moon that Her essence is best experienced.

The Full Moon ritual is the means by which we of the Willow Path form of Traditional Witchcraft relate to, celebrate and engage with the Queen. The rite is specifically designed to align the Witch's awareness to the forces of the Moon while aiding in drawing the Lady's presence to the ritual space. Further, because of the abundance of nephesh energy, sprowl or Serpent's Breath available at this time, magic and most occult arts are strongest when performed then. It is for all of these reasons that we recognize and practice some form of ritual at each Full Moon.

Having explained this, it is important to know that the Full Moon ritual can and should vary depending on which Moon is occurring at the time. As such the incantations, offerings, and even the magical workings themselves will change in accord with the season. The monthly names and meanings of each Moon are clearly discussed elsewhere in this series. The ritual presented here is meant to be a template which can be adapted to the different Moons as needed.

The Ritual
Whether held indoors or out under the night sky, the Full Moon ritual always begins with preparation of the site itself. If indoors this is held in front of the hearth, no matter in which direction the hearth may happen to be placed. In the Willow Path system of magic, the hearth is the spiritual center of the building, and it is here that the local spirits gather. Whether this is a working hearth or one that has long been closed, we still honor it as the focal point for our Art and so it is here that we set our tools of the trade. Usually, we will put those tools which tend to be identified as masculine to the right, and those that are normally thought of as feminine to the left. Of course, the Stang and Besom both have feminine and masculine attributes. Nevertheless the Stang is generally placed to the right and the Besom to the left of the hearth. The Cauldron can be placed inside the hearth except when used as a central focal point in the circle itself. On such occasions it is placed in the center of the Roth Fail.

If working outdoors, or if indoors but in a space that has no apparent hearth, we set the hearthstone/altar in the north leaving enough room to move around this. At the northern edge of the Roth Fail set the Stang, placing the male end, or the hoof of the shaft in the ground. If desired, a holder made of local stones can be used for this. Indoors you may want to build an actual 'holder' of some kind, a stand that you can place the Stang in. In many cases we will have more than one Stang present. One placed permanently in the north, while another (usually the Master or Mistress' Stang) will be used to trace the compass and invite the Watchers of the Night.

Once the area is prepared, the Roth Fail ritual is always performed before we move on to the Full Moon. We use the exact ritual noted in chapter twenty-seven of The Willow Path without fail, except for one caveat. We often will include the Words of Power representing the elemental forces within the evocations. As an example, in the east, the evocation begins with "Hear me O Mighty One, Ruler of the Whirlwinds, Guardian of the East Gate" . . . at this point we inject the name "Uscias" just as was done when Setting the Wards in the chapter on protection. In the south the name used is "Esrus", in the west "Semias", and in the north "Fessus". Beyond this the ritual used to set the Roth Fail is the same as in the first book. Once the Roth Fail is set and all are present within the Mistress states:

"Merry meet under Moon and stars,
As we call the ancient ones this night,
For between the horns lays the path we keep."

She then incants:

"Master of the Wild Wood,
Horned One in the night,
Janicot, Janicot,
Janicot, Janicot.
We welcome you
He who carries the light.
By our words we conjure you,
Through this rite we conjure you,
By bone and stone, water, smoke and fire we conjure you,
By crow and toad, by leaping hare,
Serpent's Breath and Dragon's lair,
Arise, awake this Full Moon night."

The Master addresses the coven:

"By moonlit night and starry sky,
The Master comes, horns held high,
Tawny hide and white moon brow,

Through glen and wood He leads us still.
We trace the path and climb the hill,
To the circle of stones under Full Moon's glow.
The silver mist veil opens to us now."

All then begin to circle in a tauthal direction as they chant:

"Round and round, throughout and about,
The wheel weaves in, the thread spins out,
By Stang, by Besom, by Cauldron deep,
We meet together in the Lady's keep!"

This is repeated while the group continues to circle until the becoming settles in on all present. Once all have stopped, the Master then invokes the Queen:

"From sacred wells,
Cool springs rise clear,
The Lady calls to all who hear.
By stang and besom,
By toad and hare,
By crow and serpent's breath,
The great Queen comes,
Silver circle is here,
She who rides the night.
By our words we conjure you,
Through this rite we conjure you,
By bone and stone we conjure you,
By water, smoke and fire we conjure you,
Serpent's Breath and Dragon's lair,
From the Hollow Hills,
In Full Moon's light,
We conjure you!
The Great Queen comes.
Mistress, we welcome you here this night."

All present enchant:

"Bandia Gelach, Bandia Gelach, Bandia Gelach!
Bandia Gelach, Bandia Gelach, Bandia Gelach!
Bandia Gelach, Bandia Gelach, Bandia Gelach!
Mistress in the night!"

The Mistress then recites:

"The Lady comes, nature's song we hear;
'For I am the Mistress who gives birth to the light,
I am She, the Lady of pleasure in the noonday Sun,
The Gods rise to greet me for I am beauty, I am power,
I am the secret name alive with potion and flame!
For I create all that is.
In the west I greet you as the young Goddess,
And from the stars my voice rings through all worlds.
I call to you,
Come, take my hand,
Rise as a falcon that you may be as the Gods.
For I am the Mistress of the northern sky and my love
is eternal.'"

Using the Fe, the Mistress traces the *Sigil of the Transformative Power of the Moon.*

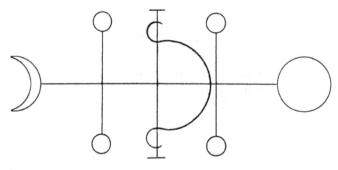

Sigil of the Transformative Power of the Moon

She then breathes life using the Charge Breath, while intoning:

282

"Iusaas"

The coven now draws in the power of Serpent and Moon, letting this gather and concentrate:

"Anál nathrach   (onal NathRack
Bandia Gelach   Banjeeah Geloch
Draiocht dénmha"   Dray-aht de-N-may)

The Mistress now leads the coven in any magic set for the evening, using the Serpent Breath gathered to assist. This point in the ritual can be used for any number of activities, from spell casting to spirit evocation, trance work and traveling in spirit, to any of the ritual dances found in Witchcraft lore to further deepen the state of becoming.[32]
When finished, the Mistress holds up a plate of food as an offering to the Great Queen saying:

"Mother, we cannot give you anything,
Because you have given us everything,
Please accept this which gives us pleasure."

This is set on the hearthstone. The Llawforwyn, Coven Maiden, then holds a goblet out before the Mistress and Master. The Mistress holds a container of mead, while the Master holds red wine. The two then simultaneously pour these into the goblet while they recite:

"Three worlds encircle the one,
Plow, tree and golden Sun,
The Lady calls from Caer Wydyr,
Cauldron deep, pool clear,
Four treasures hide in the keep,
Four realms the Wise do seek,
We call the ancient ones,

---

32. See *The Willow Path* for a description of these.

We honor them still,
In grove, in glen, on sacred hill,
So sing the songs and walk the maze,
The great stag comes through moonlit haze.
Cer and Cerri are in us found,
In the three worlds we are bound!"

A small portion of the potion is then poured into each member's own goblet, as all share in the bounty of the food and drink. The rite then concludes by closeing the Roth Fail as normal.

The rite is purposely kept simple in form, acting as a basic format which can be added to depending on the needs of the coven. This incorporates specific influences from the three different elements that we draw on. It is for this reason that in the evocation of the Master, the Basque word of power associated to the Horned God, Janicot, is used. A very specific word of power taken directly from Ancient Egyptian teachings is used in the invocation of the Lady. Too, the words spoken by the Mistress, as the Great Queen, are adapted from different Egyptian sources. Yet the entire structure, including the tools and many of the incantations throughout the ritual, are clearly drawn from Traditional Witchcraft techniques, some of which Julie had given me so long ago.

It should be noted that the entire ritual can be easily adapted for solitary work. In such cases the Witch herself will perform all parts of the ritual, repeating all of the enchantments. This can be extremely fulfilling, allowing one to experience each aspect of the ritual in personal and powerful ways.

Chapter Fourteen

✤ SPOKES AND FLAME ✤
THE FOUR FIRE FESTIVALS

For the Witch there is nothing more important than becoming one with the land, with the natural tides of power and forming relationships with the spirits that flow through these. Beyond the monthly Full Moon cycle, many Traditional Witches recognize tides that flow through the year. These are directly linked to the journey of the Sun as experienced in the round of the seasons while traveling through key points in zodiac. This was discussed in detail in the first book of the series. Here I would like to present four key rituals which we use as a means to experience these tides in deep and profound ways while renewing our power as Witches.

There is considerable controversy surrounding the various festivals that Witches recognize. From the names assigned to these, the actual number of festivals in the year, how they should be recognized, the dates that these fall on, to whether these were celebrated at all.[33] For us, as practicing members of the Art today, these arguments are a moot point. The simple fact is that we recognize specific crucial events in the year which mark very clear changes in the occult tides of energies. Those of the Art have always been very aware of these changes and how to use these to their advantage.

It should be noted that, as Julie had taught me, in our system we do recognize eight points of power in the solar year. These revolve around the cycle of the solstices and

---

33. Many of these concerns were addressed in the chapter entitled "Sun Tides" in the first book *The Willow Path*.

equinoxes. However, where the solstices and equinoxes mark periods in which one elemental force gives way to another, the four Fire Festivals represent the apex of the elemental tide in which it falls. As such, these are considered to be stronger and very important to our way of practicing the Art.

Interestingly, as one reads through Sybil Leek's writings, it is clear that she felt that the four Fire Festivals were essential elements of the system she and her coven followed. She spoke of the great lengths members would go to in order practice these rites, even if done solitary. In several interviews she stated that the four greater festivals were times when the Witch's powers were renewed. Sybil also spoke of the solstices and equinoxes as points in the year that rituals were performed. Yet, one gets the clear impression that these did not hold the same significance for her as the Fire Festivals did.

The following are our rituals used at each of the Fire Festivals. Like the rest of the material in this system they incorporate historical material drawn from Pagan European sources, Traditional Witchcraft and Hermetics. When appropriate we also introduce key components from Egyptian sources. This is important as I have found that there is a correspondence between some Ancient Egyptian observances and the overall meanings inherent within the tides manifesting in the Fire Festivals. This merging of traditions is in keeping with the realization that an underlying impulse deep in nature did manifest in multiple cultures, holding remarkably similar meanings and views. This is especially so of indigenous magical/ shamanic practices that involved the participants in directly experiencing otherworld forces for themselves. This, then is the goal of our rituals: to create a vehicle through which the Witch engages, experiences, merges and forms relationships with these tides and the otherworld beings who manifest in these. In this way each of these are meant to be seen as part of a four-fold ritual process that occurs throughout the year. They are quite literally meant to create a deep, spiritual, alchemical resonance within the Witch herself. In this way she is aligning her true self to the natural rhythm of the season and these tides of power.

To understand the intent of these rites on a deeper, esoteric level, it is important to realize that these four ceremonies carry within them a representation of the journey of the Master as the Sun moving through the Worlds of the Witch: the Annwn, Abred, Gwynfyd and Caer Wydyr. In this way we journey with Him encountering the beings within each realm. Remember that He is of the land, the wild wind rider, master of the woodlands, the thunder in the storm. He can be found in the gentle caress of the Sun's warmth bringing life, the wise counselor, yet the powerful sorcerer and Witch, from the babe born of the mother, to the virile wild goat foot lover, then as the face of death. He is the lord of the underworld, yet the Green Man of Summer. For He is regeneration. The Master lives in the spirit of every kernel of grain, the whiskey in the glass bringing intoxication, and wild abandon. Yet we see Him in the seeker, the hermit and as the noble knight on a sacred quest. Whether King of Elphame, the great ram of Egypt, Janicot of the Basque, or the forest stag of Pagan Europe, the Master is the very call of nature itself, alive in the wild places for all who listen for the piper's call.

Throughout this annual journey, the Witch, whether female or male, moves with the Master in each cycle, experiencing the energy of the seasons. However, in all four of the rituals presented, it is the Lady who remains as the force within the tide, and the very reason for His journey. She is the cause and source, while He is the expression of the tide. As such, She is highly prominent, being evoked in very powerful ways in each of these rites, for it is She that He seeks.

As noted in the first book, we calculate the timing of the Fire Festivals in two ways. The Full Moon that falls nearest the midpoint between the equinox and solstice is the strongest occult point in the season. Ideally the Full Moon should fall within two weeks of the actual midpoint. In those cases when the Full Moon falls outside of a two-week period of the exact midpoint, we will often hold two rituals: one on the midpoint itself and one on the nearest Full Moon. In these cases, the Full Moon rite tends to be focused more on ritual magic and initiation rites.

You will see that we use the Celtic names for these festivals even though some of these names are considered by certain purists to be more regional. In fact, some Traditional Witches vehemently argue against using these names altogether. For us, it really doesn't matter what names they go by. The energies are the same no matter the title. I can say that these are the names that were taught to me through various teachers, including Julie. They each appear in Celtic myth and lore. For us these are the names that work well with this system of the Art.[34]

Samhain

This ritual should be performed either on the night when the Sun reaches fifteen degrees of Scorpio, which is the exact midpoint between the fall equinox and the winter solstice, or on the night of the Full Moon that falls nearest to this event.

Ideally this should be held outdoors in a secluded area. However, for our area of the world, the weather at Samhain rarely allows this. Rather we conduct this in front of the hearth, being sure to have wood in place that we can light during the rite. If no actual functioning fireplace or woodstove exists, a red pillar candle may be used to represent the fires of Samhain.

You will need two red candles for the corners of the hearthstone, apple cider steeped with Vervain in the goblet. An offering of food should be prepared which should include breads, honey and freshly picked apples. The hearthstone itself should be draped in black. On this lay a

---

34. For an in-depth discussion on the meaning, myth and symbolism of all eight festivals please see *The Willow Path*.

Triangle of Art made from dried oak leaves. In the center place a crystal ball, black mirror or scrying bowl. If available bones, horns and antlers should adorn the hearthstone. The cauldron should be placed in the center of the Roth Fail. Inside this you will want to place a smaller fire pot which will need to be prepared in advance with a layer of salt, a layer of combustible alcohol, and by adding dried Vervain and Wormwood atop this. In addition, all normal tools of the trade should be present.

The Ritual

Begin by calling the spirits and setting the Roth Fail as normal. Following this the Master recites:

> "The cold winds of Samhain whisper through the trees.
> The veil is thin, the gates of Annwn swing open this night.
> The Great Queen comes cloaked in black.
> The Raven caws and the wolf howls.
> For this is the season of death."

The Master then recites the invocation of the Mistress:

> "By stang and besom,
> By toad and hare,
> By crow and serpent's breath,
> The great Queen comes,
> Silver circle is here,
> She who rides the night.
> By our words we conjure you,
> Through this rite we conjure you,
> By bone and stone we conjure you,
> By water, smoke and fire we conjure you,
> Serpent's breath and Dragon's lair,
> From the Hollow Hills,
> In Samhain fire light,
> We conjure you!

The Great Queen comes.

Mistress, we welcome you here this night."

The Mistress recites:

"The Lady calls to the land where Her lover lies.
Deep in dark forest, through mountain crevice.
There She descends in caverns deep to the doors of Annwn."

The Mistress recites the invocation of the God:

"Master of the Wild Wood,
Horned One in the night,
Janicot, Janicot,
Janicot, Janicot.
We welcome you
He who carries the light.
By our words we conjure you,
Through this rite we conjure you,
By bone and stone, water, smoke and fire we conjure you,
By crow and toad, by leaping hare,
Serpent's breath and Dragon's lair,
Arise, awake this Samhain night."

The Master recites:

"Tonight we journey with the Lady,
Across the threshold, into the Annwn.
Deep into the hidden labyrinth of Rostau,
We traverse the secret path to the cauldron deep."

The Mistress picks up the crystal or scrying tool and carries this as she circles nine times around the inside of the Roth Fail in a tuathal direction. All present follow her. She then replaces this in the center of the Triangle of Art.

The Master recites:

"By Stang, By besom,
By Silver Moon's glow,
The hearth fire awaits,
The cauldron full.
We call the Ancient Ones by this stone,
Keepers of the sacred bond,
Secrets untold.
The way is open, the path is clear,
The Ancient traditions are before us,
Revealed here.
In stone circle,
In mountain cottage, or forest deep,
By Balefire and the hearth's warm light,
Come to us O Ancient Ones.
Let us learn the Old Ways revealed this Samhain night."

The Master lights the cauldron and then recites:

"The secret path descends ever on,
The Queen's black cloak falls away.
Deep in Rostau the cauldron awaits.
Nine maidens attend the sacred flame.
Nine steps to the fire light.
For deep in the Annwn,
Caer Wydyr comes into sight.
Here between the Horns Lord and Lady unite.
In passion's flame, the Benu's fire burns bright.
That which is outworn is removed,
As our spirits take flight.
All that is unwanted burns away.
So that prosperity and good fortune
Come our way."

All join hands around the cauldron and chant the following
while raising power:

"Samhain fire, burning bright
Removal all obstacles,
Bring success this night!"

After some reflection the Mistress holds the crystal up as the Master recites:

"Keepers of the sacred bond,
Through woodland and stone circle,
In mountain cottage, forest deep.
As you return through the gates this Samhain night, we ask that the secret traditions of the Ancient Way open before us, in dream, in vision, in voice and thought, in word and deed your secret teachings open to us now."

The Master now lights the hearth fire reciting:

"By this flame the Ancient Ones return,
The light of Samhain beckons them on,
For Between the Horns,
Lays the path we keep.
The warmth of this fire
Guides those who seek.
By horn and bone,
Riders on the wind,
The Horned One appears!
The Lady leads us ever on,
That through death's season,
All is renewed, bringing prosperity and abundance in the year to come,
Drawn by the hearth's flame this Samhain Night!"

The Mistress recites:

"With the Mistress and Master
We walk the Maze,
Through Rostau and Annwn

The ascent is made.
The paths of ancient wisdom
Open to us now,
Gods and spirits return with us this hour."

With the Mistress in the lead, the group begins the ascent out of the Annwn, circling nine times deosil or Sunwise.

The Mistress and Master hold the apple cider as they recite:

"Three worlds encircle the one,
Plow, tree and golden Sun,
The Lady calls from Caer Wydyr,
Cauldron deep, pool clear,
Four treasures hide in the keep,
Four realms the Wise do seek,
We call the ancient ones,
We honor them still,
In grove, in glen, on sacred hill,
So sing the songs and walk the maze,
The great stag comes through moonlit haze.
Cer and Cerri are in us found,
In the three worlds we are bound!"

Finish by thanking the Gods, spirits and ancient ones, offering the cider and food. Then dismiss the Guardians.

Imbolc

In our system, the ritual of Imbolc is held on the evening when the Sun reaches fifteen degrees of Aquarius and/or on night of the Full Moon closest in time to this date. All normal tools needed for laying the Roth Fail will be present. In addition, the cauldron should be placed in the center of the circle. In this one may prepare a small fire. If working indoors we recommend the use of candles placed in the cauldron as they won't give off excessive smoke. Unlike

Samhain, we don't use the salt and alcohol for this fire as
this doesn't burn long, and salt and alcohol are employed
in rites of purification and removing old influences, as was
seen in the previous ceremony. The Imbolc the fire is lit
prior to the beginning of the ritual as the primary theme is
one of sustained and growing light.

On the hearthstone place a small container of mead and
another of red wine. You will also want an offering of sweet
cakes. The hearthstone candles may be white. The Cauldron
fire should be lit.

The Ritual
Lay the Roth Fail. When completed the Master recites:

> "The Great Queen comes,
> Clothed in White and Gold,
> Lady of stars and silver Moon.
> By stag and falcon,
> By raven, serpent, hare and toad.
> We call to the Lady,
> We welcome you here."

The Master recites the invocation of the Goddess:

> "By stang and besom,
> By toad and hare,
> By crow and serpent's breath,
> The great Queen comes,
> Silver circle is here,
> She who rides the night.
> By our words we conjure you,
> Through this rite we conjure you,
> By bone and stone we conjure you,
> By water, smoke and fire we conjure you,
> Serpent's breath and Dragon's lair,
> From the Hollow Hills,
> In Imbolc's light,

We conjure you!
The Great Queen comes.
Mistress, we welcome you here this night."

The Mistress recites:

"Deep in the Annwn,
Through the caverns of the
Rostau we travel.
With cauldron and distaff,
Stang and broom.
The Maiden calls to Her lover.
Come to me."

The Mistress recites the invocation of the God:

"Master of the Wild Wood,
Horned One in the night,
Janicot, Janicot,
Janicot, Janicot.
We welcome you
He who carries the light.
By our words we conjure you,
Through this rite we conjure you,
By bone and stone, water, smoke and fire we conjure
you,
By crow and toad, by leaping hare,
Serpent's breath and Dragon's lair,
Arise, awake this Imbolc night."

The Master recites:

"From the Castle of Glass
The young Master ascends,
Renewed by lake and cauldron,
He now wends.
Across red and white,

295

The twin rivers bend.
Through ancient lands and caverns deep.
With the twin dragons,
They, who are the essence of the Keep!
For it is She, the Lady,
Whom He does seek!"

The Master takes the Stang, and the Mistress the Besom. They stand to either side of the Cauldron as they both recite:

"We call on the dragons,
Red and White that sleep.
Across the two rivers,
Hidden in the deep,
Awake great power within the land,
Entwined serpents,
The time is at hand!"

Looking across the light of the cauldron at each other, the Mistress and Master circle the cauldron in a deosil direction, as they chant the following back and forth, alternatively as if calling to one another. They should circle the cauldron a minimum of nine times.

The Master chants:

"Anál nathrach"

The Mistress enchants:

"Bandia Gelach"

When finished, the two return the Stang and Besom to their normal places. The Mistress then recites:
"Imbolc is upon us,
Through passion and flame!
The light returns,

In the Great Queen's name!"

Taking hands around the cauldron all chant the following while raising power:

"Imbolc Fire burning bright,
Passion and desire light the night!"

Returning to the hearthstone. The Master will take up the flasks of mead and red wine. The Mistress holds the goblet and faces the Master. The Master pours the mead and wine into the goblet as he recites:

"The red and white roses,
Merge as one."

The Mistress then recites:

"Through this drink,
The twin dragons awake,
Their essence of which,
We now partake!"

The Lady and Master each sip the wine.

The Mistress and Master hold the wine as they recite:

"Three worlds encircle the one,
Plow, tree and golden Sun,
The Lady calls from Caer Wydyr,
Cauldron deep, pool clear,
Four treasures hide in the keep,
Four realms the Wise do seek,
We call the ancient ones,
We honor them still,
In grove, in glen, on sacred hill,
So sing the songs and walk the maze,

The great stag comes through moonlit haze.
Cer and Cerri are in us found,
In the three worlds we are bound!"

This is then shared with all present. Finish by thanking the Gods, spirits and ancient ones offering the wine and food. Then dismiss the Guardians.

Beltane

This ritual should be performed either on the night in which the Sun reaches fifteen degrees of Taurus, which is the exact midpoint between the spring equinox and the summer solstice, or on the night of the Full Moon that falls nearest to this event. Ideally this should be performed outdoors. However, in our situation, Beltane is almost always still too inclement. As such, we usually conduct this rite before the hearth. Whether outside or indoors, a fire should be laid at the center of the circle. Indoors, this will be in the cauldron placed in the center. As with Imbolc, when indoors, we will use candles in the cauldron as they don't smoke much.

For Beltane we place two green candles at the corners of the hearthstone. Mead and red wine as well as sweet bread or cakes will serve as offerings to be presented. The hearth itself is normally draped with a green cloth. On this a Triangle of Art made of fresh flowers and greenery should be set. In the center place a bowl of fresh well or spring water.

The stang and besom should be set to either side of the hearthstone. If indoors the cauldron will act as the Balefire. As always, all normal tools used in the setting of the Roth Fail will need to be present. The central fire should be lit prior to beginning.

The Ritual

Begin by setting the Roth Fail.

Facing the hearthstone the Mistress recites:

"There is power in the land,
Renewed this night.
For this is Beltane,
The season of Light.
By serpent and hare,
The twin dragons in flight,
The veil is thin,
The gates swing open this night!
The Great Queen comes crowned in Green and Gold,
The Green Man calls to Her as of old.
Banu, Banu, Great Goddess of Life.
Banu, Banu, Lady of the starry night!"

The Master recites the invocation of the Goddess:

"By stang and besom,
By toad and hare,
By crow and serpent's breath,
The great Queen comes,
Silver circle is here,
She who rides the night.
By our words we conjure you,
Through this rite we conjure you,
By bone and stone we conjure you,
By water, smoke and fire we conjure you,
Serpent's Breath and Dragon's lair,
From the Hollow Hills,
In Beltane's light,
We conjure you!
The Great Queen comes.
Mistress, we welcome you here this night."

The Master recites:

"The Master calls to His lover,
The Lady cloaked in Green and Gold,
Deep in forest and flowering field,

In starry night and moonlit haze.
The veil opens,
He rises to meet Her gaze."

The Mistress recites the invocation of the God:

"Master of the Wild Wood,
Horned One in the night,
Janicot, Janicot,
Janicot, Janicot.
We welcome you
He who carries the light.
By our words we conjure you,
Through this rite we conjure you,
By bone and stone, water, smoke and fire we conjure you,
By crow and toad, by leaping hare,
Serpent's breath and Dragon's lair,
Arise, awake this Beltane night."

The Mistress recites:

"Tonight we journey with the Lady,
Through the mists of Abred,
Deep in forest and field,
By sacred well and woodland glen.
With nature's secret folk as our kin,
We traverse the paths to
Cauldron and flame,
The sacred water that lies within."

The Mistress takes up the bowl of water and carries this around the circle nine times deosil as all present follow. She then places this in the center of the Triangle of Art. The Mistress then recites:

"By Stang and Besom,
By Silver Moon's Glow,

The Earth awakens
The Dragon Power now flows,
Red and White join this night.
We call the Ancient Ones
Through water, flame and light.
Keepers of the sacred Bond,
The way is open,
The path is clear,
The ancient traditions are before us,
Revealed here."

The Master faces the Balefire as he recites:

"Seed and sprout,
Flower and fruit,
The Great Queen comes,
Life bursts forth,
The wheel weaves in, the thread spins out.
The nine maidens tend the flame,
Nine steps to the Cauldron of Spring,
The twin dragons merge,
Their power reclaimed."

The Mistress lifts the broom, while the Master lifts the Stang. Looking across the light of the cauldron at each other, the Mistress and Master circle the cauldron as they chant the following back and forth, alternatively as if calling to one another. They should circle the cauldron a minimum of nine times.

The Master chants:

"Anál nathrach"

The Mistress enchants:

"Bandia Gelach"

301

When finished, they step in front of the Balefire and then place the brush of the broom through the forks of the Stang as the two recite:

"Red and White,
Sun and Moon,
The twin dragons now are one.
For between the Horns
Lady and Lord unite,
All comes to life this Beltane night."

Returning to the hearthstone the Mistress holds the bowl of water aloft as the Master recites:

"Keepers of the Sacred Bond,
Nature's secret folk.
In mountain hallow, forest keep,
Sacred well, waters deep.
The gates swing open,
The spirits of the land now come.
Our scared Bond remains as one.
For Between the Horns,
Lays the path we keep.
Your ancient wisdom we now seek.
This water of life we now share,
For it is through our Art that we welcome you here."

The bowl is set back within the triangle. The Mistress traces the Crossroad Sigil over the water with the Fe.

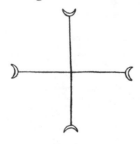

She then says:

"Balefire burning bright,
Banu Queen of Elphame,
Banu Fe in the night.
With your aid,
Prosperity comes this Beltane night!"

Linking hands everyone chants as they circle the fire:

"Queen of Elphame,
Fe in the night,
Prosperity comes this Beltane Night!"

The Mistress and Master hold the wine as they recite:

"Three worlds encircle the one,
Plow, tree and golden Sun,
The Lady calls from Caer Wydyr,
Cauldron deep, pool clear,
Four treasures hide in the keep,
Four realms the Wise do seek,
We call the ancient ones,
We honor them still,
In grove, in glen, on sacred hill,
So sing the songs and walk the maze,
The great stag comes through moonlit haze.
Cer and Cerri are in us found,
In the three worlds we are bound!"

This is shared with all present. Then finish by thanking the Gods, offering the wine and food. Then dismiss the Guardians.

Lughnasadh

In our system, the festival of Lughnasadh is held as near to the date on which the Sun reaches fifteen degrees of Leo as possible, or like the others, on the Full Moon closest to the midpoint. Falling as it does so near the annual rising of the star Sirius at dawn, we incorporate certain esoteric elements from the Ancient Egyptian festival of Wep Renpet which occurs at this time. For the Egyptians, this was perhaps the single most important point in the year. For us, we have found the themes contained in both events fit very well together, representing yet another way that the Geassa, the bond, manifests in different cultures.

For this you will need to prepare two important items in advance. The first of these is what is commonly called a 'corn dolly'. Essentially this is a doll made from the first cut sheaves of grain of the season. This can also be made from a combination of fresh cut herbs and flowers. In the Americas, it is common to use the husks from freshly harvested corn for this. Whatever you choose, feel free to be creative. We will often use a combination of herbs and flowers combined with grain stalks such as wheat if available. In choosing the ingredients for this we are careful to ensure that they resonate with prosperity and abundance. This is important as after the Lughnasadh ritual this will be placed in the home near one's door to attract luck and good fortune through the coming year.

The second item that you will want is a plate of bread, cake or cookies, made from whole grain, honey and wine - representing the "corn king". It is possible to use a whole grain bread with a mixture of honey and wine as a spread over this. In our coven we will often bake a special bread containing these ingredients, modeling this into the shape of a man.[35]

Beyond these, you will need all normal ritual equipment for the setting of the Roth Fail. The hearthstone should be decorated with grains and fruit, as signs of the season's

---

35. In the coven which I was initiated in the women would bake this specially, being certain to give the Corn King an erect phallus. Interestingly, barley cakes from Ancient Egypt have been found in tombs formed in an effigy of Osiris with an erect phallus.

first harvest. If desired, the hearthstone may be covered with a gold cloth. You will also want separate flasks of mead and red wine.

The Ritual

The Roth Fail is set as normal. Then the Mistress recites:
"Banu, Banu
The radiance of the Sun caresses the Earth,
The Great Queen's bounty comes forth this night!
The twin serpents unite,
Dragons Red and White.
For this is the feast of the first harvest!"

The Master recites:

"By stang and besom,
By toad and hare,
By crow and serpent's breath,
The great Queen comes,
Silver circle is here,
She who rides the night.
By our words we conjure you,
Through this rite we conjure you,
By bone and stone we conjure you,
By water, smoke and fire we conjure you,
Serpent's breath and dragon's lair,
From the Hollow Hills,
The Great Queen comes.
Clothed in amber and in gold.
The Lady of Stars, of Earth, and Moon!
Lady, we welcome you here!"

The Mistress recites:

"Across the golden fields of Gwynfyd,
Rich in fruit, herb and grain,
We travel with stang and besom.

For the Great Queen calls to the Sun,
That together they become one!"

The Mistress recites the invocation of the God:

"Master of the Wild Wood,
Horned One who carries the light,
Janicot, Janicot,
Janicot, Janicot.
We welcome you.
By our words we conjure you,
Through this rite we conjure you,
By bone and stone, water, smoke and fire we conjure you,
By crow and toad, by leaping hare,
Serpent's breath and dragon's lair,
With this harvest we call to you,
Welcome Great Lord of light!"

The Master takes up the Grain bread:

"By Lugh and Nuada,
By the sacrifice of Ausir,
The Harvest is upon us!
The Corn King is here!
We give thanks to the land!"

The Master carries the grain bread to each quarter, beginning in the east and circling Sunwise, stopping at each quarter, and holding the bread up intones:

"Banu the Corn King,
Banu the sacrifice He made!"

The bread is replaced on the hearthstone. The Mistress picks up the Corn Dolly. Holding this aloft she recites:

"By Queen and Mistress,
The dream wrought by Morgan,
By the gift of Aset and Hwt-Hrw
The Harvest is upon us!
The Lady of the Corn is here!
We give thanks for the bounty She provides.
We give thanks to the land!"

The Mistress carries the Corn Dolly to each quarter, beginning in the east and circling Sunwise, stopping at each quarter, and holding the Corn Dolly up intones:

"Banu the Lady of the Corn,
Banu the bounty She provides!"

Returning to the hearthstone the Master faces the north and with arms raised in invocation he recites:

"Em Hotep Hwt-Hrw wret,
nebet pet,
hnwet neteru nbw,
sat ir-ta khpr heref,
shd tawy idb m stwts.
Between the Horns Lays the Path We Keep!"

The Mistress faces the north and recites:

"The Great Queen comes
Clad in Her brilliance.
The Star that joins with the Sun,
Ind hret Hwt-Hrw!
She who brings the harvest!
Between the Horns Lays the Path We Keep!"

Joining hands the group chants as they raise the serpent power:

"Hail the Harvest!
Prosperity comes!"

After the energy has been released, the Master and
Mistress lift the grain bread and Corn Dolly respectively.
The Master recites:

"Red Dragon,
Sacred Rose,
The Sun at Lughnasadh!
The sacrifice of the God is made!"

The Mistress recites:

"White Dragon,
Sacred Rose,
The Star that rises at Lughnasadh!
The bounty of the Goddess comes to us!"

Replacing the grain bread and the Corn Dolly, the Mistress
and Master hold the goblet while reciting:

"Three worlds encircle the one,
Plough, Tree and Golden Sun.
The Lady calls from Caer Wydyr,
Cauldron deep and pool clear.
Four treasures hide in the keep.
Four realms the wise do seek.
We call the Ancient Ones.
We honor them still.
In grove, in glen, on sacred hill.
So sing the songs and walk the Maze.
The great stag bounds through moonlit haze.
Cer and Cerri are in us found.
In the three worlds we are bound."

All present share in the bounty. Finish by thanking the Gods, spirits and ancient ones. Then dismiss the Guardians and all retire to the feast.

Chapter Fifteen

❖ BETWEEN HAND AND FOOT ❖

In most valid esoteric paths there are otherworld contacts, beings who act as guides or forces within the system. Traditional Witchcraft is no exception. Throughout these books I have spoken of the Witch Queen and Witch King, the Lady and Master, or the Mistress and the Master. These titles are consistent with texts from medieval and pre-industrial Europe which often refer to the Queen and King of Elphame, as well as the Maiden and Magister. Suffice it to say that these refer to those otherworld beings who are the primary guides for this path. Yet, as we have seen, there are also others who aid the Witch: the spirits of certain elders and teachers who, while existing beyond the hedge, remain aware of those who practice in this realm. Then there are also those beings linked to the natural environment one lives in.

One of the first steps one can take when beginning to venture on the Willow Path is to perform a rite of dedication. This is meant to invite these forces into one's life, opening the connection to these beings while also creating a bond with them. In doing so, one is directly asking for their guidance.

It is important to understand that this is not a 'self' initiation. Initiation is a very different and powerful rite that, in our system, can only be conveyed by those living members who have already gone through the process and are trained in the techniques involved. Yet, keep in mind that, in my opinion, it isn't absolutely essential that one undergoes initiation to be a Witch or to practice the

Art. Rather, initiation is a very personal and life changing ritual. Initiation at once represents the culmination of a period of training, but more importantly, it marks a point of transition and transformation that many people may not want to go through. For those who do chose to cross that threshold, initiation does open doors to other realms, bringing to the surface abilities and potential that otherwise would have stayed dormant. Yet, I am convinced that it is not needed in order to practice the Art or to follow this way of life.

Whether you seek initiation or not, it is almost certain that at some point in your development you will reach a point when it will be important to reach out to the beings who are directly tied to this system; for they are the keepers of the deeper teachings and wisdom. Beyond the books, beyond the classes or even the instruction of a personal teacher, lie those forces that sit at the heart of the Willow Path. In such cases the dedication ritual becomes a fundamental step one can take on one's own to make this connection. The following is the ritual we recommend.

For this you will need a cord that can be worn as a belt. This should be long enough to tie around the waist and still have one end extend down in front approximately to the knees. One end will need to terminate in a loop, while the other will have a knot the end of which will want to be frayed into a tassel. When worn, the end with the knot is pulled through the loop and then tied, securing cord around the waist. Normally the cord is of a neutral color - tan or beige, sometimes green. Having said this, you will find that some covens, as well as Hermetic Orders, use specific-colored cords to designate different offices in the group. We tend to avoid these as we don't want there to be any sense of elitism, degree or class. For us a Witch is a Witch. Yes, there are different offices as well as leaders, teachers and elders in the group. But essentially, we are all traveling the path together with each of us learning as we go.

For this rite you will also need wine and a food offering, a bowl of water, your stone and bone, incense and a vial of natural oil. Once again, as a good all-purpose oil, we prefer Vervain. In addition to these you will want a white candle. Ideally this should be a pillar candle as you will want to use this in the future to help form the connection with these beings later, so you want this to last.

The best time for this is the night of the Full Moon. If you can time this at a time that also aligns with one of the Fire Festivals, so much the better. Prepare by fasting four to six hours before the rite. You should not have had any red meat or dairy foods within the past 24 hours. Nor should you have engaged in any sexual activity for two to three days beforehand either. If weather and personal circumstances permit, do the rite outside. This should be in a liminal, secluded place in nature far from the prying eyes of neighbors or those who may pass by. Keep in mind that you will be naked for this so consider your surroundings carefully. If an outdoor setting isn't possible this can easily be performed in your normal ritual space. Then, one hour beforehand, take a ritual bath as described earlier.

The rite itself should be done in private, unless you prefer to have your teacher present to assist. Keep in mind that this is between you, the Lady and Master, as well as the otherworld beings tied directly to this system. It is not a binding to any group or single person. As noted, this rite should be performed naked as you will be anointing various parts of body during the rite. Place two white candles in the far corners of the hearthstone. The white pillar candle should be set in the center of the hearthstone. Place the bowl of water in front of the pillar candle. All other normal tools used to set the Roth Fail should be present as well.

In advance write out and memorize your thoughts on why you want to step onto this path. Keep in mind that you are beginning a journey that will change your life forever, forming a partnership with the elder beings of the tradition, so be absolutely certain why you want to do this. Keep your reasons simple, clear and sincere. It is important that you are not overly verbose in your reason, nor should there be any sense of bartering. Do not approach this as "I will give you this, if you provide that". There is no 'selling of the soul', no bargaining. If anything, it is the opposite. For you are about to open yourself to these forces in a partnership, forming a relationship with these beings, becoming 'familiar' with them. They are not there for you to command, nor are you enslaved to them or by them. While this is a dedication and with it a recognition of your commitment to the bond, this is also a partnership, more though, it is an alliance and friendship that will reach beyond time and across worlds.

Once the Roth Fail is set, take some time to let yourself move into a state of becoming. If you have a familiar spirit call on him or her to be with you. Perform the Serpent, Cloak and Star techniques. Then take some time to merge with the light of the Full Moon itself. Even if indoors let this envelop you, fill you. When ready recite:

"I conjure you, I conjure you,
Elders of the Willow Path.
By these words I conjure you,
By will and breath I conjure you.
By smoke and fire I conjure you,
By stone and bone I conjure you,
By the waters of life I conjure you.
Come good spirits of the Art!
By the Lady of the Silver Circle,
By He who rides in the night,
The gate swings open!
Between the horns,
Lays the path we keep!"

With the middle finger of your dominant hand trace the following Sigil in the air while visualizing this as a brilliant electric blue:

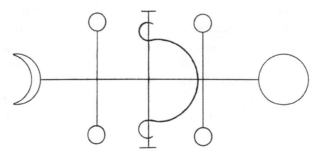

Sigil of the Transformative Power of the Moon

Then recite your dedication, your reason for seeking to walk the Willow Path. Be sure that this opens with a call or recognition of the elders, spirits and Gods of the tradition. And, again, keep this simple.

When finished, anoint your body with the oil in the following places: feet, knees, buttocks, genitals, palms, solar plexus, nipples, under the chin and back of the neck, followed by the forehead and crown of the head.

Then crouch down enough so that you can place your left hand under your feet and your right hand on top of your head. If one is physically unable to crouch, have a chair present and sit on this to do the same. Then state:

"Mistress, Master, there is no part of me that is not of thee."

Take a moment to envision the Moon's light following in through the top of your head, filling you and flowing out through your feet into you left hand. It is helpful to allow this energy to complete a circuit flowing from the right hand through the body to the left, and back up to the right, over and over, all the while allowing the Moon's light to continue to add to this. Eventually stand.

314

At this point pick up the pillar candle. Then, with your knife carve the *Sigil of the Transformative Power of the Moon* shown earlier into this. When done, anoint the candle with the oil. Set this on the hearthstone and light this as you state:

"By this flame the bond is made,
The doors are open,
For the Path they laid,
The company of the Ancient Ones I now join
Through spirit light, Serpent's Breath
And the Lady who wends this way."

Next pick up the bowl of water and hold this up. In doing so, draw the Dragon's Breath and power of the Moon into the water by reciting the formula of *Making the Enchantment* chanting repeatedly as you gather the power:

"Anál nathrach
Bandia Gelach
Draiocht dénmha"

Once the water is filled with the Dragon's Breath, drink some of this. Then set the bowl back on the hearthstone in front of the candle. Now take up the cord as you hold this out in front of you before the candle and water, then recite:

"By this Cord,
The Bond is made.
Between the Horns
The path is Laid.
I dedicate myself to thee
The Lady's tow,
The Master's steed."

Pass the cord over the flame of the candle, then anoint this with the water. Now tie the cord around your waist and recite:

"Spirits of the Willow Path,
The link is made,
The thread does pass.
For bound and bound,
Throughout and about,
The Wheel weaves in,
The thread spins out,
I dedicate myself to the Art,
Both within and throughout!"

Next, make an offering of food and wine to the elders, spirits and Gods to thank them. You need to consume a portion of this. However, some should be left in nature, buried, scattered or poured on the Earth.

The candle should be allowed to burn for one hour. Then it can be put out and kept secret, to be used whenever you seek to reinforce the connection with the elders in the future. The cord, too, should be kept secret with your other tools.

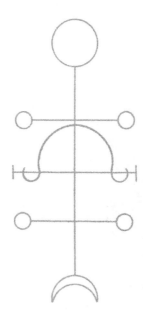

Chapter Sixteen

❖ INVOCATIONS ❖
CHARMS AND WORDS OF POWER

In *Horns of the Moon*, I presented clear instruction on the purpose and ways in which different musical tones, charms and words of power are used. Here I would like to offer a series of invocations, enchantments and Words of Power that we have found to be useful and powerful in our workings. These are drawn from a variety of sources including ancient texts, historical records, personal teachings presented to me as well as enchantments which I have composed. By now it should come as no surprise that you will find a mix reaching across the three primary occult traditions that I have been trained in:

- Traditional Witchcraft including Welch, Gaelic and Basque myth and folkloric practices;
  - Hermetics including influences from Astrological and Alchemical sources;
- And a very strong influence from Ancient Egyptian texts.

While each of these are vital to this system of the Art, I find it interesting that a number of other Traditional Witches are drawing techniques from Egyptian magic. According to Cecil Williamson, certain aspects of Egyptian magic have been a steady influence in cunning practice over the past century or longer.[36] Given cunning folks' ability to adapt different systems easily into their own form of

---

36. Patterson, Steve. *Cecil Williamson's Book of Witchcraft.* 2014

practical magic I feel this is entirely plausible. But what I am finding most intriguing is that I have personally encountered several Traditional Witches who have secretly explained that for them the Witch Queen, who is one of the primary otherworld 'contacts' of this Art, often has come through (at least in part) in forms that clearly show a link to the Egyptian Goddess, Hathor. Perhaps this isn't so unusual given the long history of female otherworld beings in the Art reaching across Europe, the Levant and Egypt.

For the Egyptians, Hathor was perhaps the preeminent otherworld being who encompassed so much that is seen in the divine feminine. She was the mother, lover and daughter. Yet She was the protector, warrior, avenger and destroyer. Her love knew no bounds yet, when angered, Her wrath was swift and severe. In Her form as Iusaas, as well as Nebet Hetepet, she was the source of all, frequently equated to the unfathomable waters from which all other realms and beings emerged. It stands to reason that, for those who work with the raw forces of nature, the Witch Queen would come through in very similar ways. For us, I would even go so far as to say that She may be one and the same sentient being, making Her presence known in Traditional Witchcraft across the centuries. The Bond, the Geassa, continues through time and cultures; the wheel weaves in, the thread spins out.

As you go through these enchantments you will find that I have included many that have been introduced earlier in these writings. I am presenting these here, along with others in this chapter, because these are easily adaptable to a variety of personal and group workings. As such, they are listed (minus the visualizations that accompany these) for ease of reference in ritual and to aid with memorization.

The Serpent's Breath
"I call you Serpent of the Land,
Awake, arise ye from thy stead,
By Dragons Red and White,

By Crow, By Toad, By Leaping Hare,
Rise in me O Serpent Breath!"

Donning the Cloak

"Bandia Gelach,
Airgead Calla,
Dlúthuigh liom."

Pronounced:
"Banjeeah Geloch
Arregot Calla
Dluthuigh Liom" (similar to 'lion' but replace with the
'n' with an 'm').

Star in the Well

"Nebet Hetepet"
"Atum"
"Hwt-Hrw"
"Wadjet"
"Nekhebet"
"Ra-Horakhty"
"Iusaas"

Stirring the Well

"Round and Round
Throughout and about,
The wheel weaves in and the thread spins out.
By Stang, By Besom, By Cauldron deep,
We meet together in the Lady's keep."

Lunar Rite of Union

Form triangle overhead with hands:
"Banu, Great Queen! Goddess!
Source of Illumination.
I open my Akh to you,
And ask, may you impart your wisdom to me!"
Form triangle in front of forehead:

"Enlighten my Ba
That I may perceive clearly
All things I seek."
Form triangle in front of chest:
"Illumine my Ka,
Imparting your essence of wonder!"

Form downward triangle in front of genitals:
"Empower my Sekhem
With your essence of life,
That I shall know you through all worlds."

Spread arms:
"I reveal my true self to you,
That I may follow in your ways!
Bandia (pronounced BAHN-JEE-uh), Great Queen!"

Addressing the Besom
"O Besom, standing by hearth and Stang,
Let your shaft be strong
Your brush be fine.
Hark, O hark my horse!
Hark, O hark my mare!
Hark, O hark my horse!
Carry me into the night!
Like the winds that the Lady rides,
To the lands of Annwn we now fly.
Below and above, in the skies of the Abred.
Sweep along as the wind,
To the fields of fair Gwynfyd.
Besom, O my mare,
To the Castle of the Lady we go.
O Besom, Horse, my Mare
Carry me to and fro!"

Making the Enchantment		
Incantation	**Pronunciation**	**Translation**
Anál nathrach	Onal NathRack	Serpent's Breath
Bandia Gelach	Banjeeah Geloch	Mistress Moon
Draiocht dénmha	Dray-aht de-N-may	This Enchantment I make!

Basque Evocation of the Master

"Har, Har! Hou, Hou! (pronounced *har, har, who, who*)
Eman hetan! Eman hetan!
Har, Har! Hou, Hou!
Janicot! Janicot! Janicot! Janicot! (pronounced *Hanicot*)
Har, Har! Hou, Hou!
Jauna (pronounced *Hauna*) Gorril! Jauna Gorril!
Akhera Goiti! Akhera Beiti!"

Calling the Master

"Master of the Wild Wood,
Horned One in the night,
Janicot, Janicot,
Janicot, Janicot.
We welcome you
He who carries the light.
By our words we conjure you,
Through this rite we conjure you,
By bone and stone, water, smoke and fire we conjure you,
By crow and toad, by leaping hare,
Serpent's breath and dragon's lair,
Arise, awake this Full Moon night."

Calling the Mistress

"From sacred wells,
Cool springs rise clear,

The Lady calls to all who hear.
By stang and besom,
By toad and hare,
By crow and serpent's breath,
The great Queen comes,
Silver circle is here,
She who rides the night.
By our words we conjure you,
Through this rite we conjure you,
By bone and stone we conjure you,
By water, smoke and fire we conjure you,
Serpent's breath and dragon's lair,
From the Hollow Hills,
In Full Moon's light,
We conjure you!
The Great Queen comes.
Mistress, we welcome you here this night."

Invocation of the Lady to the Mistress
"From Sacred wells cool springs rise clear,
The Lady calls for all who hear.
As Silver Moon rising high,
Cloaked with stars in the sky.
Lady of Stars we call to you,
Your essence of honey and morning dew.
On mountains fair and caverns deep,
Cerri is found by those who seek.
Come great Lady! Come and appear!
The maze is made, the circle spins here!
By silver plough you do make,
The land fertile in its wake!
The stars of Caer Wyder guide our gaze,
Come Great Lady, hear our praise!
So by the horns of Hwt-Hrw with tousled hair,
By Arianrhod's circle,
Silver mirror held with care,
Diana's bow is strung, Her arrow swift,

We call you Lady in the mist!
Your daughter awaits you,
Her cauldron is here!
Come great Lady, Cerri, come,
We welcome you here!"

Invocation of the Horned One to the Magister

"By oak, by stone, by circles old,
The tree's sway, Cer's laughter bold!
We call to you to take our hand,
Herne of the Hunt, Green Man of the land!
The Great Wheel turns upon the years,
Faunus of the Glen and Khnum appears!
Great Bel on Hill,
Gwydn hidden in forest deep,
Arise Great Stag from your sleep!
Arise Great Stag! Come be here!
Your servant awaits, his vision clear.
Come Master Cer! We welcome you here!"

Evocation of the Crystal Mountain

"In Moon and Stars the Lady's Crown is found,
Deep in azure keep.
For the tower of glass reaches into the night,
Atop lucent crystal's rugged peak.
It is from this realm that the Lady calls,
Her voice ringing through all worlds.
While nine ladies breathe life into the flames,
And the Cauldron simmers, the potion swirls.
Apple isle and limpid mountain, rising from the lake,
The castle walls of glass aglow,
Amber fires burning bright.
We tread the mill and climb the heights,
Through hollow and cliff, past each spirit plight.
For the wheel weaves and the thread spins.
Between the Horns, Lays the path we keep.
The Lady calls from Caer Wydyr

Her song of beauty we now hear.
For crown and cauldron are what we seek,
Through the maze to the Lady's keep!"

Stiring the Spirit Mists		
Incantation	**Pronunciation**	**Translation**
Anál nathrach	onal nathrack	Serpent Breath
Taibhse brádán	tie-bsha bardan	Phantom mist

Ancient Egyptian Enchantments

Call to the Goddess Hwt-Hrw/Hathor
"Ind hr.t, Hwt-Hr nbt 'Iwnt, 'Irt-Ra,
'Itmt sat 'Itmw, hnwt wrt,
asat khprw, ankh ntrw n dgt.s!
nbt rnw m-kht tawy, n rkh.tw ssm.s, nfrt hr shbt!
mh ib n Ra m wbn.f,
wrt mrwt, hmwt,
nfrt hr m hnkswt,
tpyt pw nt Hwt-Hrw, sawy imytw Saw-n.sn,
ant nfrt an.tw n maa.s.

Greetings Hwt-Hrw, Mistress of the sky, Passionate
Lady. The sight of you causes the Gods to live! For you
are the Mistress of many names and many forms. She
who crosses the breadth of the land. You fill the heart
of Ra with brilliance.
Great of Love, Beautiful Queen with flowing hair,
First among the Gods, She who returns as a vision!"

Hwt-Hrw's reply -
"I am the Great Goddess, who gives birth to the Light! I
am the Lady of pleasure in the noonday Sun. None can
bind me, the Lady Primeval, She who lives in truth. The
Gods rise to greet me, because I am beauty, I am power!
Mine is the secret name that brings ecstasy to every

heart, the cauldron alive with potion and flame! With the twins I create all that is. Come with my horns, display my beauty,

That I may greet you in the west as the young Goddess. From the stars my voice rings through all worlds. Come to me! Take my hand! Rise as the Falcon that you may be as the Gods. For I am Mistress of the Northern Sky, and my love is eternal! I am the Great Goddess, the serpent laughing in the fields, the Great Wild Cow and the beautiful woman of flowing hair! Here I appear in my true form!"

Honoring Hwt-Hrw

"Em Hotep Hwt-Hrw wret,
nebet pet,
hnwet neteru nbw,
sat ir-ta khpr heref,
shd tawy idb m stwts."

"Welcome In Peace, Great Hathor,
Lady of the Sky, Sovereign of the Neteru,
She who created all that is,
Who illuminates the land and the shores with her rays!"

Invocation of Hwt-Hrw

"Hwt-Hrw, Hwt-Hrw, Hwt-Hrw, Hwt-Hrw
Lady of the starry sky, Lady of the night
Lady who brings forth the brilliant morning light!
Hwt-Hrw, Hwt-Hrw, Hwt-Hrw, Hwt-Hrw
You who are the Queen of heaven
You who are the Queen of earth
Conceiver, Creator, Mother to whom we owe our birth!
Hwt-Hrw, Hwt-Hrw, Hwt-Hrw, Hwt-Hrw
Goddess of pleasure, Goddess of delight
Dancer of the Gods, Lover in the night
I pray, come now my Lady, Come now my Lady
Come now my Lady, be with me from this night!

For you are the beautiful one, the Eye of Ra
Protector, Nourisher, Renewer of all!
O wonderous cow, Lady of delight
Thrust back the darkness and fill me with your light!
For I open myself unto you and
Pray now my Lady come that we shall be one!
Hwt-Hrw, Hwt-Hrw, Hwt-Hrw, Hwt-Hrw
Blue lidded goddess of the dawn, house of the Sun
I pray, descend now my Lady that we shall be as one!
For as the Sistrum does sing and the Menat does play
Fill me with your spirit
In all that I do, all that I say!
For you are the Great Goddess, Mother of all
Let your passion now fill me as you heed my call!
Hwt-Hrw, Hwt-Hrw, O beautiful Hwt-Hrw
Come into me, Come into me, Come into me Hwt-Hrw!"

Invocation of Ra

"Homage to you, Ra, at your beautiful rising.
You rise and shine at the dawn.
The company of the Ennead praise you at sunrise and
at sunset,
When, as your morning boat meets your evening boat
with fair winds,
You sail over the heights of heaven with a glad heart.
You who are the perfect one,
You who are eternal as the splendor of the noon-day
Sun,
Ruler of all who appear in your sphere.
Therefore I make homage to you.
All Hail, Ra-Harakhti!
All Hail, Atum!
All Hail, Khepra!
You great falcon, who, by your beautiful face make all
humanity to rejoice,
You renew your youth, and position yourself in
yesterday's place.

O divine youth, self-creator, Lord of heaven and earth, you who creates beings celestial and beings terrestrial. You who are the heir to eternity, everlasting and renewing ruler, as you rise your gracious light shines upon all faces and abides in every heart. I pray, live in me, and I in you, O Golden Falcon of the Sun!"

Words of Power

Gaelic & Old Irish -
- Anál nathrach – Serpent breath
- Anfa – To drive away, to repel
- Bandia – Goddess, Mistress
- Ciapog – Magically induced confusion or delusion
- Deoraidhin – To banish a spirit
- Earaid – Magical interference or hinderance
- Fare – To restrain, to bar entrance
- Feath Fiadha – Magical mists of invisibility
- Gelach - Moon
- Gorm – Blue, associated with magic and protection
- Grian – Sun
- Iallach – To cause restraint and compulsion
- Leigheas - Healing
- Lionadh – Waxing Moon
- Mallacht – To curse
- Marcaigh Mora Geala – The "Great Bright Riders", the faery riders
- Mathairdhia – Mother Goddess
- Mealladh – To place a glamour, to place a magically induced vision
- Mearnail – Light of the Sidhe
- Neamhshaolta – To evoke and draw otherworld beings into the material
- Rath – Bounty, riches and abundance
- Saighean – Creates blasts of wind, can also be used to cause lightening or flashes of light
- Seal – Phantom, spirit, ghost
- Scath – Phantom, shadow, protective spirit

- Sciath – To shield, protect
- Seabhac – Hawk
- Seansai – Traveling in spirit, projection of astral self
- Serglige – Wasting sickness caused by magic
- Sian – Whistle or sound caused by the Sidhe
- Slainte – Health, welfare
- Slan – Health, security and wholeness
- Saineann – To bring calm weather
- Taibhse – Ghost
- Tine – Fire
- Toghairm – To invoke
- Traghadh – Waning Moon
- Trean – To bring "thrice richness", strength, ability, plenty and abundance
- Tir Na Marbh – Land of the dead
- Togharmach – Conjurer, medium
- Toghairm – Summoning, invocation, to conjure
- Toitriu – Incense "empowered smoke"
- Torramh – Harvest Home
- Taur – Omen
- Tuis – Incense
- Tongu fona deibh – "I swear by the Gods"
- Tuathal – Widershins, Moonwise direction; also Pagan, invoke inward. To bind, secure or close.
- Turas – Precognition, clairvoyance, intuition
- Uaimh – Cave, crypt
- Urchar – Faery dart

Ancient Egyptian words of Power -
- Ar – To drive away, to repel
- aSty – Abundance
- baH – Abundance
- bAq – Fortunate, bright
- bAtyt - Devotee of Hwt-Hrw
- bsA – Protect
- btAt – To harm or injure
- Da – Sexual intercourse

- Dbawt – To seal or close
- dmA – To bind
- Dsr – Sacred
- HAw – Wealth, increase, surplus
- hKa – Magic
- iaH – Moon
- iAm – To bind
- iAS – To Summon
- iqr – Wealth, virtue, excellence
- mAw – A seer
- imAw – Brilliance, splendor
- mar – Fortunate, successful, to flourish
- mDab – To banish, to expel foes
- mHy – Guardian
- nfr – Beautiful, good, healthy
- rkH – Fire, light
- rkHw – Flames
- Rnnwt – Rejoice
- rwD – Prosper, succeed
- rwdt – Success
- Rx – Sexual intercourse
- Rx xt – Wisdom
- sAw – To guard or can be used to ward off evil as well as restrain evil
- Spssw – Riches, wealth
- SsA – Wisdom, skill and knowledge
- StAw – Mysteries of the Art
- waA – To curse
- wDAt – Eye of Heru, healing, protection
- wsr – Wealthy, powerful and influential
- wDAw – Amulets, protective spells, word used to bring prosperity, success and happiness.

Conclusion

❖ THE LADY AND THE FALCON ❖

Earlier in these books, I wrote at length about my encounters with the 'Lady in Red' while I was practicing *Traveling in Spirit*. Exploring the psychic terrain of the forest in which we live, this otherworld being, cloaked in red, approached me. During a series of visits, she referred to me as a 'Merlin'. After coming out of trance my 'logical' mind chalked the term up to probably being some subconscious label seeming to relate to the Arthurian legends and perhaps I had inadvertently 'injected' the term myself.

Yet, the term kept nagging at me. Why had it figured so highly in the meetings? In *Horns of the Moon*, I described how on more than one occasion I had changed my fetch into the appearance of a small falcon, flying beside the Lady as she rode wildly through the forest. It all seemed so effortless, gliding through the forest, dodging the trees with an incredible feeling of exhilaration and sheer joy. This has been a reoccurring theme in many of these encounters.

It wasn't until recently, quite by chance, that a friend pointed out that the forests here in New England are home to a small falcon: the Merlin. This is an incredible bird, a keen hunter that thrives in the forests, navigating at incredible speeds while cruising between the trees and branches. To my memory I had never heard the name 'Merlin' attached to these magnificent creatures. Yet the name that the Lady gave was so clear. I was her Merlin.

When I had set out to write these books, they were meant to be a codification and distillation of the teachings and practices that I have received over a lifetime involvement in the Art. Yet, they have become much more. They are, in my opinion, an extension of the Geassa as a living tradition. There is no doubt that while the roots of what is now called Traditional Witchcraft rest firmly in older practices, it is a deep and secret thread that is quickly becoming an important part of western occultism and spiritual development. These are occult teachings that are based in simple rural ways of living: practical magic that is real, that works, bringing solid results. Yet, there is also a deeper spiritual aspect to this system that reaches into the very heart of nature, the very heart of who we are.

I can only speak to my training and practices, yet it seems clear that this is very animistic and shamanic in its approach, reaching to the very core of existence through multiple realms and realities. As such, the system of Witchcraft that my teacher called the Willow Path represents teachings that elevate one's understanding in such a way as to recognize the real essence of consciousness and spirit in all that is. That there are multiple worlds, with beings far more advanced and complex than we may ever fully understand. I am content to be the Merlin to one such being, learning the ways of the forest, the old ways of the Willow Path, the Geassa. Some may see her as a familiar, others as local Goddess, still others may call her the Queen of Elphame. The simple fact is that when following the Willow Path of Traditional Witchcraft, inevitably the Witch does form alliances with otherworld beings, and it is from them that the Geassa is learned and manifests. I hope that is simple series of books carries that tradition forward.

There is so much more that I could have put into these books. However, I feel that enough has been written here to give the apprentice a solid understanding of the concepts, philosophy and many of the deeper practices of this Art to form a foundation of practice on which to build. Again, I want to emphasize that at no time am I saying that this is the 'only' 'right' and 'true' way to practice Traditional

Witchcraft. Far from it. Rather, all I can say is that this is what I have been taught. This is what I have learned. And this is what I and those few associates whom I have worked with have found to be effective. Take from it what you can and leave the rest for another time.

Bibliography

Baker, Jim. *The Cunning Man's Handbook*. 2013. Avalonia, London England.

Bottrell, William and Joseph Blight. *Stories and Folklore of West Cornwall (1880)*. 1880. Republished by Kessinger Publishing "Kessinger's Legacy Reprints".

Bottrell, William. *Traditions and Hearthside Stories of West Cornwall*. 1873.

Borghouts, J.R. *Ancient Egyptian Magical Texts*. 1978. E.J. Brill, Leiden, the Netherlands

Denning, Melita and Osborne Phillips. *The Magical Philosophy, Book V, Mysteria Magica*. 1981. Llewellyn Publications, Saint Paul, Minnesota, U.S.A.

Finnestad, Ragnhild Bjerre. "Temples of the Ptolemaic and Roman Periods: Ancient Traditions in New Contexts". *Temples of Ancient Egypt*. Copyright 1997. Pages 185 - 237. Cornell University Press. Ithaca, New York, U.S.A.

Fortune, Dion. *Moon Magic*. 1956 (edition referenced 1979). Samuel Weiser, Inc. New York, NY USA

Gary, Gemma. *Traditional Witchcraft: A Cornish Book of Ways*. 2008. Troy Books. London, England.

---------, *The Devil's Dozen*. 2014-2015. Troy Books. London, England.

Gettings, Fred. *Dictionary of Occult, Hermetic and Alchemical Sigils*. 1981. Routledge & Kegan Paul. London, England.

Glass, Justine. *Witchcraft, The Sixth Sense*. 1965. Melvin

Powers, Hollywood, California, USA

Hand, Robert. Project Hindsight. 2004. http://www.projecthindsight.com/archives/history.html

Harley, Marie and Joan Ingilby. *Life and Tradition in The Moorlands of North-East Yorkshire*. 1972, 1990. Dalesman Publishing Company. United Kingdom.

Harms, Daniel; James Clark; Joseph Peterson. *The Book of Oberon: A Sourcebook of Elizabethan Magic*. 2021. Llewellyn Press. Minnesota, USA.

Holzer, Hans. *The Truth about Witchcraft*. 1969. Pocket Books. U.S.A.

Howard, Michael. *Liber Nox: A Traditional Witch's Gramarye*. 2014. Skylight Press. Great Britain.

----------, *East Anglian Witches and Wizards*. 2017. Skylight Press. Great Britain.

Huson, Paul. *Mastering Witchcraft*. 1970. G.P. Putnam's Sons. New York, New York, U.S.A.

King, Francis and Stephen Skinner. *Techniques of High Magic*. 1976. Warner Destiny Books. U.S.A.

Lecouteux, Claude. *The Tradition of Household Spirits*. 2000. Inner Traditions, Rochester Vermont, USA.

Leek, Sybil. *The Sybil Leek Book of Fortune Telling*. 1969. The Macmillan Company. Toronto, Canada.

----------, *The Complete Art of Witchcraft*. 1970. World Publishing. Canada.

----------, *ESP: The Magic Within You*. 1971. Abelard-Schuman, Intext Publisher, London, New York, Toronto.

----------, *The Best of Sybil Leek*. 1974. Popular Library. U.S.A.

----------, *The Sybil Leek Book of Curses*. 1975. Prentice-Hall, Inc. Englewood Cliffs, New Jersey, USA.

----------, *Driving Out the Devils*. 1975. G.P. Putnam's Sons, New York, New York, U.S.A.

----------, *The Sybil Leek Book of the Curious and Occult*. 1976. Ballantine / Random House, Inc. New York, NY, U.S.A.

MacMullen, Ramsay. *Christianity & Paganism in the Fourth to Eighth Centuries*. 1997. Yale University Press, New Haven CT, U.S.A.

Mathers, S.L. Macgregor. *The Key of Solomon the King (Clavicula Salomonis)*. 1888 (1976 edition referenced), Samuel Weiser, Inc. New York, NY, U.S.A.

Morehouse, David. *Remote Viewing: The Complete User's Manual for Coordinate Remote Viewing*. 2007. Sounds True. U.S.A.

Newbury Library, *Book of Magical Charms*. https://collections.carli.illinois.edu/digital/collection/nby_dig/id/2848

Paice MacLeod, Sharon. *Celtic Cosmology and the Otherworld*. 2018. McFarland & Company Inc., Publishers. Jefferson, North Carolina, USA.

Parker, Richard A., "Egyptian Astronomy, Astrology and Calendarical Reckoning. *Dictionary of Scientific Biography,* vol. XV, Suppl. I, New York: Charles Scribner's Sons, 1978, pp.706 - 727.

Patterson, Steve. *Cecil Williamson's Book of Witchcraft*. 2014. Troy Books. London, England.

Richards, Jake. *Backwoods Witchcraft: Conjure & Folk Magic From Appalachia*. 2019. Weiser Books. Newburyport, Massachusetts, USA

Roberts, Alison. *My Heart My Mother: Death and Rebirth in Ancient Egypt*. 2000. Northgate Publishers, England.

Scot, Reginald. *The Discoverie of Witchcraft*. 1584/1972 Dover Publication edition.

Wilby, Emma. *The Visions of Isobel Gowdie*. 2013. Sussex Academic Press

Wilkinson, Richard. *The Complete Temples of Ancient Egypt*. Copyright 2000. Thames and Hudson Ltd. London, England.

Index

Abraxas, 121, 125, 134, 137

Abred, 70, 77, 108, 148, 190-193, 197-198, 215, 231, 243, 248, 258, 273, 277, 289, 302, 322

Acbalaz, 269-270

Agathodaimon, 31

Alale, 134

Anaktor, 121

Angus, 134

Annwn, 30, 70, 215, 231, 289, 291-295, 297, 322

Anukis, 124, 134

Araithron, Aratron, 137

Archon, 115, 121, 125, 128, 131, 134, 137

Aspis, 115

Atum, 45, 114, 321, 328

Azamor, 167

Balen, 131

Banishing Powder, 250

Basque, 15-16, 114, 273, 286, 289, 319, 323

Bayberry, 64, 204, 255, 259, 271, 271

Becoming, 21, 37-38, 42-43, 45-46, 59, 94, 97-98, 118, 159, 161, 167, 195, 222, 224, 226, 228, 283, 285, 287, 315

Beltane, 79, 300-302, 304-305

Bes, 134

Besom, 80, 194, 240, 281, 283, 291, 293, 296, 298, 300-302, 307, 321-322, 324

Bethor, 130

Binding, 67-69, 223, 225, 314

Black Salt, 251

Burning time, 152, 214

Caer Wydyr, 215, 285, 289, 293, 295, 299, 305, 310, 325

Candle Reading, 219

Castle of Glass, 30, 297

Çatal Hüyük, 160

Cauldrons of Poesy, 37

Cernowain, 114

Cernunnos, 124

Charged Breath, 49, 183, 186, 196, 208, 228, 242, 272

Cloak, 27, 38-44, 46, 48-49, 78, 82, 93, 150, 164, 177, 180, 183, 185,

201, 272, 293, 315, 321

Cockle bread, 187

Colonial America, 61, 67, 117

Crossroads, 127, 169, 228

Crow, 35-37, 127, 282-283, 291-291, 296-297, 301-302, 307-308, 321, 323-324

Crown of Venus, 263

Crystal Mountain, 325

Crystal Well, 56-57, 197

Daisy Wheel, 117

Danu, 120, 130

Djehuty, Thoth, 89, 95, 121

Dragon, 16, 27-34, 36, 38, 42, 52-57, 77, 86, 159, 165, 167, 170, 177, 181-182, 185-91, 193-194, 197, 199, 211, 214, 216, 227, 243, 249-250, 269, 272, 282-283, 291, 292, 296-299, 301-304, 307-308, 310, 317, 320, 323-324

Dua, 48, 56, 64, 68, 83, 92, 145, 148, 170, 177, 272

Egypt, 14, 31, 33, 61, 74, 89, 110-112, 124, 160-161, 186, 188, 202, 252, 289, 320

Elphame, 14, 113, 120, 279, 289, 305, 312, 333

Epona, 121

Esrus, 101-103, 282

Falias, 105-108

Familiar, 17, 21, 34, 38, 46, 55, 58, 127, 164, 174, 192, 207, 272, 276-277, 315

Fe, wand, 21-22, 52-53, 55-57, 59, 98-102, 104, 106-107, 149-150, 167, 196, 208-209, 240, 243-244, 248, 272, 284, 304

Fertility, 37, 62, 81, 121, 133, 140-141, 186, 215, 253

Fessus, 106-107, 282

Findias, 98-100

Fire Cauldron, 86-87, 89, 240

Firey Wall of Protection, 250

Four Thieves Vinegar, 201

Garlic, 89-90, 95, 201, 251, 255, 258

Gary, Gemma, 70

Genitals, 36-37, 51, 182, 186-187, 316, 322

Gods Gwyn Ap Nudd, 114

Gorias, 101-103

Graveyard Dirt, 236-239, 242

Graveyard Smoke, 237, 240

Gwynfyd , 289

Bibliography

Hag Stone, 80

Hagith 134

Hare, 35-37, 282, 291-292, 296-297, 301-302, 307-308, 321, 323-324

Hathor, Hwt-Hrw, 31, 45, 110, 114, 121, 124-125, 130, 134, 161, 188, 196, 218, 279, 309, 320, 321, 324, 326-328, 330

Haunt, haunting, 58, 72-73, 76-77, 223, 231-232, 242, 255

Hearth, 35, 44, 58, 61, 69-71, 79, 84, 148, 206, 211, 218, 228, 240, 248, 252, 254, 260, 270, 281, 290, 293-294, 300, 322

Heka, 31, 52

High Magic, 146

Holda, 120

Holzer, Hans, 40

Hood Lamp, 70, 219

Horseshoe, 70, 160, 253, 254, 258

Hot Foot Powder, 251

Howard, Michael, 32-33, 40, 109

Imbolc, 295, 296-300

Invisibility, 200, 329

Isobel Gowdie, 17-18

Iusaas, 46, 124, 134, 285, 320-321

Janicot, 55-56, 114, 130, 197, 286, 289, 292, 297, 302, 308, 323

Julie, 14, 16, 19, 23, 25, 39, 42, 51, 69-70, 89, 174, 202, 202, 211, 218, 279, 286-287, 290

Juniper, 64, 201, 255, 259, 263-264, 271, 273

Jupiter's Reward, 264

Kamea, 91, 117-119, 122-123, 125-126, 129, 132, 135, 138, 273

Keppen, 52

Khnum, 114, 124, 130, 325

Knouphis, 31

Lampblack, 163

Lecouteux, Claude, 38

Leek, Sybil, 19, 29, 40-42, 90, 109, 120, 173, 203, 213, 217, 219-220, 225, 233-236, 254, 263, 279, 288

Loadstone, 145, 258

Low Magic, 11, 13

Lughnasadh, 305-306, 310

Mare, 66, 121, 122, 322

Master, 49, 53-55, 57, 84, 88, 113, 114, 120, 124, 127, 130, 137, 147, 197, 280-283, 285-286, 289, 291-299, 301-305, 307-310, 312, 314, 316-317, 323, 325

Min, 134

Mirror Box, 171, 173-174

Mistress, 40, 43, 49, 56-57, 120, 147, 175, 195-197, 216, 224, 226, 233, 279, 281-286, 291-292, 294-295, 297-305, 307-310, 312, 316, 323-324, 326-327, 329

Moon Cord, 226, 228

Moon Rake, 160

Morrigan, 114, 120, 124, 134

Murias, 103-105

Nata Bag, 78, 91, 145, 249, 259-260, 273

Natron, 24

Nebet Hetepet, 45, 124, 134, 320-321

Nekhbet, 33

New England, 40, 53, 59, 84, 97, 171, 198, 204, 260, 262, 332

Nowl, 254-255

Oak, 52-53, 55, 79, 86, 291, 325

Och, 115

Olive Oil, 64, 249, 255, 271

Olympic Spirits, 114-115, 121, 130, 147

Onion, 89-90

Ophiel, 127

Overlooking, Evil Eye, 44, 187-189

Pan, 114, 124, 255

Passing the Power, 47-48, 213, 274-275

Pellar, 18-19

Persia, 110, 160

Phaleg, 125

Phallic, Phallus, 53, 186

Phul, 121

Poppet, 71, 183, 204-210

Prosperity, 27, 47, 62-65, 71, 133-134, 139, 141, 145-146, 155, 199, 214-216, 218, 220, 248, 253-255, 257-263, 265, 267, 270-273, 275, 293-294, 305-306, 310, 331

Pythagorean, 111

Qabbala, 111

Ra-Horakhty, 46, 321

Red Luck Oil, 264

Revenant, 58

Rowan, 67, 84-86, 251, 254

Rutor, 125

Samhain, 113, 290-294, 296

Sator, 167

Séance, 232, 233-236

Sebile, 29-30, 120, 134

Second Skin, 24, 41-42, 75, 78, 90, 136, 180-181, 183, 189, 199-201, 248

Sekhmet, 31, 114, 202

Semias, 103-105, 282

Serpent, 16, 27-37, 42, 46, 48-49, 52-53, 55-57, 78, 82, 89, 93, 97-98, 164, 177, 181, 183, 188-189, 194-195, 197, 205, 208, 226, 242, 280, 282-283, 285, 291-292, 296-298, 302, 307-309, 315, 317, 320-321, 323-324, 326-327, 329

Seshat, 127

Sex, 37, 51, 124, 134, 142, 186

Shape-Shifting, 199-200

Shoes, 62

Sidh, 39, 60-61

Silver, 43, 56, 77-79, 90, 104-105, 107, 160-162, 168, 195, 197, 242, 245, 267, 283, 291, 293, 296, 301-302, 307, 315, 324

Spirit Mist, 241, 243, 244

Stang, 55, 70, 81-82, 97-99, 101, 103-106, 113, 148, 150, 175-176, 195, 240, 248, 281, 283, 291, 293, 296-298, 300-304, 307, 321-322, 324

Sthenos, 128

Strega, 15, 114, 120, 237

Sybille, 29

Tana, 120

Tanat/Tanit, 120

Tanus, 114

Tlachtga, 120

Toad, 35-37, 282-283, 291-292, 296-296, 301-302, 307-308, 321, 323-324

Trillium, 145, 249, 262

Tuatha de Danann, 114

Uscias, 98-100, 282

Vampiric, 75, 77, 250

Vervain, 50, 53, 64, 79, 81-82, 86-87, 90, 98, 145, 165, 169, 207, 236, 250, 255, 259-260, 263, 269, 271, 273, 290-291, 314

Vulva, 62, 186-187

Wadjet, 33, 45, 321

Warding, 66-67, 85, 109

Wealth, 63, 131, 143, 214, 257, 271, 273, 331

Williamson, Cecil, 144, 319

Witch Bottle, 92

Witch Marks, 65, 69, 121, 190

Witch Queen, 40, 46, 56, 66, 78, 84, 120, 124, 175, 197, 279, 280, 312, 320
Wormwood, 165, 169, 201, 236-237, 291
Wytcha, 227
Xais, 137
Yparon, 128, 269

Printed in the USA
CPSIA information can be obtained
at www.ICGtesting.com
JSHW022209031223
53085JS00002B/82